Full of Beans

Kay Spicer & Violet Currie

MIGHTON HOUSE

Canadian Cataloguing in Publication Data

Spicer, Kay
    Full of beans

Includes Index.
ISBN 0–9695688–1–9

1. Cookery (Beans). 2. Low-calorie diet – Recipes.
3. Low-fat diet – Recipes. 4. Gluten-free diet – Recipes.
I. Currie, Violet   II. Title.

TX803.B4576 1993   641.6'565   C93–094065–2

Sponsored by the Ontario Coloured Bean Growers Association.
Published in co-operation with the Canadian Celiac Association.

10

Published by:
Mighton House
Box 399,
Campbellville, Ontario
L0P 1B0

Distributed by **Gordon Soules Book Publishers Ltd**. ● 1359 Ambleside Lane, West Vancouver, BC, Canada V7T 2Y9 ● PMB 620, 1916 Pike Place #12, Seattle, WA 98101-1097 US
E-mail: books@gordonsoules.com
Web site: http://www.gordonsoules.com
(604) 922 6588 Fax: (604) 688 5442

Printed and bound in Canada
Cover & Design: Mary O'Neil
Recipe Editing: Bev Renahan
Illustrations & Typography: Martin Crawford
Photography: Fred Bird
Printing and Binding: Friesen Printers

The Crossed Grain symbol is the registered Trade-mark of the Canadian Celiac Association and Mighton House is a licensed user.

Front cover: Mixed Vegetable Bean Soup
Back cover: Strawberry Cream Roll

TABLE OF CONTENTS

Authors' Acknowledgements

Many people – colleagues, friends, associations, ministries – contributed to the development of this book. We are grateful to the Ontario Coloured Bean Growers Association for their sponsorship of this work, to the chairman and board of directors of the association for their assistance and to Bernadine Wolfe, secretary treasurer, who was always enthusiastic and ready to help us.

The research facilities at Centralia College, Ministry of Agriculture and Food, were used for the initial work (Dr. Currie's) on whole bean flour and many of the bean recipes. For that we are grateful.

We wish to thank the Canadian Celiac Association and their executive director, Rosie Wartecker, for co-operating and consulting with us as we created this cookbook.

A big thank you to George Birinyi, Sr. and George Berinyi, Jr., Grain Process Enterprises, for helping develop the new whole bean flour and making bags of it available to develop our recipes.

Many thanks to all our helpers who made the production of this book possible:

Gwen Dykeman, technician, and Deb Campbell, lecturer, Foods Technology Section, Centralia College, for their assistance in developing and testing some of the recipes.

Clara Paul, for testing some of the recipes.

Patricia Spicer and Carrie Parsons, secretary, Foods Technology Section, Centralia College, for doing some of the computer input of recipes.

Susan Spicer, for sharing a few of her recipe ideas for this book.

Kathy Younker, KEYS Nutrition Services, for her expertise in doing all of the nutrient analysis of the recipes and the Canadian Diabetes Association Food Choice Value calculations.

Bev Renahan, for deligently editing our recipes.

Mary O'Neil, for the creative design.

Fred Bird, for the pleasing photography.

Martin Crawford, for setting up the page formatting and illustrations.

Best Foods Canada Inc., for the inspiration for Chocolate Mocha Cake and Orange Date Loaf and the use of their pictures.

Canada Pork, for the recipe for New-Style Pork and Bean Salad and the use of the photograph.

Mighton House, for publishing our book and arranging for its distribution.

And, a special thanks from Kay to her husband, Jim Mighton, for his endurance, steady support and love through all the months, days and hours of testing, tasting and typing.

To all of you who own this book, thank you for your interest. We have enjoyed creating these recipes for good-tasting, healthful "full of beans" dishes for you, your family and friends to enjoy regularly.

FROM THE COLOURED BEAN GROWERS ASSOCIATION

Coloured beans have long been an important crop on many Ontario family farms. Traditionally most edible beans were grown in the Southwestern counties of the Province. Now the primary growing region is in a 50 mile radius of London, Ontario.

The fertile soils and warm growing season combined with growers good management have resulted in Ontario grown beans being some of the best produced in the world.

Primary varieties grown are dark and light red kidney, white kidney, and Romano/cranberry beans. Dutch brown, black turtle, yellow eyes, and pintos make up the balance of production.

It is interesting to note that approximately 75% of the Ontario crop is exported to worldwide destinations such as the United Kingdom, Europe, the Caribbean, and Africa.

In the mid-1980s several growers gathered to explore the potential of forming a growers' association. Today the Ontario Coloured Bean Growers Association is a very active group with nearly 300 growers participating in various functions that are organized. The mandate of the association is to disperse crop management information to growers to enable the production of high quality beans. The second part of the mandate is to promote domestic consumption of our bean product. The association has also sponsored researchers to promote the product as well as explore alternative uses.

Dried beans are increasingly playing a bigger role in many health conscious consumers' diets.

The Ontario Coloured Bean Growers Association is proud to have sponsored this exciting new cookbook. We hope that you enjoy the assorted delicious dishes that can be made from the recipes that have been developed for it.

Bruce Cruickshank,
Chairman
Ontario Coloured Bean Growers Association

FROM THE CANADIAN CELIAC ASSOCIATION

The Canadian Celiac Association is a national organization dedicated to providing support to persons with celiac disease and dermatitis herpetiformis through programs of awareness, advocacy, education and research.

Celiac disease is a medical condition in which the absorptive surface of the small intestine is damaged by a substance called gluten. This results in an inability of the body to absorb nutrients: protein, fat, carbohydrate, vitamins and minerals; necessary for good health.

Common symptoms include, but are not limited to: chronic diarrhea, weight loss, anemia, cramps, bloating, fatigue and irritability. These symtoms also occur in many other conditions, making a proper diagnosis necessary. Celiac disease is hereditary and can surface at any age. In some cases, the symptoms listed may or may not be evident, but sufferers develop an intense burning and itching rash called dermatitis herpetiformis. It can be treated with a gluten-free diet.

Contrary to previous misconceptions celiac disease can not be outgrown. It is a life long condition. The only known treatment for it is a gluten-free diet.

It is estimated that 13,000 Canadians suffer from this condition, many of whom have not been diagnosed. A small bowel biopsy is necessary for a definitive diagnosis. A trial of the gluten-free diet is not recommended before the diagnosis is made; it could jeopardize the results.

The substance called gluten is found in wheat, rye, oats, triticale, barley and any products made from these grains. Gluten helps bread and other baked goods bind and prevents crumbling, so it is widely used in the production of many processed and packaged foods.

The whole bean flour called for in recipes in this cook-book is gluten-free and provides the user with an alternative to the other gluten-free flours that are available. The added fibre and nutrients are a bonus.

The Canadian Celiac Asssociation is pleased to have been involved with this project.

Rosie Wartecker
Executive Director
Canadian Celiac Association

NOTE FROM THE AUTHORS:

For **gluten-free food**, we expect all of you cooks to use only gluten-free ingredients, such as gluten-free sausages, gluten-free peanut butter, gluten-free baking powder, etc. And, when a bread or another food is suggested as an accompaniment, we trust that only a gluten-free item will be consumed.

Please note: Our recipes for <u>gluten-free</u> appetizers to desserts are marked with ⒼⒻ .

The recipes that are <u>not gluten-free</u> are marked with ⊗ .

NUTRIENT ANALYSIS OF RECIPES

Nutrient analysis of recipes was performed by KEYS Nutrition Services using the 1991 Canadian Nutrient File Nutrient Analysis Program, copyright Elizabeth Warwick, B.H.Sc., P.Dt. Fibre values for red and white kidney beans were obtained from personal communication with Dr. R. Mongeau, Ph.D. Food Directorate, Health and Welfare, Ottawa, Ontario. Fibre values for black and cranberry beans were obtained from Plant Fibre in Foods, 2nd edition, Anderson, J.W., 1990.

Analysis was based on Imperial measures. The analysis accounted for cooking methods, yields and resultant changes in nutrient profile. Recipe variations were averaged when the energy difference was minimal (less than 10 calories).

Food Choices values were assigned using the *Guidelines for Calculating Canadian Diabetes Association Food Choice Values and Symbols*. Carbohydrate values are calculated as total carbohydrate minus dietary fibre.

As some dessert recipes contain significant amounts of carbohydrate, (as added sugars) it may be prudent for the person with diabetes to reduce the portion size to correspond with individual meal plans. The Canadian Diabetes Association position statement on the *Role of Dietary Sugars in Diabetes Mellitus* (1992), suggests that up to 10% of total energy may be consumed in the form of added sugars.

The Canadian Diabetes Association Food Choice Values and Symbols contained in the book (above the nutrient information on each page), are part of the Good Health Eating Guide system, (1979) of meal planning. Each of the six food choice groups, ☐ Starchy Foods, ◆ Milk, ◢ Fruit and Vegetables, ◢ Protein Foods, ▲ Fats and Oils and ✛ Extras, identifies foods with common macronutrients, (carbohydrate, protein, fat) and energy.

The person with diabetes using the Good Health Eating Guide system will have an individualized meal plan which identifies how many of each choice to make at each meal and snack. They can choose foods within each choice or "fit" in one of the many delicious recipes found in the book into their plan. Choices from each of the food choice groups are shown below:

☐ **Starchy Foods**
- 1 slice bread
- 1/2 cup (125 mL) noodles
- 1/2 cup (125 mL) corn

◆ **Milk Products**
- 1/2 cup (125 mL) milk
- 1/2 cup (125 mL) plain yogurt
- 1/4 cup (50 mL) canned milk

◢ **Fruit and Vegetables**
- 1 orange
- 1/2 cup (125 mL) peas
- 1/3 cup (75 mL) apple juice

◢ **Protein Foods**
- 1 egg
- 1/4 cup (50 mL) fish
- 1 tbsp (15 mL) peanut butter

▲ **Fats and Oils**
- 1 tsp (5 mL) margarine or butter
- 1 tsp (5 mL) oil
- 2 tsp (10 mL) salad dressing

✛ **Extras**
- Beans, yellow or green
- broccoli
- peppers, red or green

For more information, see page 216 for contact, and page 224 for comparison with American Diabetes Association Exchange System.

Kathy Younker, P.Dt.

NUTRITIOUS BEANS

The nutrient profile of dried beans is impeccable. They rate as the richest source of vegetable protein, a very high source of both insoluble and soluble dietary fibre and a fabulous source of non-sweet complex carbohydrate, making them a marvelous source of energy. They supply impressive amounts of the B-vitamins (niacin, riboflavin, thiamine and folic acid), calcium, iron, phosphorous, potassium, zinc and some trace elements. All are positive nutritional qualities that health professionals recommend for healthy choices.

In addition, beans contain no cholesterol or gluten and very little sodium and fat. They are definitely a boon when it comes to healthy eating and maintaining a healthy weight. As well, with all those positive qualities, they are important for special diets such as gluten-free, diabetic, low-salt, low-fat, low-calorie, low-cholesterol, high fibre and high iron diets.

Dried beans can be eaten as a healthy substitute for animal protein in anyone's diet. However, it is true that legumes like other plant sources of protein do not contain all the essential amino acids as meat, fish, poultry, eggs and dairy products do. The blessing is that the amino acid, methionine, that is low in dried beans is high in cereal protein. In turn, the one (lysine) low in grains such as rice and corn, is high in dried beans. Happily the two complement each other and when eaten together provide complete protein in the diet.

For a complete protein balance from plant sources combine dried beans with:
- Grain and cereal protein (rice, millet, corn, wheat, barley)
- Seed and nut protein (sesame seeds, sunflower seeds, cashew nuts)
- Dairy protein (milk, cheese, yogurt)
- Egg protein

Some great examples from international cuisines of combinations that work include:

Mexican beans with corn tortillas

Cuban black beans with rice

Hummus with tahini (sesame seed paste)

Indian Dal with rice

Boston baked beans with bread

VEGETARIAN BEANS

Meatless meals have increased in popularity since the sixties and seventies. Since then, the focus of a healthy diet has switched from protein and higher fat foods to the consumption of foods rich in complex carbohydrate-grains, cereals, fruits and vegetables, dried beans. In addition, these foods are naturally low in fat, high in fibre, and are rich sources of vitamins and minerals, qualities that health professionals recommend for healthy food choices.

A review of scientific literature on vegetarian and near-vegetarian diets has indicated that in spite of widely differing dietary practices, a reasonably well-chosen plant source diet, supplemented with dairy products and eggs or without eggs, is adequate for every nutritional requirement of all age groups. It is the quality of the protein in such a diet which determines whether the diet will maintain life or not.

Fibre in beans

Dietary fibre has been around forever. However, in the past three to four decades interest in this indigestible food component and its impact on the risk and control of some chronic health problems has intensified.

It was in the '60s, when Dr. Denis Burkitt reported on studies of the diet (high fibre) of some rural African tribes and the low incidence of colonic cancers. Subsequent research shows that a high fibre diet may have beneficial effects on some abnormal physiological conditions such as, diabetes, obesity, certain intestinal irregularities (diverticulosis) and cardiovascular disease.

Dietary fibre remains in the colon after carbohydrate, protein and fat have been digested. It aids passage of food through the intestines by increasing its volume and fluid content and helping to prevent constipation. It may also interact with certain bacteria to produce chemicals that help inhibit the growth of cancer cells in the colon.

There are two types of dietary fibre: water-insoluble and water-soluble. Insoluble fibre (roughage) does not dissolve but can bind and hold onto water. Rich food sources of insoluble fibre are wheat bran, corn bran, nuts, and some fruits and vegetables.

Soluble fibre such as the guar gum in dried beans, dissolves in water, forming gels. As such, it displays important metabolic functions. It helps to regulate the serum glucose level and reduce serum triglycerides, as seen, in research, in people with diabetes. Also, it helps to lower serum cholesterol by binding with low density lipoproteins. Sources of water-soluble fibre include dried beans and legumes, oat bran, barley bran, as well as, some fruits such as apples and oranges.

Dietary fibre may also help to maintain a healthy weight. Certainly dishes made with dried beans satisfy the appetite with their great staying power and so help control over eating.

Both the Canadian Cancer Society and Health and Welfare Canada recommend we consume 20 to 30 grams of dietary fibre per day for optimum good health.

Gas-Free Beans?

Unfortunately, beans do have the reputation of causing varying degrees of uncomfortable and sometimes embarrassing intestinal gas. It is because some unusual saccharides (raffinose, stachyose and verbacose) in beans may not be digested sufficiently. When they enter the large intestine they are consumed by bacteria and this produces gas and bloating (flatulence) in some people.

To eliminate at least 80 per cent of the problem, follow all the steps given for precooking dried beans. That is: always discard the soaking water, rinse the soaked beans, cover them with plenty of fresh water for cooking, discard the cooking water and then rinse the cooked beans again. As well, drain and rinse canned beans. A large amount of the gas-producing components (but very little of the essential nutrients) head down the drain.

Fortunately, as beans are eaten on a more regular basis the digestive system adapts and the intestinal gas problem decreases.

The Bean Family

Dried beans, peas and lentils are known as pulses and belong to one of the plant world's largest families, Leguminosae, or legumes family. All the members, and there are hundreds, have five-petalled flowers and seeds carried in pods. As in every family, different strains have distinct and subtle nuances of size, color, flavor and texture.

They come in assorted sizes and colors. Delicate to more earthy and robust describe their flavor. Their texture runs from creamy to mealy but it is comforting. The one characteristic common to all varieties is their capacity to absorb the flavors of other foods. It is no wonder then that it is possible to make an infinite number of tasty dishes "full of beans". They love company.

The following describes seven of the most common colored beans: (see photograph opposite page 32)

RED KIDNEY BEANS: These kidney-shaped beans, popular in Mexican-style cooking, have a smashing brownish-red color. Their mealy texture is perfect for both salads and casseroles. Tons of them are canned and available on store shelves.

DARK RED KIDNEY BEANS: Color and flavor seem to be more vibrant than in lighter red kidney beans. Other features are the same.

WHITE KIDNEY BEANS: Italian cooks call these cannellini beans. They have white- to cream-colored skins and interiors and cook up to be very tender with a delicate flavor. Pureed, they are similar to creamy mashed potatoes and make a perfect low-fat base for dips and spreads. Use them in place of any of the white beans called for in recipes.

ROMANO BEANS: Known also as cranberry beans, Romano beans are pretty with deep cranberry-colored striations running through their pinkish-beige shell. During cooking the color fades to greyish-beige. They are popular in Italian cooking but can also be substituted in any dishes calling for kidney beans, such as chili.

BLACK BEANS: The size of black beans (turtle beans, tiger beans, black haricots) varies from small to large. When cooked they maintain their roundish shape and satiny black color. The inside stays creamy-colored even though some black leaches into the cooking water. Their flavor is nut-like, their texture, mealy. They are popular in Caribbean, Mexican and South American cookery.

DUTCH BROWN BEANS: These evenly-colored, golden brown beans maintain their lovely color in cooking. They are the mellow fellows with a gentle earthy character about them, in both texture and taste.

YELLOW EYE BEANS: There is a distinctive golden brown spot or eye on these cream-colored rounded beans that are a little smaller than kidney beans. Their skin seems thinner and it takes less time to cook them and develop their pleasant slightly smoky flavor. Use them in place of any colored bean called for in a recipe.

All of the colored beans mentioned above are interchangeable in the recipes in this cookbook.

CONVENIENT BEANS

Beans are user-friendly. It is true, cooking them from scratch takes time but very little work is involved. For the ultimate in convenience, beans can also be purchased canned.

BUYING BEANS

Smooth whole beans with a satin sheen and ones without cracks or shrivelled skins indicate top-quality beans. Cracked and broken, old and dull beans may never soak or cook properly. Bulk beans are usually fresher and in good shape, besides you can see what you are getting.

Today, there are great assortments of dried beans in bulk food stores, health food centres and specialty shops dealing in ethnic foods. Supermarket and grocery stores are beginning to display more choices in their bulk food sections and on their shelves. To make the selection even broader, ask for varieties that are not there and encourage the manager to add to his stock. There are also more and more varieties available canned but they are expensive compared to the same kinds in their dried form.

STORING

Dried colored beans seem to last forever but **do** deteriorate on long storage. The longer the storage the drier the bean and the harder it is to cook. Beans that are several years old take much longer to cook than beans from a recent harvest.

They are certainly easy to store at home. Simply keep them in a moisture-proof container or bag. They endure all temperature variations from warm to room temperature to freezing. However, that is not a reason to buy bushels more than you will use in a reasonable time unless for some strange reason you have to stock up like our pioneers did when they could only buy supplies one or two times a year. Try to cook dried beans within a year of their purchase and always replenish your supply from a store where you know there is a fast turnover of the commodity.

If you do end up with an assortment that is years old pour them into glass jars. Display them where you will enjoy their pretty colors and shapes plus the homey touch they add to the decor.

PREPARING BEANS FOR THE TABLE

Transforming the hard, dried legume into a tender, edible bean takes four easy steps---cleaning and washing, soaking, rinsing, cooking. Each one is simple. (A large sieve or colander for rinsing, a few large bowls for soaking and a big deep pot or two for cooking help facilitate the process.)

1. Cleaning and Washing:

   First pick over the dried beans, removing broken and cracked ones and foreign matter like the odd little stick or pebble. Place in a colander or sieve and then swish running water through the beans.

2. Soaking:

Dried beans need to be soaked before cooking to replace some of the water lost in drying, to help speed up the cooking time and to leach out some of the substances that cause flatulence. There are two methods for soaking beans:

a) The Long Cold Soak:

Cover dried beans with about 3 cups (750 mL) water, preferrably soft, to each cup of beans. Let stand for 6 to 10 hours or overnight in a cool place. (In warm weather place the container in the refrigerator to prevent the beans from turning sour which can happen if they are left out too long before boiling.)

b) The Quick Hot Soak:

Cover dried beans with about 3 cups (750 mL) water, preferrably soft, per cup of beans. Bring to boil for 2 to 3 minutes. Remove from heat and let stand for 1 hour.

3. Rinsing:

Drain the beans of their soaking water by pouring them into a large colander or sieve placed over the sink. Then rinse them thoroughly with cold, running water.

4. Cooking:

In a pot large enough to allow for expansion and foaming, cover the rinsed soaked beans with fresh cold water, preferably soft. Add 1 teaspoon (5 mL) cooking oil (a little helps to reduce foaming while cooking). Bring to boil; boil for 5 minutes. (At this point drain and rinse again under cold running water, if you wish, to further improve digestibility and remove any scum. Return beans to pot, cover them with cold water and bring to a boil.) Reduce heat and, with lid ajar to prevent boiling over, gently simmer beans until they are just tender but not mushy.

Add herbs, garlic, onion to season the beans while they are cooking. However, **do not** add salt, sugar, lemon juice, vinegar or tomato products since the acid in them inhibits the cooking that tenderizes the bean. Add them once the beans are nearly tender and cook for an additional 10 to 15 minutes for the seasonings to permeate the beans.

Cooking times depend on the type, age and quality of the dried beans, the altitude and whether hard or soft water is used. Thin skinned, recently harvested beans cook faster than thicker skinned or older beans. It take longer to soak and cook them at high altitudes. Hard water can cause toughness. Some cooks add baking soda to speed up the cooking time, however, we **do not** recommend the practice. It impacts negatively on both the flavor and nutritional value of the cooked beans.

The best way to test their doneness is to taste them. Cooked beans are free of any raw starch taste, tender and easy to squash in your mouth.

During the change from dried to cooked, the beans double in bulk (sometimes just a bit more). To get two cups (500 mL) cooked beans you have to soak then cook one cup (250 mL) dried beans.

COOKING TIMES

BEAN	SOAK	SUGGESTED COOKING TIME
Dark red kidney	yes	approximately 50 minutes
Red kidney	yes	50 minutes
White kidney	yes	50 minutes
Romano	yes	45 minutes
Dutch brown	yes	45 minutes
Yellow-eye	yes	45 minutes
Black bean	yes	40 minutes

1 cup (250 mL) dried = 2 to 2 1/2 cups (500 to 625 mL) cooked

OTHER COOKING METHODS:

Slow Cooker Cooking: Follow manufacturer's directions.

Pressure Cooker: A newer model with clog-proof vent will cut down on cooking time. Follow manufacturer's directions.

Microwave Oven: Cooking dried beans in a microwave oven is not recommended and even if it were, the cooking time is virtually the same as the conventional method.

STORING COOKED BEANS

Cooked beans store well in plastic bags or covered containers in the refrigerator for up to five days, or in the freezer for up to six months.

Having home-cooked beans stashed away is like having convenience foods on hand and for much less than it costs to buy the same varieties canned. It is a good idea to pack them in measured amounts---1 cup (250 mL), 2 cup (500 mL), etc – that are usually called for in recipes.

Nutritional and energy information for cooked kidney beans: Ⓖ

Each serving: 1/2 cup (125 mL)

1	☐ Starchy	111	calories	GOOD: Iron, Magnesium
1/2	⊘ Protein	464	kilojoules	EXCELLENT: Folate
		0 g	total fat	HIGH: Fibre
		0 g	saturated fat	
		0 mg	cholesterol	
		7 g	protein	
		20 g	carbohydrate	
		5.4 g	fibre	
		1 mg	sodium	
		319 mg	potassium	

WHOLE BEAN FLOUR

All of the recipes for gluten-free baked goods in this cookbook call for whole bean flour. It is made from natural, Ontario-grown, whole dried Romano (cranberry) beans. First, they are precooked (micronized) in their dry state and then, they are stone-ground to a uniform fine flour in the milling process. Nothing is wasted.

Nutritionally, whole bean flour is impressive. It provides more calcium, iron, potassium, thiamine, riboflavin, folate and far more dietary fibre than all-purpose flour and other gluten-free flours except for soybean flour. There is not a trace of gluten in this flour, making it wonderful for individuals who are gluten- and wheat-sensitive or have celiac disease. It is a top-notch alternative to use in place of other gluten-free flours available today.

Because gluten is missing, whole bean flour lacks the holding power or strength found in flours made from grains where gluten is present such as wheat, rye, triticale, barley and oats. This means the cell structure in breads, muffins and cakes made from whole bean flour is more dense than it would be if the same products were made using wheat flour. However, the leavening agents (gluten-free baking powder, baking soda, yeast and stiffly beaten egg whites) used in our recipes, in the quantities or combinations suggested, do lighten the gluten-free doughs.

Yeast breads, for example, call for yeast and also baking powder. Both work to produce a good palatable, robust bread. If you choose to use whole bean flour as a substitute for all-purpose flour in recipes from other cookbooks, expect to do some experimenting. You may find a little less whole bean flour will give the best results. Measure for measure the whole bean flour seems to absorb more moisture than wheat flour.

Before measuring whole bean flour from its container or bag, stir it lightly with a fork or spoon to aerate and lighten it. Lightly spoon it into the appropriate dry measure and smooth off the top with a straight edge.

To buy whole bean flour, refer to page 216 and ask for it at your local grocery stores and supermarkets.

APPETIZERS

Low-Fat Hummus

Hummus with Hot Mushrooms and Onions

Hummus

Falafel

Sesame Cream Sauce

Black Bean Salsa

Peanutty Bean Dip

Chili Dip

Creamy Spinach and Bean Dip

Chicken Crisps

Ham and Cheese Puffs

Layered Appetizer Pie

Tortilla Bean Pinwheels

Bean and Pecan Paté

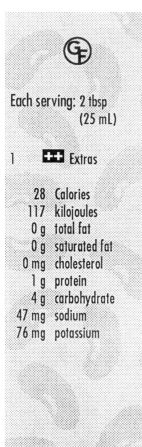

Each serving: 2 tbsp
(25 mL)

1	![Extras] Extras	
28	Calories	
117	kilojoules	
0 g	total fat	
0 g	saturated fat	
0 mg	cholesterol	
1 g	protein	
4 g	carbohydrate	
47 mg	sodium	
76 mg	potassium	

LOW-FAT HUMMUS

Tahini is sesame seed paste and gives hummus its distinct flavor. It is available in specialty food stores where ingredients for Mediterranean and Israeli-style cooking are available. However, if tahini is unavailable use 1 tbsp (15 mL) peanut butter plus 1 tbsp (15 mL) sesame oil.

1 1/2 cups	cooked Romano, white kidney or Dutch brown beans	375 mL
2	cloves garlic	2
2 tbsp	tahini	25 mL
2 tbsp	lemon juice	25 mL
1/2 tsp	salt	2 mL
6	drops hot pepper sauce	6
	Hot water	
	Chopped fresh chives or parsley	

• Set aside about 7 whole beans. In food processor or blender, combine beans, garlic, tahini, lemon juice, salt and hot pepper sauce. Process until pureed adding hot water to thin to consistency desired.

• Garnish with chives and reserved beans.

Makes about 1 3/4 cups (425 mL).

Hummus with Hot Mushrooms and Onions

At a beach restaurant along the Mediterranean in Tel Aviv matzos instead of pita bread accompanied this wonderful concoction because it was the Sabbath. Eat it with a fork or serve it with Seed and Nut Crackers (pg. 153) for scooping the mixture from its plate.

1 3/4 cups	Low-Fat Hummus (p.16)	425 mL
1	white onion	1
1/2 lb	button mushrooms	250 g
1 tsp	canola oil	5 mL
1 tsp	turmeric	5 mL
1/2 tsp	ground cumin	2 mL
1/4 tsp	ground thyme	1 mL
1/4 tsp	salt	1 mL
Pinch	freshly ground black pepper	Pinch
	Chopped fresh mint or parsley	

• Prepare hummus. (If stored in refrigerator, let come to room temperature.)

• Cut onion in half lengthwise; cut each half into slices. Cut mushrooms in half.

• In nonstick skillet, heat oil over medium heat; cook onion and mushrooms, stirring occasionally, for about 7 minutes or until onion is translucent and moisture from mushrooms has nearly evaporated. Stir in turmeric, cumin, thyme, salt and pepper.

• Divide hummus among 4 small plates. Spread in circle on each plate, creating raised edge and indentation in the centre. Spoon hot mushroom mixture into centre.

• Serve immediately sprinkled with parsley.

Makes 4 servings.

GF

Each serving: 1/4 of recipe

1	☐	Starchy
1	⊘	Protein
1	✚✚	Extras

146	calories
610	kilojoules
4 g	total fat
1 g	saturated fat
0 mg	cholesterol
8 g	protein
20 g	carbohydrate
398 mg	sodium
400 mg	potassium

GOOD: Phosphorus, Iron, Magnesium
EXCELLENT: Folate
HIGH: Fibre

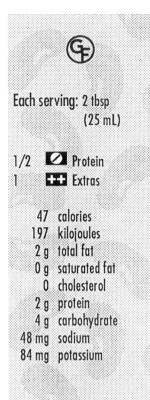

Hummus

Hummus is nicest when it holds its shape like whipped cream. Serve surrounded with broccoli florets, carrot sticks and cucumber spears for dipping. It is also wonderful as a filling for celery sticks, mushroom caps or snow peas.

1 1/2 cups	cooked Romano, white kidney or Dutch brown beans	375 mL
2	cloves garlic	2
1/4 cup	tahini	50 mL
2 tbsp	lemon juice	25 mL
1 tbsp	olive oil	15 mL
1/2 tsp	salt	2 mL
6	drops hot pepper sauce	6
	Hot water	
	Chopped fresh chives or parsley	
	Paprika	

• Set aside about 7 whole beans for garnish.

• In food processor or blender, combine remaining beans, garlic, tahini, lemon juice, olive oil, salt and hot pepper sauce. Process until pureed, adding hot water to thin to consistency desired.

• Transfer to serving plate or shallow bowl. Spread in circle, creating a raised edge and indentation in centre. Garnish with chives, paprika and reserved beans.

Makes 1 3/4 cups (425 mL).

FALAFEL

*If you love garlic, increase it to three cloves in the falafels.
Serve them hot or at room temperature with Sesami (Tahini)
Cream Sauce (p.20) on their own, wrapped up in a
Gluten-Free Tortilla (p.178) or in the pocket of pita bread
with lettuce, relish and tomatoes (a snack that will not be
gluten-free).*

1 cup	Romano or white kidney beans	250 mL
2	cloves garlic, finely chopped	2
1/4 cup	packed fresh parsley OR 1 tbsp (15 mL) dried	50 mL
1/4 cup	packed fresh cilantro OR 1 tbsp (15 mL) dried	50 mL
2 tbsp	chopped onion	25 mL
1/2 tsp	ground cumin	2 mL
1/2 tsp	salt	2 mL
1/4 tsp	freshly ground black pepper	1 mL
1/4 tsp	baking soda	1 mL
	Canola oil	
	Sesame Cream Sauce (p.20)	

• In saucepan, combine beans and 4 cups (1 L) water. Bring to
boil over medium heat; boil for 3 minutes. Remove from heat
and set aside to soak for about 45 minutes or until beans are
soaked right through and fairly soft but still crunchy. Drain
well.

• In food processor, combine beans, garlic, parsley, cilantro,
onion, cumin, salt and pepper. Process, scraping down sides of
container several times, for 2 to 3 minutes or until texture of
ground almonds. Add baking soda; process for a few seconds
longer. With damp hands, form 1 tbsp (15 mL) bean mixture
at a time into patties.

• In non stick skillet, heat a few drops oil over medium heat.
Cook 6 to 8 patties at a time for about 5 minutes on each side
or until golden brown. Repeat with remaining patties, adding
one or two more drops oil to skillet, if necessary.

• Serve hot or cold with Sesame Cream Sauce.

Makes 8 servings, 24 patties.

GF

Each serving: 3 patties

1	▢	Starchy
1/2	▨	Protein

82	Calories
343	kilojoules
1 g	total fat
0 g	saturated fat
0 mg	cholesterol
5 g	protein
14 g	carbohydrate
135 mg	sodium
330 mg	potassium

GOOD: Iron, Magnesium
EXCELLENT: Folate

Sesame Cream Sauce

Make about 30 minutes before serving, since the texture improves on standing.

1/4 cup	lemon juice	50 mL
1/4 cup	water	50 mL
2 tbsp	tahini	25 mL
	Salt	
	Hot pepper sauce	

• In small bowl, whisk together lemon juice, water and tahini into thin creamy sauce. Season to taste with salt and hot pepper sauce.

Makes 1/2 cup (125 mL).

Black Bean Salsa

For a snappy low-calorie first course serve this fat-free concoction on lettuce-lined plates garnished with low-fat yogurt and a sprinkle of hard-cooked egg. For a buffet, place in a bowl surrounded by rice crackers or corn chips with a spoon to lift salsa onto crackers.

2 cups	cooked black beans	500 mL
2	tomatoes, seeded, diced and drained	2
2	green onions, thinly sliced	2
1	clove garlic, minced	1
1/3 cup	chopped fresh cilantro OR 2 tbsp (25 mL) dried	75 mL
2 tbsp	chopped red sweet pepper	25 mL
2 tbsp	chopped green sweet pepper	25 mL
1 tbsp	chopped pickled jalapeño pepper	15 mL
1 tbsp	balsamic vinegar	15 mL
Pinch	granulated sugar	Pinch
	Salt and freshly ground black pepper	

• In glass bowl, combine beans, tomatoes, green onions, garlic, cilantro, red, green and jalapeño peppers, vinegar and sugar; mix well. Season to taste with salt and black pepper.

• Let stand, stirring occasionally, for 1 hour, before serving.

Makes 12 servings, about 3 cups (750 mL).

Peanutty Bean Dip or Spread

Serve with crunchy corn chips or crisp veggies for dipping or spread on pieces of pita or soda crackers.

1 1/2 cups	cooked Romano or Dutch brown beans	375 mL
1/4 cup	smooth peanut butter	50 mL
2 tbsp	lemon juice	25 mL
1	clove garlic, finely chopped	1
1/2 tsp	salt	2 mL
6	drops hot pepper sauce	6
Pinch	granulated sugar	Pinch

• In food processor or blender, combine beans, peanut butter, lemon juice, garlic, salt, hot pepper sauce and sugar. Process, scraping down sides of container occasionally, for 2 to 3 minutes or until very smooth.

• Transfer to small dish or pot. Cover and refrigerate for up to 5 days or freeze for up to 3 months.

Makes 1 3/4 cups (425 mL).

Each serving: 2 tbsp (25 mL)

1/2 Fruits & Vegetables

43 calories
180 kilojoules
1 g total fat
0 g saturated fat
0 mg cholesterol
2 g protein
4 g carbohydrate
63 mg sodium
89 mg potassium

GOOD: Folate

Chili Dip

Serve with crisp raw vegetables or corn chips for a snappy starter or snack.

1 tsp	canola oil	5 mL
1	small onion, chopped	1
1	clove garlic, minced	1
1 1/2 tsp	chili powder	7 mL
1 tsp	ground cumin	5 mL
1 tbsp	tomato paste	15 mL
2 tsp	red wine vinegar	10 mL
2 cups	cooked red kidney, or Dutch brown beans	500 mL
1 cup	light cream cheese (250 g package)	250 mL
	Salt and freshly ground black pepper	

• In small nonstick skillet, heat oil over medium heat; cook onion and garlic for about 4 minutes or until onion is translucent. Stir in chili powder and cumin; cook for 1 minute. Stir in tomato paste and vinegar.

• In food processor or blender, combine beans, cream cheese and onion mixture. Process, scraping down sides of container occasionally, for about 2 minutes or until as smooth as mayonnaise. If too thick, add hot water, a little at a time, until desired consistency.

• Season to taste with salt and pepper.

• Transfer to small bowl or pot. Serve immediately or cover and refrigerate for up to 5 days or freeze for up to 4 months.

Makes about 3 cups (750 mL).

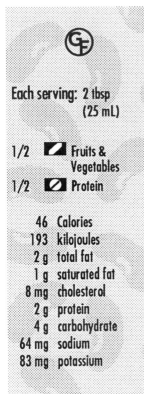

Each serving: 2 tbsp
(25 mL)

1/2 Fruits &
Vegetables
1/2 Protein

46 Calories
193 kilojoules
2 g total fat
1 g saturated fat
8 mg cholesterol
2 g protein
4 g carbohydrate
64 mg sodium
83 mg potassium

CREAMY SPINACH AND BEAN DIP

This dip proves how beautifully cooked beans can replace part of the cottage cheese, sour cream or yogurt usually called for in a dip recipe such as this one. The creamy quality of the more expensive dairy products is maintained, fat is reduced and fibre increased.

Half	pkg (10 oz/300 g) frozen chopped spinach	Half
1 cup	cooked white kidney beans	250 mL
1 cup	1% cottage cheese	250 mL
1	small clove garlic, halved	1
1 tsp	chopped onion	1
1/2 tsp	dried basil	2 mL
1/2 tsp	Worcestershire sauce	2 mL
Pinch	ground nutmeg	Pinch
	Salt and freshly ground black pepper	

• Squeeze excess moisture out of spinach. Set aside.

• In food processor or blender, process beans, cottage cheese, garlic, onion, basil, Worcestershire sauce and nutmeg, scraping down sides of container several times, for 2 to 3 minutes or until puréed. Add spinach; process until well mixed. Season to taste with salt and pepper.

• Transfer to bowl or container. Cover and refrigerate for at least 4 hours or up to 2 days.

Makes 2 cups, 10 servings.

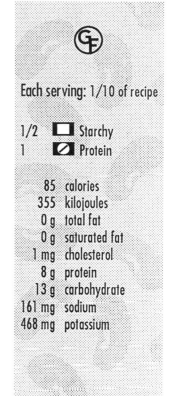

Each serving: 1/10 of recipe

1/2	☐	Starchy
1	☑	Protein

85	calories
355	kilojoules
0 g	total fat
0 g	saturated fat
1 mg	cholesterol
8 g	protein
13 g	carbohydrate
161 mg	sodium
468 mg	potassium

GOOD: Iron, Magnesium, Vitamin A

EXCELLENT: Folate

HIGH: Fibre

CHICKEN CRISPS

Move over meatballs, these could be your replacement at cocktail parties. They are great dipped in salsa.

Each serving: 2 crisps

1   Protein

60	calories
251	kilojoules
2 g	total fat
0 g	saturated fat
17 mg	cholesterol
7 g	protein
2 g	carbohydrate
174 mg	sodium
127 mg	potassium

GOOD: Niacin

2 tbsp	soft margarine OR butter	25 mL
1 tbsp	grated onion	15 mL
1/3 cup	whole bean flour	75 mL
1/2 tsp	salt	2 mL
Pinch	freshly ground black pepper	Pinch
1 cup	chicken broth	250 mL
1 tsp	Worcestershire sauce	5 mL
1 1/2 cups	ground cooked chicken OR turkey	375 mL
1 tbsp	chopped fresh parsley	15 mL

• In saucepan melt margarine over medium heat; cook onion for 1 minute. Stir in bean flour, salt and pepper until well mixed. Gradually add broth and Worcestershire sauce, stirring constantly; cook for about 4 minutes or until sauce is thick and smooth. Stir in chicken and parsley. Chill for 1 hour.

• Shape 1 tablespoonful (15 mL) at a time into small balls. Place 2 inches (5 cm) apart on nonstick baking sheet. With back of spoon, flatten to 1/4 inch (5 mm) thickness.

• Bake in 375°F (190°C) oven for 15 minutes or until golden.

Makes 12 servings, 24 crisps.

Ham and Cheese Puffs

These savory little ham and cheese-flecked buns disappear so quickly at parties it is smart to make a double batch to make sure you have enough. Freeze the extras, two in a package, to tuck in lunch boxes to go with salad, soup or Chili with Corn (p.96).

1/4 cup	whole bean flour	50 mL
1/4 cup	rice flour	50 mL
1/2 tsp	salt	2 mL
1/2 cup	water	125 mL
1/4 cup	soft margarine OR butter	50 mL
3	egg whites	3
1/2 cup	finely chopped cooked ham	125 mL
2 tbsp	grated Parmesan cheese	25 mL

• In small dish, stir together bean flour, rice flour and salt.

• In saucepan over medium high heat, bring water and margarine to rolling boil. Stir in flour all at once and continue stirring for about 30 seconds or until mixture leaves side of pan and forms a ball. Remove from heat.

• Beat in egg whites, one at a time, until thoroughly blended and mixture is smooth and velvety. Stir in ham and Parmesan cheese.

• Drop by heaping teaspoonfuls (5 mL) into 24 mounds about 1 inch (2.5 cm) apart on nonstick baking sheet.

• Bake in 375°F(190°C) oven for 25 minutes or until puffed and golden brown.

• Serve warm or at room temperature.

Makes 6 servings, 24 puffs.

Each serving: 4 puffs

1/2	□	Starchy
1	▨	Protein
1	▲	Fats & Oils

138	calories
576	kilojoules
8 g	total fat
1.8 g	saturated fat
6 mg	cholesterol
6 g	protein
8 g	carbohydrate
462 mg	sodium
128 mg	potassium

LAYERED APPETIZER PIE

Offer a tray of cucumber slices, red and green pepper squares and celery sticks for scooping up a portion of each of the layers for a serving. Rice crackers and corn chips are also just right for the job.

2 cups	Refried Beans, (p.144)	500 mL
1 cup	light sour cream	250 mL
1 tbsp	chopped pickled jalapeño pepper	15 mL
1	ripe avocado, peeled	1
1 tbsp	chopped fresh cilantro OR 1 tsp (5 mL) dried	15 mL
1 tbsp	light mayonnaise	15 mL
1 tbsp	lime juice	15 mL
1/2 cup	chopped pitted black olives	125 mL
6	green onions, thinly sliced	6
2	tomatoes, seeded and chopped	2
3/4 cup	shredded Cheddar OR Monterey Jack cheese	175 mL
72	Crisp Corn and Bean Chips (p.178)	72

• In bowl, stir together refried beans, 2 tbsp (25 mL) light sour cream and jalapeño peppers until well blended. Spread in 9-inch (23 cm) pie plate or quiche dish.

• In bowl, mash together avocado, cilantro, mayonnaise and lime juice; spread over bean layer.

• Beat remaining light sour cream until creamy. Spread over avocado layer right to edge of plate.

• Garnish top with concentric circles or diagonal stripes of black olives, green onions, tomatoes and cheese.

Makes 12 servings.

Tortilla Bean Pinwheels

Use make-your-own Gluten-Free Tortillas (p.178) rather than store-bought flour tortillas, if you wish, to make these hors d'oeuvres gluten-free .

1 cup	cooked kidney beans	250 mL
2 tsp	molasses	10 mL
1 tsp	chili powder	5 mL
1 tsp	Dijon mustard	5 mL
Pinch	freshly ground black pepper	Pinch
3	8-inch (20 cm) tortillas	3
1/2 cup	light cream cheese	125 mL
4	green onions, thinly sliced	4

• In small bowl or food processor, mash together or process beans, molasses, chili powder, mustard and pepper until smooth.

• Spread each tortilla with one-third of the cream cheese. Spread bean mixture over cheese. Sprinkle with green onions.

• Roll up each tortilla, jelly-roll fashion, to make a log. Trim thin ends from each roll. Wrap snugly in plastic wrap or waxed paper. Refrigerate for at least 3 hours or up to 24 hours.

• At serving time, cut into slices about 1/2 inch (1 cm) thick.

Makes 9 servings, 36 pinwheels.

Each serving: 4 pinwheels

1/2 ☐ Starchy
1/2 ◪ Protein

82	calories
342	kilojoules
1 g	total fat
0 g	saturated fat
8 mg	cholesterol
2 g	protein
10 g	carbohydrate
102 mg	sodium
144 mg	potassium

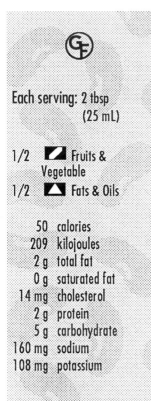

Each serving: 2 tbsp
(25 mL)

1/2 Fruits &
Vegetable
1/2 Fats & Oils

50 calories
209 kilojoules
2 g total fat
0 g saturated fat
14 mg cholesterol
2 g protein
5 g carbohydrate
160 mg sodium
108 mg potassium

BEAN AND PECAN PATÉ

Nuts, mushrooms and beans are a team in this low-calorie curry-scented paté. Serve it surrounded by rice crackers and Seed and Nut Crackers (p.153). Place a small knife on the side for spreading the paté.

1 tsp	canola oil	5 mL
1	medium onion, diced	1
1/3 cup	chopped pecans or walnuts	75 mL
8	medium mushrooms, chopped	8
1 tsp	curry powder	5 mL
1 tsp	salt	5 mL
1/4 tsp	freshly ground black pepper	1 mL
1 1/2 cups	cooked Romano or kidney beans	375 mL
1	hard-cooked egg	1
2 tbsp	dry red wine	25 mL
Pinch	granulated sugar	Pinch
	Chopped chives or green onions	

• In nonstick skillet, heat oil over medium heat; cook onion and pecans, stirring occasionally, for about 5 minutes or until onion is translucent and pecans toasted.

• Stir in mushrooms; cook for about 4 minutes longer or until liquid from mushrooms evaporates. Stir in curry powder, salt and pepper; cook for 1 minute longer.

• Transfer to food processor fitted with metal blade. Add beans, hard-cooked egg, wine and sugar. Process, scraping down sides of container several times, for 2 to 3 minutes or until nearly smooth.

• Pack into serving dish container. Cover and refrigerate for up to 3 days. At serving time, garnish with chives.

Makes 1 1/2 cups (375 mL).

SOUPS

Camper's Six-Bean Soup

Camper's Six-Bean Soup Mix

Bacon and Bean Soup

Classic Black Bean Soup

Mixed Vegetable Bean Soup

Creamy Broccoli & Bean Soup

Cream of Mushroom & Bean Soup

Corn and Bean Chowder

Oxtail Bean Soup

Mexican Vegetable, Beef and Bean Soup

Chicken, Rice and Bean Soup

Hearty Bean Hot Pot

Country Cabbage & Bean Soup

Island Bean Soup

Minestrone

Pistou

Paste e Fagioli

Spanish Bean Soup with Garlic and Mint

Hungarian Bean Soup

Greek Bean Soup (Fassoulada)

Light Black Bean Soup with Cheese

Tomato, Spinach & Bean Soup

Harvest Squash & Bean Soup

Country-Style Bean Soup

CAMPER'S SIX-BEAN SOUP

Dried beans are much lighter than canned ones to carry in a backpack. A bag of this easy-to-prepare soup weighs in at about a pound (500 g) and has enough in it for a great nutritious bean feast.

| 1 | bag Camper's Six-Bean Soup Mix (below) | 1 |
| 8 cups | water | 2 L |

• Remove bag of seasoning from soup mix; set aside.

• Rinse bean mixture. Add to large heavy soup kettle; stir in water. Bring to boil over campfire, grill or burner; reduce heat and simmer, covered and stirring occasionally, for 30 minutes or until beans are almost tender.

• Stir in seasonings; simmer, stirring frequently and adding more water as liquid evaporates, for 45 to 60 minutes or until beans are tender. (Some of them will be mushy and thicken the soup.)

Makes 8 servings, about 8 cups (2 L).

CAMPER'S SIX-BEAN SOUP MIX

2 cups	each dried white, red and dark red kidney, black, yellow-eyed and Romano beans	500 mL
1 1/2 cups	millet OR long grain rice	375 mL
1/4 cup	chili powder	50 mL
2 tbsp	each dried basil and parsley	25 mL
1 tbsp	each ground thyme, marjoram and sage	15 mL
1 tbsp	ground celery seed	15 mL
1 tbsp	dehydrated granulated garlic	15 mL
1 tsp	freshly ground black pepper	5 mL
1 tsp	crushed red chili pepper	5 mL
1 1/2 cups	chopped sun-dried tomatoes	375 mL
1 1/2 cups	dehydrated chopped onions	375 mL
2 tbsp	salt	25 mL
1 tbsp	granulated sugar	15 mL
6	bay leaves	6

• In large bowl, thoroughly mix white, red and dark red kidney, black, yellow-eyed and Romano beans. Measure 2 cups (500 mL) into each of six plastic storage bags. Add 1/4 cup (50 mL) millet to each bag.

• In small processor or mortar with pestle, combine chili powder, basil, parsley, thyme, marjoram, sage, celery seed, garlic, black and red pepper. Process or grind until well blended. Divide evenly among 6 small plastic bags. To each one, add 1/4 cup (50 mL) each tomatoes and onions, 1 tsp (5 mL) salt, 1/2 tsp (2 mL) sugar and 1 bay leaf, crumbled. Close and seal bags.

• Tuck 1 bag of seasonings into each bag of beans. Seal, label and store in dry place.

Makes 6 bags, each enough for 8 servings.

BACON AND BEAN SOUP

The tantalizing flavor of this compatible combination certainly jump starts the appetite when it is served as the starter of a meal.

3	slices side bacon, cut into strips	3
1	carrot, finely chopped	1
2 cups	cooked Romano, kidney or Dutch brown beans	500 mL
2 cups	chicken stock	500 mL
2 cups	water	500 mL
1	bay leaf	1
	salt and freshly ground pepper	

• In saucepan, cook bacon over medium heat for about 7 minutes or until just crisp. Drain away all drippings.

• Add carrot, beans, stock, water and bay leaf; bring to boil. Reduce heat and simmer, partly covered, for 20 minutes or until carrot is tender. Discard bay leaf. Season to taste with salt, if desired, and pepper.

Makes 4 servings, about 4 cups (1 L).

Each serving: 1/4 of recipe

1	☐ Starchy	
1 1/2	⊘ Protein	

186	calories
779	kilojoules
4 g	total fat
1 g	saturated fat
3 mg	cholesterol
14 g	protein
23 g	carbohydrate
424 mg	sodium
539 mg	potassium

GOOD: Phosphorus, Iron, Zinc, Magnesium, Vitamin B12

EXCELLENT: Vitamin A, Niacin, Folate

VERY HIGH: Fibre

CLASSIC BLACK BEAN SOUP

This lighthearted rendition of a classic from the American south is made with no added fat. The smidgen of fat mentioned comes from the low-fat yogurt garnish.

3 cups	cooked black beans	750 mL
2 cups	strong vegetable OR beef stock	500 mL
1	can (14 oz/398 mL) tomato sauce	1
2	cloves garlic, minced	2
1	onion, chopped	1
1	stalk celery, chopped	1
1	bay leaf	1
1/2 tsp	each ground thyme, cumin and oregano	2 mL
1/4 tsp	freshly ground black pepper	1 mL
6	drops hot pepper sauce	6
2 tsp	lemon juice	10 mL
1 tsp	brown sugar	5 mL
	Salt	
1/4 cup	low-fat yogurt	50 mL
6	thin slices lemon	6

• In large heavy saucepan, combine beans, stock, tomato sauce, garlic, onion, celery, bay leaf, thyme, cumin, oregano, pepper and hot pepper sauce; bring to boil over medium heat.

• Reduce heat and simmer, covered, for 45 minutes or until vegetables are tender.

• Discard bay leaf. Stir in lemon juice and brown sugar.

• In batches, transfer to container of food processor or blender; puree until smooth. Return to saucepan and heat through. Season to taste with salt, if desired.

• Ladle into warm soup bowls. Garnish with yogurt and lemon slices.

Makes 6 servings, about 6 cups (1.5 L).

Colored Bean Varieties: *(from top to bottom)*
Romano (cranberry), dark red kidney, white kidney,
Dutch brown, black (turtle), yellow eye and red kidney beans.

MIXED VEGETABLE BEAN SOUP

Beans, assorted vegetables, rice and good stock are what great colorful soups are made of and this one proves that is true.

1 cup	dried white or red kidney beans or other colored beans, soaked (p.12)	250 mL
6 cups	chicken or beef stock	1.5 L
3	strips side bacon, cut into 1/2 inch (1 cm) pieces	3
1	onion, coarsely chopped	1
1	clove garlic, minced	1
1	stalk celery, diced	1
1/2 cup	dry red wine	125 mL
1	carrot, diced	1
1	scrubbed potato, diced	1
1	tomato, peeled and coarsely chopped	1
1 cup	diced peeled rutabaga OR white turnip	250 mL
1 cup	shredded cabbage	250 mL
1 tsp	chopped fresh thyme OR 1/4 tsp (1 mL) dried	5 mL
1/2 tsp	freshly ground black pepper	2 mL
1/3 cup	long-grain rice	75 mL
1/4 cup	chopped fresh parsley	50 mL
1/2 cup	low-fat yogurt	125 mL

• Drain and rinse soaked beans.

• In large soup kettle or Dutch oven, combine beans and 8 cups (2L) water; bring to boil. Reduce heat and simmer, partly covered, for 40 minutes or until tender. Drain and rinse. Pour stock over beans.

• In skillet, cook bacon over medium heat until just crisp. Drain on paper towels. Remove all but 1 tsp (5 mL) drippings from pan; cook onion, garlic and celery for 5 minutes or until onion is translucent. Add to beans.

• Pour wine into skillet; deglaze skillet by stirring to scrape up any brown bits. Pour into bean mixture.

• Add carrot, potato, tomato, rutabaga, cabbage, thyme and pepper; bring to boil. Reduce heat and simmer, partly covered and stirring once or twice, for 40 minutes.

• Stir in rice; simmer for 20 minutes longer or until rice is tender. Stir in parsley.

. Ladle into warm soup bowls; garnish each with yogurt.

Makes 8 servings, about 8 cups (2 L).

EACH SERVING: 1/8 of recipe

1	☐	Starchy
1/2	◪	Fruits & Vegetables
1	⊘	Protein
1	✛	Extras

200	Calories
837	kilojoules
2 g	total fat
0 g	saturated fat
1 mg	cholesterol
11 g	protein
29 g	carbohydrate
639 mg	sodium
708 mg	potassium

GOOD: Phosphorus, Iron, Magnesium, Niacin

EXCELLENT: Vitamin A, Folate

VERY HIGH: Fibre

CREAMY BROCCOLI & BEAN SOUP

This low-calorie, fat-free, easy-to-prepare soup makes a great warming winter soup. It also is a super chilled soup for warm days especially when the nutmeg is doubled.

2 cups	chopped broccoli	500 mL
1 1/2 cups	cooked Romano or white kidney beans	375 mL
1	stalk celery, finely chopped	1
1	leek (white part only) OR small onion, thinly sliced	1
1	bay leaf	1
2 cups	chicken stock	500 mL
1/4 tsp	ground nutmeg	1 mL
1 cup	skim milk	250 mL
	Salt and white pepper	
2 tbsp	low-fat yogurt OR light sour cream	25 mL
	Paprika	

• In large saucepan, combine broccoli, beans, celery, leek, bay leaf and chicken stock; bring to boil. Reduce heat and simmer, covered, for 15 minutes or until broccoli is tender. Discard bay leaf.

• Transfer half of mixture to blender or food processor; add nutmeg. Process until smooth. Pour into clean saucepan. Puree remaining bean mixture; add to saucepan. Stir in milk. Season to taste with salt and white pepper. Heat just to simmering.

• Ladle into warm soup bowls OR refrigerate for at least 3 hours and serve chilled.

• Garnish each bowlful with dollop of yogurt (about 1 tsp / 5 mL total) and sprinkle of paprika. With tip of knife, cut through yogurt to create swirls.

Makes 6 servings, about 6 cups (1.5 L).

Each serving: 1/6 of recipe

1/2		Starchy
1		Protein
1		Extras

97	calories
406	kilojoules
0 g	total fat
0 g	saturated fat
0 mg	cholesterol
8 g	protein
15 g	carbohydrate
293 mg	sodium
407 mg	potassium

GOOD: Vitamin C
EXCELLENT: Folate
HIGH: Fibre

CREAM OF MUSHROOM & BEAN SOUP

Add a green mixed vegetable salad and a square of cornbread to make a satisfying soup and salad meal.

1 tsp	butter or soft margarine	5 mL
1/4 cup	finely chopped onion	50 mL
1/2 lb	mushrooms, halved and thinly sliced	250 g
1/2 tsp	salt	2 mL
1/4 tsp	white pepper	1 mL
2 cups	chicken stock	500 mL
1 cup	cooked white kidney or Romano beans	250 mL
1/2 cup	milk	125 mL
2 tbsp	cornstarch OR arrowroot flour	25 mL
	Chopped fresh chives OR parsley	

• In large saucepan, heat butter over medium heat; cook onion and mushrooms, stirring occasionally, for about 7 minutes or until liquid from mushrooms has nearly disappeared. Season with salt and pepper.

• Stir in stock and beans; bring to boil. Reduce heat and simmer, partly covered, for about 10 minutes or until beans are heated through.

• Stir cornstarch into milk until smooth. Add to mushroom mixture and cook, stirrring constantly, until thickened.

• Serve immediately in warm soup bowls. Garnish with sprinkling of chives.

Makes 4 servings, about 4 cups (1 L).

Each serving: 1/4 of recipe

2 □ Starchy
1 1/2 ⊘ Protein

224	calories
938	kilojoules
2 g	total fat
1 g	saturated fat
4 mg	cholesterol
16 g	protein
36 g	carbohydrate
613 mg	sodium
962 mg	potassium

GOOD: Zinc

EXCELLENT: Phosphorus, Iron, Magnesium, Vitamin D, Riboflavin, Niacin, Folate

VERY HIGH: Fibre

CORN AND BEAN CHOWDER

For the testers this was a hands-down favorite. Using pre-cooked beans, canned ones, if you wish, it takes only about 20 minutes to prepare and ladle into bowls.

2	slices side bacon	2
1	onion, finely chopped	1
1	stalk celery, thinly sliced	1
1	can (19 oz/540 mL) cream-style corn	1
1 cup	cooked Romano, Dutch brown or white kidney beans, mashed	250 mL
2 cups	skim milk	500 mL
1/2 tsp	salt	2 mL
1/4 tsp	white pepper	1 mL
Pinch	ground nutmeg	Pinch
	chopped chives	

• In large saucepan over medium heat, cook bacon until crisp. Drain on paper towels; crumble and set aside. Remove all but 1 tsp (5 mL) drippings from saucepan.

• Add onion and celery; cook, stirring occasionally, for 5 minutes or until onion is translucent.

• Stir in corn, mashed beans, milk, salt, white pepper and nutmeg; bring to boil. Reduce heat and simmer, uncovered, for 5 minutes or until thoroughly heated.

• Ladle into warm soup bowls. Garnish with crumbled bacon and chives.

Makes 6 servings, about 6 cups (1.5 L).

OXTAIL BEAN SOUP

Here is a soup to satisfy hearty appetites. Add a crunchy salad and warm bread to have a great meal.

2 cups	mixed dried colored beans, washed	500 mL
12 cups	water	3 L
1 lb	lean oxtail, cut in pieces	500 g
2	onions, chopped	2
1 cup	chopped celery	250 mL
1 cup	finely chopped carrots	250 mL
1 cup	finely chopped turnip (rutabaga)	250 mL
1 tsp	salt	5 mL
1/2 tsp	dry mustard	2 mL
1/2 tsp	ground thyme	2 mL
1/4 tsp	freshly ground black pepper	1 mL
	Chopped fresh parsley	

• In large soup kettle or Dutch oven, combine beans, water, oxtail and onions; bring to boil. Reduce heat and simmer, covered, for 1 1/2 to 2 hours or until beans are tender enough to be mashed with a spoon. With large spoon, skim off and discard any foam.

• Remove oxtail. Cut meat from bone; dice meat and discard bones. Set aside.

• With potato masher or large spoon, mash beans in kettle. Add reserved meat, celery, carrots, turnip, salt, mustard, thyme and pepper. Simmer, partly covered, for 20 minutes or until vegetables are tender.

• Ladle into warm soup bowls. Garnish with parsley.

Makes 8 servings, about 8 cups (2 L).

Each serving: 1/8 of recipe

2	☐	Starchy
2	▨	Protein
1 1/2	▲	Fats & Oils
1	➕	Extras

332 calories
1390 kilojoules
13 g total fat
5 g saturated fat
25 mg cholesterol
18 g protein
34 g carbohydrate
335 mg sodium
1035 mg potassium

GOOD: Phosphorus, Niacin, Vitamin B₆

EXCELLENT: Iron, Zinc, Magnesium, Vitamin A, Folate, Vitamin B₁₂

MODERATE: Fibre

Mexican Vegetable, Beef and Bean Soup

Another name for this meal-in-a-bowl could be "Chili Bean Soup". It is chock full of the same foods that give chili its characteristic Mexican taste and good-for-you nutrients.

1/2 lb	lean ground beef	250 g
1 cup	chopped onions	250 mL
1	clove garlic, minced	1
2 tsp	chili powder	10 mL
1/2 tsp	salt	2 mL
1/4 tsp	freshly ground black pepper	1 mL
1	can (19 oz/540 mL) tomatoes	1
2 cups	beef stock	500 mL
1 cup	diced carrots	250 mL
1 cup	diced celery	250 mL
1	can (7 oz/199 mL) kernel corn	1
2 cups	cooked red kidney beans	500 mL
1	small green sweet pepper, finely chopped	1
6 tbsp	shredded Cheddar cheese	90 mL
	Chopped fresh cilantro or parsley	

• In large saucepan, cook ground beef, onions and garlic over medium heat, stirring to break up meat, for 7 to 10 minutes or until beef is no longer pink and onion is translucent. Spoon off any fat. Stir in chili powder, salt and pepper. Cook for 1 minute longer.

• Stir in tomatoes, stock, carrots, celery, corn and beans; bring to boil, breaking up tomatoes with fork. Reduce heat and simmer, partly covered, for 30 minutes or until carrots are soft.

• Stir in green pepper. Ladle into warm soup bowls. Garnish with sprinkling of cheese and cilantro.

Makes 6 servings, 6 cups (1.5 L).

CHICKEN, RICE AND BEAN SOUP

This is a great make-ahead soup to feed a crowd. It can be refrigerated in covered containers for up to four days or frozen for up to two months.

6 cups	strong chicken stock	1.5 L
2 cups	water	500 mL
2	stalks celery, diced	2
1	onion, finely chopped	1
1	carrot, diced	1
1	can (19 oz/540 mL) tomatoes	1
1/2 cup	long-grain rice	125 mL
1 tsp	Worcestershire sauce	5 mL
1/4 tsp	freshly ground black pepper	1 mL
1 tbsp	chopped mixed fresh herbs (parsley, thyme, oregano and basil) OR 1 tsp (5 mL) dried herbs	15 mL
1 cup	diced cooked chicken	250 mL
1 1/2 cups	cooked white kidney or Dutch brown beans	375 mL
	Salt	

• In large soup kettle or Dutch oven, combine chicken stock, water, celery, onion, carrot, tomatoes, breaking up tomatoes with fork, rice, Worcestershire sauce and pepper; bring to boil.

• Reduce heat and simmer, covered, for 15 minutes or until rice is nearly tender.

• Stir in herbs, chicken and beans; simmer, uncovered, for 10 minutes or until heated through. Season to taste with salt, if desired.

Makes 10 servings, 10 cups (2.5 L).

Each serving: 1/10 of recipe

1	▢	Starchy
2	◪	Protein
1	⊞	Extras

166 calories
695 kilojoules
2 g total fat
0 g saturated fat
21 mg cholesterol
15 g protein
19 g carbohydrate
750 mg sodium
512 mg potassium

GOOD: Phosphorus, Iron, Magnesium, Vitamin A, Folate, Vitamin B6
EXCELLENT: Niacin
MODERATE: Fibre

HEARTY BEAN HOT POT

Hearty soups like this one make substantial one-pot meals. The fresh garnishes add a wonderful finishing touch.

3 cups	dried white kidney, Romano or Dutch brown beans, soaked (p.12)	750 mL
1	leftover ham bone with meat OR smoked ham hock (1 3/4 lb/875 g)	1
3	onions, chopped	3
3	carrots, chopped	3
2	stalks celery, chopped	2
2	cloves garlic, minced	2
1	bay leaf	1
1/2 tsp	freshly ground black pepper	2 mL
1/2 tsp	ground cloves	2 mL
1/2 cup	dry white wine	125 mL

GARNISH:

1 cup	finely chopped celery	250 mL
1 cup	finely chopped green OR red sweet pepper	250 mL
1 cup	finely chopped mushrooms	250 mL
1 cup	light sour cream	250 mL

• In large soup kettle or Dutch oven, combine beans, ham bone, onions, carrots, celery, garlic, bay leaf, pepper and cloves. Pour in 10 cups (2.5 L) water; bring to boil. Reduce heat and simmer, uncovered, for 1 1/2 hours or until beans are tender.

• Remove hambone. Cut meat from bone; dice meat to make about 2 cups (500 mL) and set aside. Discard bone and bay leaf. If desired, puree in batches; return to pan. Add reserved ham; bring to simmer. Stir in wine.

• Garnish: Ladle into warm soup bowls. Pass celery, green pepper, mushrooms and sour cream in separate small bowls for individuals to sprinkle over their soup.

Makes 10 servings, about 10 cups (2.5 L).

Each serving: 1/10 of recipe

1 1/2 ☐ Starchy
4 ∅ Protein
1 ✚✚ Extras

314	calories
1315	kilojoules
5 g	total fat
1 g	saturated fat
45 mg	cholesterol
31 g	protein
32 g	carbohydrate
801 mg	sodium
1030 mg	potassium

GOOD: Riboflavin, Vitamin C
EXCELLENT: Phosphorus, Iron, Zinc, Magnesium, Vitamin A, Thiamin, Niacin, Folate, Vitamin B$_6$, Vitamin B$_{12}$

VERY HIGH: Fibre

COUNTRY CABBAGE & BEAN SOUP

Keep this soup in the refrigerator for up to three days to reheat at a moment's notice. It can also be frozen for up to two months.

1 1/2 cups	dried Romano or Dutch brown beans, soaked (p.12)	375 mL
8 cups	water	2 L
2 cups	beef stock	500 mL
1/4 lb	cooked smoked sausage, cubed	125 g
4 cups	coarsely chopped cabbage	1 L
2	potatoes, peeled and chopped	2
1	onion, coarsely chopped	1
1/4 tsp	freshly ground black pepper	1 mL
2 tsp	olive oil	10 mL
1 tsp	paprika	5 mL
	Salt	
Pinch	cayenne	Pinch
2 tbsp	chopped fresh chives OR 2 tsp (10 mL) dried	25 mL
2	tomatoes, seeded and finely chopped	2

• Drain and rinse soaked beans.

• In soup kettle or Dutch oven, combine beans, water, stock, sausage, cabbage, potatoes, onion and pepper; bring to boil. Reduce heat and simmer, covered, stirring occasionally, for 1 1/2 hours or until beans are tender and vegetables very soft.

• Stir in olive oil and paprika; season to taste with salt, if desired, and cayenne. Simmer for 10 minutes longer.

• Stir in chives. Ladle into warm soup bowls. Garnish each with 1 tbsp (15 mL) chopped tomato.

Makes 10 servings, about 10 cups (2.5 L).

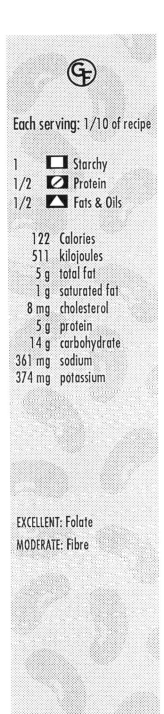

Each serving: 1/10 of recipe

1 ☐ Starchy
1/2 ∅ Protein
1/2 ▲ Fats & Oils

122 Calories
511 kilojoules
5 g total fat
1 g saturated fat
8 mg cholesterol
5 g protein
14 g carbohydrate
361 mg sodium
374 mg potassium

EXCELLENT: Folate
MODERATE: Fibre

ISLAND BEAN SOUP

Cans of coconut cream are available at specialty food stores that stock foods from the West Indies. Keep several on hand to make this great soup typical of that part of our world.

2 cups	mixed dried colored beans, washed	500 mL
10 cups	water	2.5 L
1	medium smoked ham hock (1/2 lb/ 250 g)	1
1	bay leaf	1
3	stalks celery, diced	3
1	potato, peeled and diced	1
1	onion, chopped	1
1	clove garlic, minced	1
1	can (19 oz/540 mL) tomatoes	1
1	can (5 1/2 oz/156 mL) tomato paste	1
1	can (3 1/2 oz/100 g) coconut cream	1
1 tsp	ground sage	5 mL
1/2 tsp	dried basil	2 mL
1/4 tsp	freshly ground black pepper	1
Pinch	each crushed red chili pepper, ground oregano and ground ginger	Pinch
1	small green sweet pepper, chopped	1

• In large soup kettle or Dutch oven, bring beans, water, ham hock and bay leaf to boil; cook for 10 minutes. Reduce heat and simmer, covered, for about 1 1/4 hours or until beans are tender enough to be mashed with a spoon. Skim off any foam.

• Remove ham hock. Cut meat from bone; dice meat and discard bone.

• Add meat, celery, potato, onion, garlic, tomatoes, tomato paste, coconut cream, sage, basil, pepper, chili pepper, oregano and ginger to beans. Stir well, breaking up tomatoes with fork.

• Cook, partly covered, stirring occasionally, for 25 minutes or until vegetables are tender. Discard bay leaf.

• Ladle into warm soup bowls. Garnish with green pepper.

Makes 8 servings, about 8 cups (2 L).

MINESTRONE

Perfect for a crowd, this minestrone keeps well in the refrigerator for four days or in the freezer for up to two months. Make gluten-free ⊕ by using gluten-free macaroni.

2 tsp	olive oil	10 mL
1/4 lb	salt pork or side bacon, cubed	125 g
2	cloves garlic, minced	2
1	Spanish onion, coarsely chopped	1
4 cups	beef stock	1 L
3	carrots, thinly sliced	3
3	stalks celery, thinly sliced	3
2 cups	shredded cabbage	500 mL
1	potato, cubed	1
1	can (19 oz/540 mL) Italian plum tomatoes	1
2 cups	cooked red kidney beans	500 mL
1 cup	macaroni	250 mL
1 cup	frozen peas	250 mL
2 tbsp	chopped fresh parsley OR 2 tsp (10 mL) dried	25 mL
1 tbsp	chopped fresh basil OR 1 tsp (5 mL) dried	15 mL
1 tsp	salt	5 mL
1/2 tsp	each dried oregano and thyme	2 mL
1/4 tsp	freshly ground black pepper	1 mL
1/3 cup	grated Parmesan cheese	75 mL

• In large soup kettle or Dutch oven, heat oil over medium heat; cook salt pork until golden. Drain well on paper towels.

• Remove all but 1 tsp (5 mL) drippings from kettle. Cook garlic and onion, stirring occasionally, for 5 minutes or until translucent.

• Stir in stock, carrots, celery, cabbage, potato, beans and tomatoes, breaking tomatoes up with fork; bring to boil. Reduce heat, cover and simmer for 30 minutes or until potatoes are tender.

• Add macaroni, peas, parsley, basil, salt, oregano, thyme and pepper. Simmer for 15 minutes or until macaroni is al dente, tender but still firm.

• Ladle into warm soup bowls; top each with 1 tsp (5 mL) Parmesan cheese.

Makes 15 servings, about 15 cups (3.75 L).

PISTOU

Compared to traditional pesto the one created for this pistou is low-fat but its flavor is still lively.

1 tsp	olive oil	5 mL
1	onion, finely chopped	1
1	stalk celery, thinly sliced	1
1	potato, peeled and diced	1
1	medium zucchini, diced	1
1 lb	tomatoes, skinned and chopped	500 g
2 cups	cooked white kidney or Dutch brown beans	500 mL
4 cups	vegetable stock OR water	1 L
1/4 tsp	freshly ground black pepper	1 mL
1/2 lb	green beans, cut into 1 inch (2.5 cm) pieces	250 g
1 cup	broken vermicelli	250 mL
	Salt	
1 tbsp	chopped fresh parsley	15 mL
Pesto:		
2	cloves garlic	2
1 cup	coarsely chopped fresh basil OR 3/4 cup (175 mL) chopped fresh parsley with 1 tbsp (15 mL) dried sweet basil	250 mL
2 tbsp	pine nuts or walnuts	25 mL
1/4 cup	olive oil	50 mL
1/4 cup	grated Parmesan cheese	50 mL

• In large saucepan or soup kettle, heat oil over medium heat. Cook onion and celery for 5 minutes or until onion is tender.

• Add potato, zucchini, tomatoes, kidney beans, stock and pepper. Bring to boil, reduce heat and simmer, partly covered, for 20 minutes.

• Add vermicelli and green beans. Continue cooking for 15 minutes or until vermicelli and green beans are tender. Season to taste with salt, if desired. Stir in parsley.

• Pesto: While soup is simmering. in food processor or blender, combine garlic, basil, pine nuts, olive oil and Parmesan cheese. Process, stopping and scraping down container several times, for 3 to 4 minutes or until mixture is smooth. (This pesto is low-fat and thicker than those using more oil.) Store in covered jar or bowl in refrigerator until serving time.

• Stir 1/6 of Pesto (about 1 tbsp/15 mL) into each bowl of soup.

Makes 6 servings, about 6 cups (1.5L).

Pasta e Fagioli
(Bean and Pasta Soup)

In this low-fat, high-fibre version of the popular Italin soup the pasta and beans complement each other and provide complete protein. For a gluten-free 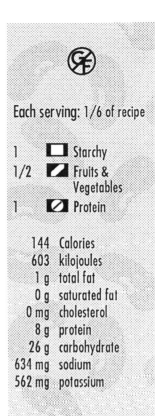 *variation use rice or gluten-free pasta.*

1 tsp	canola oil	5 mL
2 cups	thinly sliced celery OR diced zucchini	500 mL
2	cloves garlic, minced	2
1	onion, chopped	1
2 cups	beef OR vegetable stock	500 mL
1	can (7 1/2 oz/213 mL) tomato sauce	1
2 cups	cooked white kidney or Romano beans	500 mL
1 cup	water	250 mL
1/2 cup	macaroni	125 mL
1/2 tsp	salt	2 mL
1/4 tsp	freshly ground black pepper	1 mL

• In large saucepan, heat oil over medium heat. Cook celery, garlic and onion, stirring occasionally, for about 7 minutes or until onion is translucent.

• Add stock, tomato sauce, beans and water; bring to boil. Reduce heat and simmer, partly covered, for 15 minutes for flavors to blend.

• Stir in macaroni, salt and pepper; simmer for 15 minutes or until macaroni is tender. Season to taste with more salt and pepper, if desired.

Makes 6 servings, about 6 cups (1.5 L).

Each serving: 1/6 of recipe

1	☐ Starchy
1/2	◪ Fruits & Vegetables
1	◨ Protein

144 Calories
603 kilojoules
1 g total fat
0 g saturated fat
0 mg cholesterol
8 g protein
26 g carbohydrate
634 mg sodium
562 mg potassium

GOOD: Iron, Magnesium
EXCELLENT: Folate
VERY HIGH: Fibre

Spanish Bean Soup with Garlic and Mint

Four out of five tasters liked this herb-scented soup better cold than hot. And, it is best in the summer when mint flourishes in herb gardens everywhere.

2 tbsp	olive oil	25 mL
2	cloves garlic, minced	2
2 cups	cooked kidney or Romano beans	500 mL
2 1/2 cups	chicken OR vegetable stock	625 mL
1/2 tsp	salt	2 mL
4	drops hot pepper sauce	4
1 cup	fresh mint leaves OR 1/3 cup (75 mL) dried	250 mL
1/2 cup	fresh parsley sprigs OR 1/4 cup (50 mL) dried	125 mL
1	rice cake, broken into 12 pieces	1

• In large saucepan, heat oil over medium heat; cook garlic for 2 minutes to release flavor.

• Add beans, stock, salt and hot pepper sauce; bring to boil. Reduce heat and simmer, uncovered, for 15 minutes or until beans are tender. Stir in mint and parsley.

• Transfer to food processor or blender; process for 2 to 3 minutes or until pureed. Return to saucepan and bring to simmer.

• Ladle into warm soup bowls to serve hot OR refrigerate for at least 3 hours and serve chilled.

• Garnish each bowlful with 3 pieces of rice cake.

Makes 4 servings, about 4cups (1 L).

HUNGARIAN BEAN SOUP

It is the paprika that is indispensable in this Hungarian-style soup which is a light, low-fat rendition of goulash. The beans replace most of the meat called for in traditional goulash recipes.

1 tsp	canola oil	5 mL
1	onion, coarsely chopped	1
1	clove garlic, minced	1
2 tbsp	Hungarian paprika	25 mL
2 cups	chicken stock	500 mL
2 cups	cooked red kidney or Dutch brown beans, mashed	500 mL
1/4 lb	smoked sausage, ham or pepperoni, diced	125 g
1/2 tsp	salt	2 mL
1/4 tsp	freshly ground black pepper	1 mL
1/4 cup	low-fat yogurt	50 mL
1	green onion, thinly sliced	1

• In large saucepan, heat oil over medium heat; cook onion and garlic, stirring occasionally, for 4 minutes or until onion is nearly translucent. Stir in paprika; cook for 1 minute longer. Stir in stock and bring to boil; boil for 1 minute.

• Add mashed beans and sausage; return to boil. Season with salt and pepper. Reduce heat and simmer, covered, for 45 minutes or until flavors are well blended.

• Just before serving, blend in yogurt. Ladle into warm soup bowls. Garnish with green onion.

Makes 4 servings, about 4 cups (1 L).

GF

Each serving: 1/4 of recipe

1 ☐ Starchy
2 ∅ Protein
1 ➕ Extras

203	Calories
850	kilojoules
5 g	total fat
1 g	saturated fat
7 mg	cholesterol
14 g	protein
25 g	carbohydrate
829 mg	sodium
614 mg	potassium

GOOD: Phosphorus, Zinc, Magnesium, Vitamin A, Thiamin, Niacin, Vitamin B$_{12}$

EXCELLENT: Iron, Folate
VERY HIGH : Fibre

FASSOULADA
(GREEK BEAN SOUP)

Bean cookery draws from cuisines all around the world. This soup originated in Greece. Its flavor virtually sings with fresh notes of lemon and garlic and it is fabulous.

2 cups	cooked Romano or white kidney beans	500 mL
2 cups	chicken stock	500 mL
3	cloves garlic, minced	3
1/4 cup	lemon juice	50 mL
2 tsp	olive oil	10 mL
	Salt and white pepper	
	Lemon zest	

• In large saucepan, combine beans, stock, garlic, lemon juice and olive oil; bring to boil. Reduce heat and simmer, uncovered, for about 5 minutes or until flavors mingle and garlic is tender.

• Transfer to food processor or blender; process for 2 to 3 minutes or until very smooth. Season to taste with salt, if desired, and pepper.

• Ladle into warm soup bowls OR refrigerate for at least 3 hours and serve chilled. Garnish with lemon zest.

Makes 4 servings, about 4 cups (1 L).

LIGHT BLACK BEAN SOUP WITH CHEESE

This is a wonderful soup for summertime when both sage and tomatoes are at their prime in the garden.

1 tsp	canola oil	5 mL
1	small onion or leek (white part), minced	1
1	clove garlic, minced	1
1 cup	cooked black beans	250 mL
2 cups	vegetable OR chicken stock	500 mL
2 cups	water	500 mL
1 1/2 tsp	chopped fresh sage OR 1/2 tsp (2 mL) dried	7 mL
1 tsp	brown sugar	5 mL
1/4 tsp	freshly ground black pepper	1 mL
1	tomato, peeled, seeded and diced	1
1/3 cup	grated Parmesan cheese	75 mL

• In large saucepan, heat oil over medium heat; cook onion and garlic, stirring occasionally, for about 4 minutes or until translucent.

• With fork, crush about one-third of the beans; add to pan along with remaining beans, stock, water, sage, brown sugar, salt and pepper. Bring to boil; reduce heat, and simmer, uncovered, for 15 minutes until liquid is slightly reduced.

• Add diced tomato; simmer, uncovered, for 5 minutes longer or until tomato is just cooked and no longer floats.

• Ladle into warm soup bowls. Garnish with Parmesan cheese.

Makes 5 servings, about 5 cups (1.25 L).

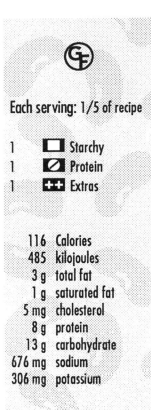

Each serving: 1/5 of recipe

1	☐	Starchy
1	⊘	Protein
1	✚✚	Extras

116	Calories
485	kilojoules
3 g	total fat
1 g	saturated fat
5 mg	cholesterol
8 g	protein
13 g	carbohydrate
676 mg	sodium
306 mg	potassium

GOOD: Folate
MODERATE: Fibre

Each serving: 1/4 of soup

1   ▢ Starchy
1/2   ◪ Fruits &
         Vegetables
1   ⊘ Protein
1   ◮ Fats & Oils

173   calories
723   kilojoules
3 g   total fat
0 g   saturated fat
0 mg   cholesterol
11 g   protein
27 g   carbohydrate
673 mg   sodium
1002 mg   potassium

GOOD: Calcium, Phosphorus,
       Niacin, Vitamin B$_6$

EXCELLENT: Iron, Magnesium,
           Vitamin A,
           Vitamin C, Folate

VERY HIGH: Fibre

TOMATO, SPINACH & BEAN SOUP

This is an all-seasons soup. In summer, replace the canned tomatoes with four ripe ones from the garden and use just-picked spinach, if possible, for a zestful soup full of color.

2 tsp	canola oil	10 mL
1	onion, chopped	1
1	clove garlic, minced	1
1	can (19 oz/540 mL) tomatoes	1
1 1/2 cups	cooked white kidney beans	375 mL
1 cup	vegetable OR chicken stock	250 mL
1/2 tsp	salt	2 mL
1/4 tsp	freshly ground black pepper	1 mL
1/4 tsp	ground nutmeg	1 mL
1/4 tsp	ground cumin	1 mL
1/4 tsp	granulated sugar	1 mL
5 drops	hot pepper sauce	5
1 pkg	(10 oz/300 g) fresh OR frozen spinach, chopped	1
	Juice and zest of half an orange	

• In large saucepan, heat oil over medium heat. Cook onion and garlic for 5 minutes or until onion is translucent.

• Add tomatoes, beans, stock, salt, pepper, nutmeg, cumin, sugar and hot pepper sauce; bring to boil. Reduce heat and simmer, uncovered, for 10 minutes. Stir in spinach; simmer for 3 minutes or until spinach is tender.

• Just before serving, stir in orange juice and zest. Ladle into warm soup bowls.

Makes 4 servings.

Harvest Squash & Bean Soup

This is a soup you can make ahead to take to the cottage or cabin for the week-end but hold the milk and orange juice. Stir them into the puréed bean mixture just before serving.

3 cups	chicken stock	750 mL
2 cups	diced peeled butternut squash OR pumpkin	500 mL
2 cups	cooked Romano, Dutch brown or white kidney beans	500 mL
1	orange, sectioned and seeded	1
1	small clove garlic	1
1 tsp	ground cardamom	5 mL
1/2 tsp	ground cinnamon	2 mL
1/4 tsp	each ground cloves and allspice	1 mL
4	drops hot pepper sauce	4
1/4 cup	orange juice	50 mL
1 cup	2% milk	250 mL
	Grated rind of 1 orange	

• In large saucepan, combine stock, squash, beans, orange sections, garlic, cardamom, cinnamon, cloves, allspice and hot pepper sauce; bring to boil. Reduce heat and simmer, uncovered, for 20 minutes or until squash is tender and soft.

• Process in food processor or blender, in two batches if necessary and scraping down sides once or twice, for about 3 minutes or until well puréed. Add orange juice and milk; process until blended.

• Serve hot, at room temperature or chilled. Garnish with sprinkle of orange rind.

Makes 6 servings, about 6 cups (1.5 L).

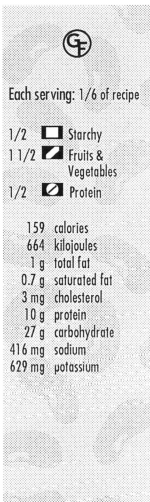

Each serving: 1/6 of recipe

1/2 ☐ Starchy
1 1/2 ◪ Fruits & Vegetables
1/2 ◙ Protein

159	calories
664	kilojoules
1 g	total fat
0.7 g	saturated fat
3 mg	cholesterol
10 g	protein
27 g	carbohydrate
416 mg	sodium
629 mg	potassium

GOOD: Phosphorus, Iron, Magnesium, Niacin

EXCELLENT: Folate

HIGH: Fibre

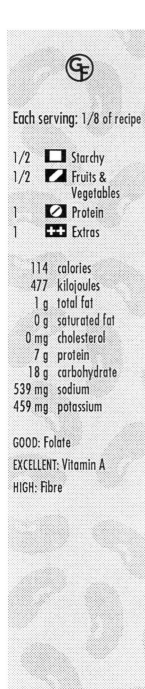

Each serving: 1/8 of recipe

1/2 ▢ Starchy
1/2 ◩ Fruits &
          Vegetables
1 ⊘ Protein
1 ⊞ Extras

114 calories
477 kilojoules
1 g total fat
0 g saturated fat
0 mg cholesterol
7 g protein
18 g carbohydrate
539 mg sodium
459 mg potassium

GOOD: Folate
EXCELLENT: Vitamin A
HIGH: Fibre

COUNTRY-STYLE BEAN SOUP

When the beans are cooked in advance and are ready to be a convenience food or if there is a can of beans on the cupboard shelf waiting to be opened, this comforting soup takes about half an hour to make.

1 tsp	canola oil	5 mL
1 cup	chopped onion	250 mL
1 cup	sliced carrots	250 mL
1 cup	sliced celery	250 mL
2 cups	cooked black (turtle) beans	500 mL
3 cups	chicken OR vegetable stock	750 mL
1/2 tsp	salt	2 mL
1/4 tsp	crushed dried basil	1 mL
1/4 tsp	freshly ground black pepper	1 mL
Pinch	each ground ginger and crumbled sage	Pinch
1 cup	skim milk	250 mL

• In large soup kettle or Dutch oven, heat oil over medium heat; cook onion, stirring occasionally, for 5 minutes or until translucent.

• Add carrots, celery, beans and stock; bring to boil. Reduce heat and simmer, partly covered, for 25 minutes or until carrots are soft.

• In batches, transfer to food processor or blender and process for 1 to 2 minutes or until smooth. Return to saucepan.

• Add salt, basil, pepper, ginger and sage; bring to boil. Stir in milk and heat just to simmering.

Makes 8 servings, about 8 cups (2 L).

SALADS

Kidney Bean & Pineapple Salad

Romano Beans Vinaigrette

Red Beans and Rice with Cilantro

Bean Potato Salad

Broccoli, Bean & Cheese Salad

Pasta, Sun-Dried Tomato and Bean Salad

Winter Salad

Beans à la Grecque

Coleslaw with Beans

Taco Bean Salad

Four Bean Salad

New-Style Pork & Bean Salad

Spinach Salad with Beans and Mushrooms

Dilly Bean Salad

Tex-Mex Corn & Bean Salad

Tomato Bean Mould

Tuna, Pasta and Bean Salad

Bean Salad Supreme

Caesar Bean Salad

Stuffed Tomatoes

Black Bean, Roasted Peppers and Capers Salad

Georgian Bean Salad with Walnuts

Tuscan Bean Salad

Frankly Fake Mayonnaise

Yogurt and Bean Salad Dressing

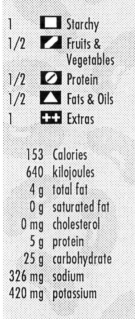
KIDNEY BEAN & PINEAPPLE SALAD

The salads in this collection make colorful, flavorful side salads. As well, like this one, they are hearty enough to be served as main courses particularly when the serving size is increased.

2 cups	cooked white or red kidney beans	500 mL
2	stalks celery, thinly sliced	2
2	green onions, thinly sliced	2
1	small red sweet pepper, coarsely chopped	1
1	can (14 oz/398 mL) pineapple chunks, drained	1
1/4 cup	drained pickled jalapeño pepper, seeded and chopped	50 mL
1/4 cup	chopped fresh cilantro OR 1 tbsp (15 mL) dried	50 mL
1/4 cup	balsamic vinegar	50 mL
2 tbsp	olive oil	25 mL
1 tbsp	Dijon mustard	15 mL
1/2 tsp	salt	2 mL
1/4 tsp	freshly ground black pepper	1 mL
Pinch	granulated sugar	Pinch
	Spinach leaves	
	Cilantro OR parsley leaves	

• In large bowl, combine kidney beans, celery, green onions, red sweet pepper, pineapple, jalapeño pepper and cilantro.

• In bowl or jar with tight-fitting lid, whisk or shake together vinegar, oil, mustard, salt, black pepper and sugar.

• Pour dressing over bean mixture; toss to coat.

• Cover and refrigerate, stirring occasionally, for at least 4 hours or overnight.

• Serve in spinach-lined salad bowl. Garnish with cilantro leaves.

Makes 6 servings.

ROMANO BEANS VINAIGRETTE

Once the beans are cooked this salad could hardly be simpler to prepare. When freshly cooked hot beans are added to the dressing and other vegetables, as in this recipe, they seem to absorb the flavors more readily.

1 cup	dried Romano beans, soaked (p.12)	250 mL
1	small red sweet pepper	1
1	small green sweet pepper	1
1	small onion, minced	1
1	small clove garlic, minced	1
1/2 cup	red wine vinegar	125 mL
1 tbsp	olive oil	15 mL
1/2 tsp	salt	2 mL
1/4 tsp	freshly ground black pepper	1 mL
1/4 cup	chopped fresh parsley	50 mL

• Drain and rinse soaked beans.

• In large sauce pan, combine beans and 8 cups (2 L) fresh water; bring to boil. Reduce heat and simmer for 20 to 25 minutes or until just tender. Drain well.

• Meanwhile, seed and coarsely chop red and green peppers. Combine with onion and garlic in salad bowl.

• In bowl or jar with tight-fitting lid, whisk or shake together vinegar, oil, salt and pepper. Pour over pepper mixture.

• Add drained hot beans to pepper mixture, stirring to thoroughly coat.

• Cover and refrigerate, stirring occasionally, for at least 3 hours or up to 5 days. At serving time, stir in parsley.

Makes 4 servings.

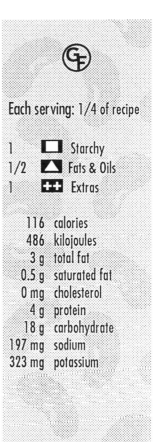

Each serving: 1/4 of recipe

1	☐	Starchy
1/2	▲	Fats & Oils
1	✚✚	Extras

116	calories
486	kilojoules
3 g	total fat
0.5 g	saturated fat
0 mg	cholesterol
4 g	protein
18 g	carbohydrate
197 mg	sodium
323 mg	potassium

GOOD: Magnesium
EXCELLENT: Vitamin C, Folate
MODERATE: Fibre

Each serving: 1/8 of recipe

1 1/2 ☐ Starchy
1 1/2 ▲ Fats & Oils
1 ➕ Extras

194 calories
812 kilojoules
7 g total fat
0 g saturated fat
0 mg cholesterol
5 g protein
27 g carbohydrate
111 mg sodium
279 mg potassium

GOOD: Vitamin C
EXCELLENT: Folate
HIGH: Fibre

RED BEANS AND RICE WITH CILANTRO

The rice is added to complement the beans and produce a salad that provides complete protein. Mexican flavors — cilantro, chili powder and cumin — make it a popular palate-pleaser.

2 cups	cooked red kidney or black beans	500 mL
2 cups	cooked long-grain white or brown rice	500 mL
4	green onions, thinly sliced	4
2	stalks celery, thinly sliced	2
1	small red sweet pepper, diced	1
1/4 cup	canola oil	50 mL
1/4 cup	lime juice	50 mL
1 tbsp	white vinegar	15 mL
1/4 cup	finely chopped fresh cilantro OR 1 tbsp (15 mL) dried	50 mL
1 tsp	chili powder	5 mL
1 tsp	ground cumin	5 mL
1 tsp	granulated sugar	5 mL
1/2 tsp	salt	2 mL
1/4 tsp	freshly ground black pepper	1 mL

• In salad bowl, combine kidney beans, rice, green onions, celery and red sweet pepper.

• In bowl or jar with tight-fitting lid, whisk or shake together oil, lime juice, vinegar, cilantro, chili powder, cumin, sugar, salt and pepper.

• Pour over bean mixture; toss lightly to thoroughly coat.

• Cover and refrigerate for at least 3 hours or up to 3 days, stirring occasionally.

Makes 8 servings.

BEAN POTATO SALAD

Perhaps beans and potatoes seem like an unlikely couple, but in this update of an old-style family favorite they do go together. The combination carts easily to a picnic or pot luck supper.

2 cups	cubed peeled potatoes	500 mL
1	bay leaf	1
2 cups	cooked red kidney or Dutch brown beans	500 mL
4	green onions, thinly sliced	4
2 tbsp	white vinegar	25 mL
2 tsp	canola oil	10 mL
1/2 tsp	celery seeds	2 mL
1/2 tsp	salt	2 mL
1/4 tsp	paprika	1 mL
Pinch	granulated sugar	Pinch
1/2 cup	light mayonnaise	125 mL
1/4 cup	low-fat yogurt OR light sour cream	50 mL
1 tsp	Dijon mustard	5 mL
	Thinly sliced red radishes (optional)	
	Chopped fresh parsley	

• In saucepan of lightly salted water, bring potatoes and bay leaf to boil; cook for about 10 minutes or until potatoes are tender. Drain well; discard bay leaf. In glass bowl or non-reactive container, combine potatoes, beans and green onions.

• In small bowl or jar with tight-fitting lid, whisk or shake together vinegar, oil, celery seed, salt, paprika and sugar. Pour over warm potato mixture; stir gently. Cover and refrigerate, stirring occasionally, for at least 3 hours or up to 2 days.

• At serving time, blend together mayonnaise, yogurt and mustard; fold into potato mixture. Garnish with radishes (if using) and parsley.

Makes 6 servings.

GF

Each serving: 1/6 of recipe

2		Starchy
1/2		Protein
1		Fats & Oils

234	calories
980	kilojoules
8 g	total fat
0 g	saturated fat
0 mg	cholesterol
7 g	protein
34 g	carbohydrate
285 mg	sodium
601 mg	potassium

GOOD: Iron, Magnesium, Vitamin B$_6$
EXCELLENT: Folate
VERY HIGH: Fibre

BROCCOLI, BEAN & CHEESE SALAD

For a change, tuck this combo into pita bread or roll a pita bread or tortilla around it to eat out of hand in the casual way street food is handled in Israel. However, for those avoiding gluten, remember pita bread is not gluten-free GF.

2 cups	cooked red kidney beans	500 mL
1	small onion, finely chopped	1
2 cups	small broccoli OR broccoflower florets	500 mL
1/4 cup	balsamic vinegar	50 mL
1 tbsp	olive oil	15 mL
1 tsp	Dijon mustard	5 mL
1	clove garlic, minced	1
1 tsp	salt	5 mL
1/4 tsp	freshly ground black pepper	1 mL
2 tbsp	crumbled blue, old Cheddar OR goat cheese	25 mL

• In glass bowl or nonreactive container, combine kidney beans, onion and broccoli florets.

• In small bowl or jar with tight-fitting lid, whisk or shake together vinegar, olive oil, mustard, garlic, salt and pepper. Pour over bean mixture; toss to coat well. Fold in cheese.

• Cover and refrigerate, stirring occasionally, for at least 2 hours or up to 24 hours.

Makes 6 servings.

Pasta, Sun-Dried Tomato and Bean Salad

In this satisfying salad the beans and pasta combine to provide complete protein. As well, the cheese and salami add to that quality making it perfect for a main entree. Simply garnish it with fresh herbs, if possible.

1 lb	fusilli or rotini (corkscrew-shaped pasta)	500 g
1/2 cup	snipped sun-dried tomatoes	125 mL
1 cup	boiling water	250 mL
1/3 cup	red wine vinegar	75 mL
1 tbsp	Dijon mustard	15 mL
1 tbsp	water	15 mL
1	clove garlic	1
Half	onion, chopped	Half
2 tbsp	olive oil	25 mL
1/2 tsp	salt	2 mL
4	drops hot pepper sauce	4
2 cups	cooked red kidney or Romano beans	500 mL
1 cup	cubed part-skim mozzarella cheese	250 mL
1	green OR yellow sweet pepper, diced	1
1/2 cup	chopped fresh Italian (flat-leaf) parsley	125 mL
3	thin slices gluten-free salami	3

• In saucepan of lightly salted boiling water, cook fusilli for 12 minutes or until *al dente*; drain well. Rinse under cold water; drain well. Transfer to salad bowl.

• Soak sun-dried tomatoes in boiling water for 5 minutes. Drain well and add to bowl.

• In small food processor or blender, combine vinegar, mustard, water, garlic, onion, oil, salt and hot pepper sauce; process until pureed and well blended. Pour over pasta; toss gently.

• Add beans, mozzarella, green pepper and parsley; toss well. Cover and refrigerate for at least 2 hours or up to 2 days.

• At serving time, cut salami into thin strips; sprinkle over salad.

Makes 8 servings.

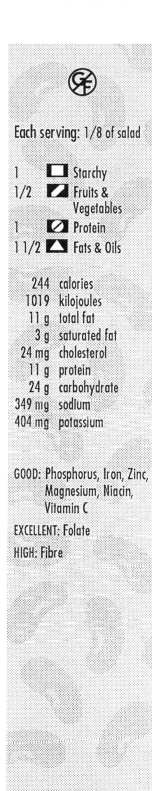

Each serving: 1/8 of salad

1	☐	Starchy
1/2	◩	Fruits & Vegetables
1	⊘	Protein
1 1/2	◪	Fats & Oils

244	calories
1019	kilojoules
11 g	total fat
3 g	saturated fat
24 mg	cholesterol
11 g	protein
24 g	carbohydrate
349 mg	sodium
404 mg	potassium

GOOD: Phosphorus, Iron, Zinc, Magnesium, Niacin, Vitamin C

EXCELLENT: Folate

HIGH: Fibre

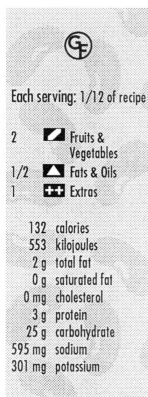

Each serving: 1/12 of recipe

2 ▨ Fruits &
Vegetables
1/2 ◣ Fats & Oils
1 ✚ Extras

132 calories
553 kilojoules
2 g total fat
0 g saturated fat
0 mg cholesterol
3 g protein
25 g carbohydrate
595 mg sodium
301 mg potassium

GOOD: Vitamin A
EXCELLENT: Folate
HIGH: Fibre

WINTER SALAD

The sauerkraut adds a tasty twist and the beans supply a nutritional boost to this cool weather salad. It fits the "keeps-a-week" category and is great to have on hand.

1/2 cup	cider vinegar	125 mL
1/2 cup	granulated sugar	125 mL
2 tbsp	canola oil	25 mL
1 tsp	salt	5 mL
1/2 tsp	dry mustard	2 mL
4	drops hot pepper sauce	4
3 cups	sauerkraut, well-drained	750 mL
2 cups	cooked red kidney or Dutch brown beans	500 mL
2	onions, halved and thinly sliced	2
2	stalks celery, thinly sliced	2
1	carrot, halved crosswise and thinly sliced	1
1	can (14 oz/398 mL) pineapple tidbits, drained	1
1 tsp	celery seeds	5 mL
	Freshly ground black pepper	

• In saucepan, combine vinegar, sugar, oil, salt, mustard and hot pepper sauce. Bring to boil, stirring constantly, until sugar is dissolved. Set aside.

• In colander or sieve, rinse sauerkraut under cold running water. Drain well and squeeze out extra liquid. With scissors, cut into pieces, about 1 inch (2.5 cm) long.

• In large bowl, combine sauerkraut, beans, onions, celery, carrot, pineapple and celery seeds. Pour vinegar mixture over top; toss to combine well. Season to taste with pepper.

• Cover and refrigerate, stirring occasionally, for at least 24 hours or up to 7 days.

Makes 12 servings.

Beans à la Grecque

It is important to allow a long chilling time for this salad to allow the flavors to meld amd mature.

1/2 cup	water	125 mL
1/4 cup	white wine vinegar	50 mL
2 tbsp	tomato paste	25 mL
1 tbsp	olive oil	15 mL
1	clove garlic, minced	1
1 tsp	ground coriander	5 mL
1/2 tsp	ground cumin	2 mL
1/2 tsp	salt	2 mL
1/2 lb	button mushrooms, halved	250 g
2	small zucchini, sliced	2
1	small onion, thinly sliced	1
2 cups	cooked white kidney or Dutch brown beans	500 mL
1/4 cup	chopped fresh parsley OR 1 tbsp (15 mL) dried	50 mL
1/4 tsp	freshly ground black pepper	1 mL
	Juice of half small lemon	
	Lemon zest	

• In large saucepan, combine water, vinegar, tomato paste, oil, garlic, coriander, cumin and salt; bring to boil. Reduce heat and simmer for 5 minutes.

• Add mushrooms, zucchini and onion; cook for about 3 minutes or until just cooked and still crunchy. Stir in beans, parsley and pepper. Transfer to glass bowl or nonreactive container. Set aside, stirring occasionally until cool.

• Cover and refrigerate for at least 6 hours or up to 3 days.

• Stir in lemon juice. Serve garnished with lemon zest.

Makes 6 servings.

Each serving: 1/6 of recipe

1 ☐ Starchy
1/2 ⊘ Protein

120	calories
502	kilojoules
2 g	total fat
0 g	saturated fat
0 mg	cholesterol
6 g	protein
19 g	carbohydrate
9 mg	sodium
515 mg	potassium

GOOD: Iron, Magnesium, Niacin
EXCELLENT: Folate
VERY HIGH: Fibre

COLESLAW WITH BEANS

This is a great "keeper" to have on hand all the time. The addition of beans makes it more robust than regular coleslaw.

6 cups	finely chopped cabbage (about half medium head)	1.5 L
1	carrot, coarsely grated	1
1	stalk celery, coarsely grated	1
1	onion, finely chopped	1
1 cup	cooked red kidney or black beans	250 mL
1/4 cup	cider vinegar	50 mL
1 tbsp	canola oil	15 mL
2 tsp	granulated sugar	10 mL
1 tsp	celery seeds	5 mL
1 tsp	salt	5 mL
1 tsp	Dijon mustard	5 mL
1/4 tsp	freshly ground black pepper	1 mL

• In large glass or nonreactive container, combine cabbage, carrot, celery and onion. Lightly stir in beans.

• In small saucepan, combine vinegar, oil, sugar, celery seeds, salt, mustard and pepper; bring to boil. Pour hot dressing over cabbage mixture; toss gently to mix well.

• Cover and refrigerate, stirring occasionally, for at least 2 hours or up to 5 days.

Makes 10 servings, about 5 cups (1.25L)

Each serving: 1/10 of recipe

1/2   Fruits & Vegetables

1   Extras

55	calories
230	kilojoules
1 g	total fat
0 g	saturated fat
0 mg	cholesterol
2 g	protein
8 g	carbohydrate
251 mg	sodium
224 mg	potassium

GOOD: Vitamin A, Vitamin C, Folate

HIGH: Fibre

Taco Bean Salad

This is adapted from the main course salads served in Mexican-style restaurants. Our version is quick-and-easy to make and it is fast food with less fat.

2 cups	bite-sized pieces iceberg lettuce	500 mL
1 cup	shredded red or green cabbage	250 mL
1 cup	cooked red kidney beans	250 mL
2	green onions, thinly sliced	2
1	carrot, shredded	1
Half	red sweet pepper, slivered	Half
1/4 cup	shredded old Cheddar cheese	50 mL
1/4 cup	chopped fresh cilantro OR	50 mL
	1 tbsp (15 mL) dried	
1/4 cup	low-fat yogurt	50 mL
1/4 cup	salsa	50 mL
2 tbsp	light mayonnaise	25 mL
1 tsp	white wine vinegar	5 mL
1 tsp	chili powder	5 mL
	Freshly ground black pepper	
2	slices cooked turkey breast (2 oz/60 g)	2
12	corn chips	12
	Cilantro OR parsley leaves	
	Half lime, cut into wedges	

• In bowl, combine lettuce, cabbage, beans, onions, carrot, red pepper, cheese and cilantro; toss well.

• In small bowl, whisk together yogurt, salsa, mayonnaise, vinegar and chili powder until well blended; season to taste with pepper. Pour over cabbage mixture; toss gently.

• Cut turkey into thin slivers. Arrange on top of salad. Tuck corn chips around salad. Garnish with cilantro leaves and lime wedges.

Makes 4 servings.

Each serving: 1/4 of recipe

1	▢ Starchy
1/2	◩ Fruits & Vegetables
1 1/2	⊘ Protein
1/2	◣ Fats & Oils
1	⊞ Extras

229 calories
957 kilojoules
8 g total fat
1 g saturated fat
20 mg cholesterol
13 g protein
27 g carbohydrate
433 mg sodium
537 mg potassium

GOOD: Phosphorous, Iron, Zinc, Magnesium, Niacin, Vitamin B$_6$

Excellent: Vitamin A, Vitamin C, Folate

High: Fibre

Four Bean Salad

You can replace the white kidney beans with more red ones, if desired, but it's not nearly as pretty.

2 cups	cooked white kidney or Romano beans	500 mL
2 cups	cooked red kidney beans	500 mL
1	can (14 oz/398 mL) cut green beans	1
1	can (14 oz/398 mL) cut yellow beans	1
1 cup	sliced celery	250 mL
5	canned sweet corn cobs, sliced	5
2	green onions, sliced	2
1/4 cup	each chopped red, green and yellow sweet pepper	50 mL
1/2 cup	white vinegar OR balsamic vinegar	125 mL
1/3 cup	canola oil	75 mL
1/4 cup	granulated sugar	50 mL
1 tsp	salt	5 mL
1 tsp	Dijon mustard	5 mL
1/2 tsp	freshly ground black pepper	2 mL
1/2 tsp	each dried tarragon and thyme	2 mL
1/2 tsp	celery seeds	2 mL
	Lettuce leaves	

• Rinse white and red kidney beans with hot water. Drain and rinse canned green and yellow beans. Drain well.

• In glass bowl or nonreactive container, combine kidney beans, green beans, yellow beans, celery, sweet corn, green onions and red and green peppers.

• In small saucepan, whisk together vinegar, oil, sugar, salt, mustard, pepper, tarragon, thyme and celery seeds; bring to boil. Boil for 1 minute or until sugar dissolves. Pour over bean mixture; toss well.

• Cover and refrigerate, stirring occasionally, for at least 8 hours or up to 2 days.

• Season to taste with more salt and pepper. Spoon into lettuce-lined salad bowl or onto individual lettuce-lined plates.

Makes 10 servings.

GF

Each serving: 1/10 of recipe

1 1/2	☐	Starchy
1/2	◩	Fruits & Vegetables
1	⊘	Protein
1	▲	Fats & Oils
1	++	Extras

240	calories
1003	kilojoules
7 g	total fat
0 g	saturated fat
0 mg	cholesterol
10 g	protein
34 g	carbohydrate
325 mg	sodium
554 mg	potassium

GOOD: Phosphorus

EXCELLENT: Iron, Magnesium, Folate

HIGH: Fibre

NEW-STYLE PORK & BEAN SALAD

The idea for this presentation of cold crunchy bean salad with hot grilled pork tenderloin comes from Canada Pork. It is good looking, great tasting and truly nutritious.

2	pork tenderloins (2 lb/1 kg total)	2
1 tsp	dry mustard	5 mL
1/3 cup	lemon juice	75 mL
1/4 cup	vegetable oil	50 mL
1 tsp	each dried thyme and basil	5 mL
1/2 tsp	salt	2 mL
1/4 tsp	freshly ground black pepper	1 mL
2 cups	cooked white kidney or Dutch brown beans	500 mL
1	carrot, diced	1
1/2 cup	finely chopped red onion	125 mL
1/4 cup	each diced red and yellow sweet pepper	50 mL
2 tbsp	chopped fresh parsley	25 mL

• Rub pork all over with mustard.

• Combine lemon juice, oil, thyme, basil, salt and pepper; sprinkle 4 tsp (20 mL) over pork. Set aside at room temperature to marinate for 30 minutes.

• Meanwhile, in bowl, combine beans, carrot, onion, red and yellow pepper and parsley; pour in remaining lemon juice mixture, stirring to coat well. Set aside at room temperature.

• Broil tenderloins or grill over medium-hot coals or on medium-high setting for 16 to 25 minutes, turning occasionally, until thermometer inserted into centre reads 160°F (70°C). (Or roast on rack in shallow roasting pan in 375°F (190°C) oven for 25 to 35 minutes.) Let stand for 5 minutes; cut crosswise into thin medallions or slices.

• Arrange bean salad on individual plates and overlap with slices of pork.

Makes 8 servings.

Photograph courtesy of *Canada Pork*

GF

Each serving: 1/8 of recipe

1/2	▢	Starchy
4	⊘	Protein
1	➕➕	Extras

240	calories
1003	kilojoules
8 g	total fat
1 g	saturated fat
63 mg	cholesterol
28 g	protein
13 g	carbohydrate
166 mg	sodium
613 mg	potassium

GOOD: Iron, Magnesium, Riboflavin, Folate

EXCELLENT: Phosphorus, Zinc, Vitamin A, Thiamin, Niacin, Vitamin B$_6$, Vitamin B$_{12}$

Moderate: Fibre

Spinach Salad with Beans and Mushrooms

Here is a traditional favorite bumped up with beans, water chestnuts and bean sprouts.

1	pkg (10 oz/300g) fresh spinach	1
6	medium mushrooms, sliced	6
1	small red onion, sliced and in rings	1
1 1/2 cups	cooked red kidney or black beans	375 mL
1	can (10 oz/284 mL) sliced water chestnuts, drained	1
1 cup	bean sprouts	250 mL
2 tbsp	white wine vinegar OR herb vinegar	25 mL
1 tbsp	olive oil	15 mL
2 tsp	soy sauce	10 mL
1	clove garlic, minced	1
1 tsp	Dijon mustard	5 mL
1/4 tsp	salt	1 mL
1/4 tsp	freshly ground black pepper	1 mL
1/4 tsp	ground nutmeg	1 mL
1	hard-cooked egg, chopped	1

• Wash spinach and pat dry. Remove and discard stems. Tear leaves into bite-sized pieces into salad bowl. Add mushrooms, onion rings, beans, water chestnuts and bean sprouts; toss gently.

• In small bowl or jar with tight-fitting lid, whisk or shake together vinegar, olive oil, soy sauce, garlic, mustard, salt, pepper and nutmeg. Pour over spinach mixture; toss well.

• Sprinkle with hard-cooked egg and toss again. Serve immediately.

Makes 6 servings.

Dilly Bean Salad

The secret to the cool, refreshing character of this glorious salad is the addition of fresh dill and mint. Dried ones will also work but the exciting greenness comes from fresh herbs.

2 cups	cooked white or red kidney beans	500 mL
1	tomato, diced	1
1	small onion, diced	1
1	large clove garlic, minced	1
1/4 cup	sunflower seeds	50 mL
1/4 cup	chopped fresh dill OR 1 tbsp (15 mL) dried	50 mL
2 tbsp	chopped fresh mint OR 1 1/2 tsp (7 mL) dried	25 mL
2 tbsp	vinegar	25 mL
1 tbsp	canola oil	15 mL
1 tbsp	soy sauce	15 mL
1 tsp	packed brown sugar	5 mL
1 tsp	Dijon mustard	5 mL
1/4 tsp	salt	1 mL
1/4 tsp	freshly ground black pepper	1 mL

• In salad bowl, combine beans, tomato, onion, garlic, sunflower seeds, dill and mint.

• In bowl or jar with tight-fitting lid, whisk or shake together vinegar, oil, soy sauce, brown sugar, mustard, salt and pepper.

• Pour over bean mixture; toss gently to coat. Cover and refrigerate, stirring occasionally, for at least 2 hours or up to 2 days.

Makes 4 servings.

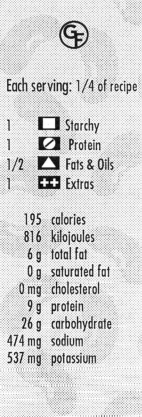

Each serving: 1/4 of recipe

1	☐	Starchy
1	⊘	Protein
1/2	△	Fats & Oils
1	⊞	Extras

195	calories
816	kilojoules
6 g	total fat
0 g	saturated fat
0 mg	cholesterol
9 g	protein
26 g	carbohydrate
474 mg	sodium
537 mg	potassium

GOOD: Phosphorus, Zinc, Thiamin

EXCELLENT: Iron, Magnesium, Folate

VERY HIGH: Fibre

Tex-Mex Corn & Bean Salad

Here is an ideal, virtually fat-free, colorful salad for a buffet—planned or potluck. Its bittersweet tang comes from the lime juice and yogurt in the dressing.

1 cup	cooked black beans	250 mL
1 cup	cooked red kidney beans	250 mL
1 cup	cooked, canned or thawed kernel corn	250 mL
1/4 cup	lime juice	50 mL
1/4 cup	low-fat yogurt	50 mL
2 tsp	granulated sugar	10 mL
1	small clove garlic, minced	1
1 tsp	chili powder	5 mL
1/2 tsp	salt	2 mL
1/4 tsp	ground cumin	1 mL
1/4 tsp	freshly ground black pepper	1 mL
6	drops hot pepper sauce	6
2	green onions, sliced	2
1	small cucumber, seeded and diced	1
1	tomato, seeded and diced	1
1	small green sweet pepper, diced	1
1	navel orange, halved and sliced crosswise	1

• In glass bowl, combine black beans, kidney beans and corn.

• In bowl or jar with tight-fitting lid, whisk or shake together lime juice, yogurt, sugar, garlic, chili powder, salt, cumin, pepper and hot pepper sauce. Pour over bean mixture; toss to coat well. Cover and refrigerate for at least 3 hours or up to 8 hours.

• At serving time, add green onions, cucumber, tomato and green pepper. Toss well. Garnish with orange slices.

Makes 8 servings.

Each serving: 1/8 of recipe

1	Starchy
1/2	Protein
1	Extras

106 calories
444 kilojoules
0 g total fat
0 g saturated fat
0 mg cholesterol
5 g protein
22 g carbohydrate
243 mg sodium
347 mg potassium

GOOD: Vitamin C
EXCELLENT: Folate
MODERATE: Fibre

Tomato Bean Mould

Lovely to look at and lovely to savor, this jellied salad is fat-free. For a finishing touch serve our Frankly Fake Mayonnaise (p. 77) with it. It is also fat-free.

2	envelopes unflavored gelatin	2
1 cup	water	250 mL
1	can (19 oz/540 mL) tomatoes	1
1 cup	cooked white or red kidney beans	250 mL
2	green onions, thinly sliced	2
1	stalk celery, thinly sliced	1
1/2 tsp	granulated sugar	2 mL
2 tbsp	tomato paste	25 mL
1 tbsp	red or white wine vinegar	15 mL
1 tsp	Worcestershire sauce	5 mL
4	drops hot pepper sauce	4
1/2 cup	orange juice	125 mL
	Lettuce leaves	

• In small dish or cup, sprinkle gelatin over 1/2 cup (125 mL) water; let stand for 5 minutes to soften.

• In saucepan, stir together tomatoes, breaking up with fork if whole, beans, onions, celery, sugar, tomato paste, vinegar, Worcestershire sauce, hot pepper sauce and remaining water; bring to boil. Reduce heat and simmer for 5 minutes. Stir in gelatin until dissolved. Stir in orange juice.

• Chill for 30 minutes or until nearly set; stir well. Pour into 4-cup (1 L) mould.

• Refrigerate for at least 4 hours or until firm or up to 3 days.

• Unmould on lettuce-lined serving plate or individual salad plates.

Makes 8 servings.

Each serving: 1/8 of recipe

1   Fruits & Vegetables

59	calories
247	kilojoules
0 g	total fat
0 g	saturated fat
0 mg	cholesterol
4 g	protein
10 g	carbohydrate
125 mg	sodium
319 mg	potassium

GOOD: Folate
MODERATE: Fibre

TUNA, PASTA AND BEAN SALAD

For a gluten-free 🍞 version of this main meal salad, rice noodles will work as well as regular pasta.

2 cups	cooked red kidney beans	500 mL
2 cups	cooked small shell pasta or macaroni	500 mL
1	medium carrot, grated	1
1	stalk celery, diagonally sliced	1
1	red onion, chopped	1
2 tbsp	red wine vinegar	25 mL
2 tbsp	lemon juice	25 mL
2 tbsp	olive oil	25 mL
1	clove garlic, minced	1
1 tsp	Dijon mustard	5 mL
1/2 tsp	salt	2 mL
1/4 tsp	freshly ground black pepper	1 mL
	Lettuce leaves	
1	can (6.5 oz/185 g) tuna, packed in water	1
	Lemon wedges	

• In large bowl, combine beans, pasta, carrot, celery and onion.

• In small bowl or jar with tight-fitting lid, whisk or shake together vinegar, lemon juice, olive oil, garlic, mustard, salt and pepper.

• Pour over bean mixture; stir gently. Cover and refrigerate, stirring occasionally, for at least 2 hours or up to 6 hours.

• At serving time, line individual plates or salad bowl with lettuce leaves. Top with bean mixture. Drain tuna and break into chunks; arrange on bean mixture. Garnish with lemon wedges.

Makes 4 servings.

Each serving: 1/4 of recipe

3 ▢ Starchy
2 1/2 ◰ Protein
1 ➕➕ Extras

360 calories
1507 kilojoules
8 g total fat
1 g saturated fat
8 mg cholesterol
25 g protein
48 g carbohydrate
460 mg sodium
722 mg potassium

GOOD: Zinc, Vitamin C, Vitamin B₆

EXCELLENT: Phosphorus, Iron, Magnesium, Vitamin A, Niacin, Folate, Vitamin B₁₂

MODERATE: Fibre

Bean Salad Supreme

The vegetable cocktail used in the dressing seems to give this colorful legume and green bean salad a special glow.

2 cups	cooked red kidney or Dutch brown beans	500 mL
1 cup	blanched green beans	250 mL
2	stalks celery, thinly sliced diagonally	2
1	medium onion, thinly sliced	1
1	medium red sweet pepper, thinly sliced	1
1/2 cup	vegetable cocktail	125 mL
1/3 cup	red wine vinegar	75 mL
2 tbsp	canola oil	25 mL
2 tsp	granulated sugar	10 mL
1/2 tsp	dry mustard	2 mL
1/4 tsp	salt	1 mL
1/4 tsp	freshly ground black pepper	1 mL

• In bowl, combine kidney and green beans, celery, onion and green pepper.

• In screw-top jar with tight-fitting lid, shake together vegetable cocktail, vinegar, oil, sugar, mustard, salt and pepper. Pour over vegetables.

• Cover and refrigerate, stirring occasionally, for at least 4 hours or up to 24 hours.

• Stir well. With slotted spoon, remove vegetables, allowing excess dressing to drain away, to serving bowl or individual plates.

Makes 8 servings.

Each serving: 1/8 of recipe

| 1 | ☐ Starchy |
| 1/2 | ▲ Fats & Oils |

104	calories
435	kilojoules
3 g	total fat
0 g	saturated fat
0 mg	cholesterol
4 g	protein
15 g	carbohydrate
172 mg	sodium
341 mg	potassium

EXCELLENT: Folate
MODERATE: Fibre

1   □ Starchy
1   ∅ Protein
1   ▲ Fats & Oils
1   ┿┿ Extras

179   calories
748   kilojoules
9 g   total fat
1 g   saturated fat
4 mg   cholesterol
8 g   protein
16 g   carbohydrate
454 mg   sodium
563 mg   potassium

GOOD: Phosphorus, Iron

EXCELLENT: Vitamin A,
             Vitamin C, Folate

HIGH: Fibre

CAESAR BEAN SALAD

The added beans go well with the robust dressing of this Caesar salad. They also provide a nutritional bonus, particularly if the salad is featured as a main course item.

1	head romaine lettuce	1
1 cup	cooked red kidney or black beans	250 mL
1/4 cup	grated Parmesan cheese	50 mL

DRESSING:

1 tbsp	canola oil	15 mL
1 tbsp	lemon juice	15 mL
2 tsp	anchovy paste	10 mL
1 tsp	Worcestershire sauce	5 mL
1/2 tsp	Dijon mustard	2 mL
1	small clove garlic, minced	1
1/4 cup	light mayonnaise	50 mL
	Salt and freshly ground black pepper	

• Wash and dry romaine leaves; remove heavy veins and tear leaves into salad bowl. Add beans and Parmesan cheese. Toss well.

• Dressing: In small bowl, whisk together oil, lemon juice, anchovy paste, Worcestershire sauce, mustard and garlic. Beat in mayonnaise.

• Just before serving, pour dressing over romaine mixture; toss well. Season to taste with salt and pepper; toss again.

Makes 4 servings.

STUFFED TOMATOES

Each of these scooped out tomatoes filled with the bean and corn concoction and perched on crisp lettuce makes a pretty individual salad for a special luncheon or supper.

4	medium tomatoes	4
2	slices side bacon	2
1 cup	cooked black beans	250 mL
1	can (7 oz/199 mL) kernel corn	1
2	green onions, sliced	2
2 tbsp	grated Parmesan cheese	25 mL
2 tsp	sunflower seeds	10 mL
1/4 cup	light mayonnaise	50 mL
1 tsp	Dijon mustard	5 mL
1 tbsp	chopped fresh basil OR 1 tsp (5 mL) dried	15 mL
1 tsp	chopped fresh dill OR 1/4 tsp (1 mL) dried dillweed	5 mL
2	drops hot pepper sauce	2
2 cups	shredded leaf OR iceberg lettuce	500 mL
1	lime, cut into wedges	1

• With sharp knife, slice stem end from tomatoes. Scoop out pulp and seeds; set aside for another use (soup or sauce). Lightly sprinkle inside of tomato shells with salt. Invert on paper towels to drain. Refrigerate for up to 2 hours.

• Meanwhile, in small nonstick skillet, cook bacon over medium heat until crisp. Remove to paper towels to drain.

• In bowl, combine beans, corn, green onions, Parmesan cheese and sunflower seeds.

• In small bowl, combine mayonnaise, mustard, basil, dill and hot pepper sauce; mix well. Pour over bean mixture; toss well.

• Crumble bacon; stir into bean mixture. Cover and refrigerate for 2 hours.

• At serving time, divide lettuce among 4 salad plates. Spoon bean mixture into tomato shells to heaping full. Place on shredded lettuce. Garnish with lime wedges.

Makes 4 servings.

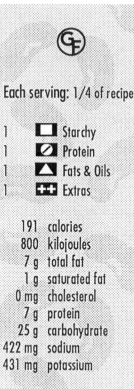

1   ☐ Starchy
1   ⊘ Protein
1   ▲ Fats & Oils
1   ➕ Extras

191 calories
800 kilojoules
7 g total fat
1 g saturated fat
0 mg cholesterol
7 g protein
25 g carbohydrate
422 mg sodium
431 mg potassium

GOOD: Iron, Magnesium,
     Vitamin C
EXCELLENT: Folate
VERY HIGH: Fibre

BLACK BEAN, ROASTED PEPPER AND CAPER SALAD

The smoky taste of the peppers and the tang from the lemon and capers makes this a lively salad. Any other colored beans may be used as a substitute for the black beans.

1	red sweet pepper	1
2 cups	cooked black beans	500 mL
2 tbsp	olive oil	25 mL
2 tbsp	red wine vinegar	25 mL
1 tbsp	lemon juice	15 mL
1	clove garlic, minced	1
1/2 tsp	granulated sugar	2 mL
1/2 tsp	salt	2 mL
1/4 tsp	freshly ground black pepper	1 mL
6	drops hot pepper sauce	6
1	stalk celery, sliced	1
1/4 cup	drained pickled capers	50 mL
	Chopped fresh parsley OR chives	

• Cut red pepper in half; place skin side up on small baking sheet. Broil for 10 minutes or until skin is brown and blistered; turn and broil for 5 minutes longer. Immediately seal in brown paper bag; let sweat for 10 minutes.

• Meanwhile, pour boiling water over beans; let stand for 1 minute. Drain well and place in salad bowl.

• In bowl or jar with tight-fitting lid, whisk or shake together olive oil, vinegar, lemon juice, garlic, sugar, salt, pepper and hot pepper sauce. Pour over beans; toss to coat well.

• Slip charred skin off peppers; dice roasted pepper and add to beans along with celery and capers. Toss well.

• Refrigerate, covered, for 3 hours or up to 5 days. Serve cold or at room temperature. Garnish with chopped parsley.

Makes 4 servings.

GEORGIAN BEAN SALAD WITH WALNUTS

Walnut oil accentuates the nutty-taste of this combination typical of a Russian dish. If it is not available, sesame oil or peanut butter make acceptable substitutes.

2 cups	cooked red kidney, Dutch brown or Romano beans	500 mL
1/4 cup	chopped walnuts	50 mL
2	green onions, thinly sliced	2
1	small clove garlic, minced	1
1 tbsp	red wine vinegar	15 mL
1 tbsp	water	15 mL
1 tsp	walnut OR olive oil	5 mL
1/2 tsp	salt	2 mL
1/4 tsp	freshly ground black pepper	1 mL
1/4 tsp	brown sugar	1 mL
2 tbsp	chopped fresh cilantro or parsley	25 mL
	Lettuce leaves	
2 tbsp	finely chopped red or green sweet pepper	25 mL

• In glass bowl or nonreactive container, combine beans, walnuts, onions and garlic.

• In small bowl or jar with tight-fitting lid, whisk or shake together vinegar, water, oil, salt, pepper and brown sugar. Pour over bean mixture; toss well.

• Cover and refrigerate, stirring occasionally, for at least 6 hours or up to 3 days.

• Spoon onto lettuce-lined bowl or plate. Garnish with red sweet pepper.

Makes 4 servings.

Each serving: 1/4 of recipe

1	☐	Starchy
1	☑	Protein
1/2	▲	Fats & Oil
1	⊞	Extras

177 calories
741 kilojoules
6 g total fat
0.5 g saturated fat
0 mg cholesterol
9 g protein
23 g carbohydrate
197 mg sodium
433 mg potassium

GOOD: Iron, Magnesium
EXCELLENT: Folate
VERY HIGH: Fibre

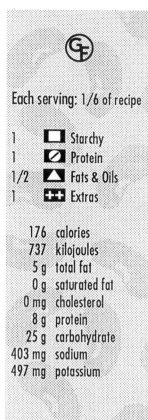

TUSCAN BEAN SALAD

The celery, carrot and onion add a pleasing crunch to this "portable" salad. It is great for a picnic and easily doubles for a crowd.

1 tsp	olive OR canola oil	5 mL
1 cup	finely chopped onion	250 mL
3 cups	cooked Romano or white kidney beans	750 mL
1	carrot, finely chopped	1
1	stalk celery, finely chopped	1
1/4 cup	rice vinegar	50 mL
2 tbsp	lemon juice	25 mL
2 tbsp	canola oil	25 mL
2 tsp	finely chopped fresh rosemary OR 1/2 tsp (2 mL) dried	10 mL
1 tsp	finely chopped fresh tarragon OR 1/4 tsp (1 mL) dried	5 mL
1 tsp	salt	5 mL
1/4 tsp	freshly ground black pepper	1 mL
	Chopped fresh parsley	

• In nonstick skillet, heat oil over medium heat; cook onion for 5 minutes or until golden brown. Transfer to bowl.

• Add beans, carrot and celery; toss to mix.

• In small bowl or jar with tight-fitting lid, whisk or shake together vinegar, lemon juice, oil, rosemary, tarragon, salt and pepper. Pour over bean mixture. Toss well.

• Cover and refrigerate, stirring occasionally, for at least 2 hours or up to 3 days.

• Serve cold or at room temperature, sprinkled with parsley.

Makes 6 servings.

FRANKLY FAKE MAYONNAISE

Without fat or cholesterol, this dressing is great to toss with salad greens or shredded cabbage.

1 cup	cooked white kidney beans	250 mL
1/4 cup	hot water	50 mL
4 tsp	white vinegar	20 mL
2 tsp	lemon juice	10 mL
1 tsp	Dijon mustard	5 mL
1	clove garlic, minced	1
1/4 tsp	salt	1 mL
1/4 tsp	granulated sugar	1 mL
3	drops hot pepper sauce	3

• In food processor or blender, combine beans, hot water, vinegar, lemon juice, mustard, garlic, salt, sugar and hot pepper sauce. Process with off/on motion, scraping down sides of container occasionally, for 2 to 3 minutes or until very smooth.

• Transfer to container with tight-fitting lid. Refrigerate for up to 2 weeks.

Makes 1 cup (250 mL).

Each serving: 1 tbsp (15 mL)

1 ➕ Extras

15 calories
61 kilojoules
0 g total fat
0 g saturated fat
0 mg cholesterol
1 g protein
3 g carbohydrate
28 mg sodium
48 mg potassium

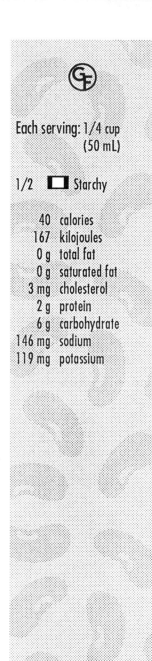

Each serving: 1/4 cup
(50 mL)

1/2 ☐☐ Starchy

40 calories
167 kilojoules
0 g total fat
0 g saturated fat
3 mg cholesterol
2 g protein
6 g carbohydrate
146 mg sodium
119 mg potassium

YOGURT AND BEAN SALAD DRESSING

To cut the fat, spoon this low-fat, low-calorie dressing on crisp greens instead of mayonnaise and high-fat salad dressings. It is also superb on hot or cold steamed asparagus and green beans.

3/4 cup	cooked white kidney or Romano beans	175 mL
1/2 cup	plain low-fat yogurt	125 mL
1/4 cup	light sour cream	50 mL
1 tsp	dried dillweed	5 mL
	Salt and freshly ground black pepper	

• In small food processor or bowl, process or mash together beans, yogurt, sour cream and dillweed. Season to taste with salt and pepper.

• Dressing can be covered and stored in refrigerator for up to 3 days.

Makes 1 1/4 cups (300 mL).

SNACKS

Mexican Joes

Vegetable & Cheese Tortilla Stacks

Nachos

Egg & Bean Salad Sandwich Filling

Chili Bean Rarebit

Ham and Bean Pizza

Salmon, Broccoli & Bean Quiche

Each serving: 1/8 of recipe

2 ▭ Starchy
1/2 ▰ Fruits & Vegetables
1 1/2 ⊘ Protein
1 ▲ Fats & Oils
1 ⊞ Extras

317 Calories
1325 kilojoules
9 g total fat
3 g saturated fat
23 mg cholesterol
15 g protein
41 g carbohydrate
589 mg sodium
476 mg potassium

GOOD: Phosphorus, Magnesium
EXCELLENT: Iron, Zinc, Niacin, Folate, Vitamin B$_{12}$
HIGH: Fibre

MEXICAN JOES

This cousin of the Sloppy Joe is served open-faced on half of a hamburger bun. For gluten-free Ⓖ *Mexican Joes spoon the beef and bean mixture over slices of Seed and Nut Bread (p.155) or rice cakes.*

1/2 lb	lean ground beef	250 g
1	onion, chopped	1
1	small green sweet pepper, chopped	1
1	clove garlic, minced	1
1	can (7 1/2 oz/213 mL) tomato sauce	1
1/2 tsp	Worcestershire sauce	2 mL
1/2 tsp	chili powder	2 mL
2	drops hot pepper sauce	2
2 cups	cooked red kidney or Romano beans	500 mL
4	hamburger buns, cut in half	4
8	tomato slices	8
1/2 cup	shredded Cheddar cheese	125 mL
1 cup	shredded lettuce	250 mL

• In nonstick skillet over medium heat, cook ground beef, onion, green pepper and garlic, stirring to crumble beef, for about 6 minutes or until meat is no longer pink. Drain off any fat.

• Stir in tomato sauce, Worcestershire sauce, chili powder and hot pepper sauce. Bring to boil; cook, stirring once or twice, for about 5 minutes or until slightly thickened.

• With wooden spoon or fork, mash half the beans. Stir into skillet with remaining beans; cook for 2 minutes or until heated through.

• Place one bun half on each serving plate. Spoon bean mixture evenly on top. Garnish with tomato slice, shredded cheese and lettuce.

Makes 8 servings.

VEGETABLE AND CHEESE TORTILLA STACK

This heart-healthy snack overflowing with the flavors of the South-west is great for entertaining at a brunch or late supper.

4	Gluten-Free Tortillas (p.178)	4
1 cup	shredded Edam cheese	250 mL
1/2 cup	1% cottage cheese	125 mL
1 cup	shredded celery	250 mL
1/2 cup	shredded carrot	125 mL
1/4 cup	finely chopped stuffed olives	50 mL
2 cups	cooked red kidney beans	500 mL
1	clove garlic, halved	1
1/4 cup	chopped fresh cilantro OR 1 tbsp (15 mL) dried	50 mL
1 tsp	chili powder	5 mL
1/2 cup	salsa	125 mL
2	green onions, thinly sliced	2
1/2 cup	light sour cream	125 mL
	Chopped green or red sweet pepper	

• Lay tortillas in single layer on ungreased baking sheet. Warm in 350°F (180°C) oven for 3 minutes.

• Meanwhile, in bowl, stir together half of the Edam cheese, the cottage cheese, celery, carrot and olives. Set aside.

• In food processor, combine beans, garlic, cilantro and chili powder. Process, scraping down sides of bowl occasionally, for about 1 minute or until smooth. Transfer to nonstick skillet. Stir in half the salsa; cook over medium heat, stirring frequently, for about 10 minutes or until heated through and slightly dry. Stir in green onions.

• Place one warmed tortilla on ungreased baking sheet. Spread with one-third of the bean mixture; top with one-third of the cheese mixture. Repeat with remaining tortillas, bean and cheese mixtures ending with fourth tortilla.

• Bake in 350°F (180°C) oven for 15 minutes. Sprinkle with remaining cheese; bake for about 2 minutes longer or until cheese just melts. Let stand for 5 minutes. Cut into 4 wedges.

• Garnish with sour cream and sweet peppers. Serve with remaining salsa.

Makes 4 servings.

Each serving: 1/4 of recipe

2 1/2 ☐ Starchy
2 1/2 ◪ Fruits & Vegetables
1 ▲ Fats & Oils
1 ⊞ Extras

368 calories
1541 kilojoules
12 g total fat
5 g saturated fat
36 mg cholesterol
22 g protein
43 g carbohydrate
526 mg sodium
836 mg potassium

GOOD: Riboflavin, Niacin, Vitamin B$_6$
EXCELLENT: Calcium, Phosphorus, Iron, Zinc, Magnesium, Vitamin A, Folate, Vitamin B$_{12}$
VERY HIGH: Fibre

NACHOS

It is hard to stop munching on nachos once you start. And, they are good for you. However, remember that each one carries with it a little more fat but not as much as ones made with canned refried beans where the fat content is much higher than in ours.

Each serving: 4 nachos

1 1/2 ▢ Starchy
1   ⊘ Protein
1 1/2 ◣ Fats & Oils

238 calories
994 kilojoules
11 g total fat
3 g saturated fat
22 mg cholesterol
9 g protein
23 g carbohydrate
352 mg sodium
306 mg potassium

GOOD: Phosphorus, Zinc, Magnesium
EXCELLENT: Folate
MODERATE: Fibre

1	tomato, finely chopped	1
1	small onion, finely chopped	1
1	clove garlic, finely chopped	1
2 tbsp	chopped fresh cilantro OR 2 tsp (10 mL) dried	25 mL
1 tbsp	finely chopped pickled jalapeno pepper	15 mL
24	round regular or blue corn chips	24
1 cup	Refried Beans (p.144)	250 mL
1/4 cup	chopped green OR red sweet pepper	50 mL
1/2 cup	shredded Cheddar OR Monterey Jack cheese	125 mL
1/2 cup	light sour cream	250 mL
1/4 cup	sliced green onions OR diced avocado	50 mL

• In small sieve, strain tomato to remove excess liquid.

• In small bowl, combine tomato pulp, onion, garlic, cilantro and jalapeño pepper.

• Arrange corn chips in single layer on baking sheets.

• Stir together Refried Beans and green pepper; spread 2 tsp (10 mL) onto each chip. Top evenly with tomato mixture; sprinkle with cheese.

• Broil for about 20 seconds or until cheese melts but does not brown. Remove from broiler.

• With fork, whip sour cream until very smooth; spoon 1 tsp (5 mL) onto each nacho. Sprinkle with green onion. Serve immediately.

Makes 6 servings, 24 nachos.

EGG AND BEAN SANDWICH FILLING

Spoon this filling onto rice cakes and garnish with capers and slivers of red or green sweet pepper for a wonderful open-faced sandwich. Or, use it for a regular sandwich, or stuff it into a pita pocket with a slice of tomato and shredded lettuce, remembering, however, that regular and pita bread are not gluten-free ⊗ *.*

2	hard-cooked eggs	2
2	green onions, thinly sliced	2
1/4 cup	finely chopped celery	50 mL
2 tbsp	light mayonnaise	25 mL
1/2 tsp	Dijon mustard	2 mL
1 cup	cooked kidney or Romano beans, roughly mashed	250 mL
	Salt and freshly ground black pepper	

• In bowl and using sharp knife or fork, chop eggs. Stir in green onions, celery, mayonnaise and mustard. Stir in mashed beans.

Season to taste with salt and pepper.

Makes 3 servings, 1 1/2 cups (375 mL).

Each serving: 1/3 of recipe

1	☐ Starchy
1	☑ Protein
1/2	▲ Fats & Oils

162	calories
678	kilojoules
6 g	total fat
1 g	saturated fat
143 mg	cholesterol
9 g	protein
16 g	carbohydrate
384 mg	sodium
307 mg	potassium

GOOD: Iron, Vitamin B_{12}
EXCELLENT: Folate
HIGH: Fibre

Each serving: 1/4 of recipe

1 1/2 ☐ Starchy
1/2 ◆ Milk (skim)
1 1/2 ∅ Protein
1 ▲ Fats & Oils

264 calories
1103 kilojoules
10 g total fat
6 g saturated fat
30 mg cholesterol
15 g protein
27 g carbohydrate
494 mg sodium
334 mg potassium

GOOD: Iron, Zinc, Magnesium,
Vitamin D, Riboflavin,
Niacin, Vitamin B$_{12}$
EXCELLENT: Calcium,
Phosphorus, Folate
MODERATE: Fibre

CHILI BEAN RAREBIT

Cooking lore tells us that the first rarebit was made because the hunter did not bring a rabbit home for dinner and his wife had to create a meal with what she had in her cupboard – cheese and bread. This version made using beans to extend the more expensive cheese supplies less fat and far more fibre. To make the dish gluten-free ⓖ serve the sauce over rice cakes.

1 cup	cooked white or red kidney beans, mashed	250 mL
1 cup	skim milk	250 mL
1 tsp	chili powder	5 mL
1/2 tsp	paprika	2 mL
1/4 tsp	salt	1 mL
3	drops hot pepper sauce	3
2	English muffins	
1 cup	shredded old (sharp) Cheddar cheese	250 mL

• In saucepan, whisk together mashed beans, milk, chili powder, paprika, salt and hot pepper sauce. Bring to boil over medium heat. Cook, stirring frequently, for about 3 minutes or until slightly thickened.

• Meanwhile, split and toast English muffins.

• Remove saucepan from heat; stir in cheese until it melts.

• Serve immediately over muffin halves.

Makes 4 servings.

Ham and Bean Pizza

The crust chosen for this pizza is the gluten-free one. It provides a thin base for the toppings used here and would be perfect for any other favorite toppings. The beans in this one give our pizza an earthy robust character.

1	unbaked 13-inch (33 cm) Gluten-Free (p.155) pizza crust	1

TOPPING:

1	can (7 1/2 oz/213 mL) tomato sauce	1
1 tsp	dried basil	5 mL
1/4 tsp	freshly ground black pepper	1 mL
3/4 cup	grated part skim mozzarella cheese	175 mL
1/2 cup	cooked red kidney or black beans	125 mL
Half	onion, thinly sliced	Half
Half	green sweet pepper, thinly sliced	Half
1/2 cup	diced cooked ham	125 mL
1/4 cup	crumbled feta cheese	50 mL
2 tbsp	thinly sliced stuffed olives OR capers	25 mL
2 tbsp	grated Parmesan cheese	25 mL

• Spread pizza crust evenly with tomato sauce; sprinkle with basil and pepper. Sprinkle evenly with mozzarella; arrange beans, onion, green pepper, ham, feta cheese and olives on top. Sprinkle with Parmesan cheese.

• Bake in 400°F (200°C) oven for 25 minutes or until crust is golden brown and cheese bubbly.

Makes 8 servings.

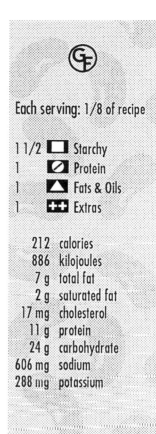

Each serving: 1/8 of recipe

1 1/2 ☐ Starchy
1 ⊘ Protein
1 ▲ Fats & Oils
1 ⊞ Extras

212 calories
886 kilojoules
7 g total fat
2 g saturated fat
17 mg cholesterol
11 g protein
24 g carbohydrate
606 mg sodium
288 mg potassium

GOOD: Phosphorus, Niacin
EXCELLENT: Folate
MODERATE: Fibre

Each Serving: 1/8 of recipe

1	⬜	Starchy
1 1/2	⊘	Protein
1	▲	Fats & Oils

222	calories
927	kilojoules
10 g	total fat
3 g	saturated fat
67 mg	cholesterol
13 g	protein
17 g	carbohydrate
302 mg	sodium
401 mg	potassium

GOOD: Calcium, Iron, Riboflavin, Niacin, Folate

EXCELLENT: Phosphorus, Vitamin D, Vitamin B$_{12}$

MODERATE: Fibre

SALMON, BROCCOLI QUICHE WITH BEANS

Here's a good-for-you, good tasting quiche. And, it is filling so an eighth of it is enough for a snack. For meal-size servings, cut into sixths and add crunchy coleslaw or garlicy Caesar salad to round out the meal.

1	unbaked 9 inch (23 cm) single crust gluten-free pie shell (p.177)	1
1/2 cup	shredded low fat mozzarella cheese	125 mL
1 1/2 cups	cooked red kidey or Romano beans	375 mL
1	can (7 1/4 oz/220 g) salmon, drained	1
1 cup	blanched broccoli florets	250 mL
3	green onions, thinly sliced	3
2	eggs	2
1 cup	2% milk	250 mL
1/2 tsp	salt	2 mL
1/2 tsp	dried dillweed	2 mL
1/4 tsp	freshly ground black pepper	1 mL

• Line pie shell with piece of foil. Bake in 400°F (200°C) oven for 10 minutes or until partly baked. Remove foil; let cool.

• Sprinkle cheese over partially baked shell. In layers arrange beans, then salmon, broccoli and onions over cheese.

• In bowl, whisk eggs; whisk in milk, salt, dillweed and pepper. Pour over layers in pie shell.

• Bake in 375°F (190°C) oven for 30 minutes or until tester inserted near centre comes out clean.

• Let stand for 5 minutes before serving.

Makes 8 servings.

MEATLESS DISHES

Meatless Lasagne

Layered Pasta & Bean Bake

Bean and Rice Cakes Parmigiana

Bean Burgers

Vegetable Bean Loaf

Baked Beans and Fruit

Curried Beans with Rice

Beans 'n' Rice

Cuban Beans and Rice

Chili

Chili with Corn

Speedy Santa Fe Beans

Polenta with Beans

Risotto with Beans

Enchiladas with Red Sauce

Vegetable Shepherd's Pie

Vegetable Bean au Gratin

Tomatoey Macaroni and Cheese with Beans

Tamale and Bean Pot Pie

Mushrooms and Beans

Potato Bean Cakes

Ratatouille

Tomato and Bean Pasta Sauce

Bean Stroganoff

Three Bean Terrine

Frittata with Zucchini and Beans

Cream Sauce ◆ Herb Sauce ◆ Mornay Sauce

Meatless Lasagne

In this vegetarian lasagne the beans and lasagne noodles complement each other to form complete protein. For a ⊕ gluten-free version, use Gluten-Free Tortillas (p.178) instead of pasta.

1 tsp	canola oil	5 mL
1	onion, chopped	1
1	stalk celery, finely chopped	1
1	carrot, grated	1
1	clove garlic, minced	1
1/3 cup	finely chopped walnuts or pecans	75 mL
2 cups	cooked red kidney beans, mashed	500 mL
1 1/4 cups	canned tomato paste	300 mL
2 cups	water	500 mL
1 tsp	ground thyme	5 mL
1/2 tsp	ground oregano	2 mL
	Salt and freshly ground black pepper	
2 cups	1% cottage cheese	500 mL
1	egg, lightly beaten	1
12	oven-ready lasagne noodles	12
2 cups	shredded mozzarella cheese (8 oz/250 g)	500 mL
1/2 cup	grated Parmesan cheese	125 mL

• In large nonstick skillet, heat oil over medium heat; cook onion, celery, carrot, garlic and nuts for about 6 minutes or until onion is translucent. Stir in mashed beans, tomato paste, water, thyme and oregano; bring to boil. Reduce heat and simmer for 15 minutes or until slightly reduced and flavors have mingled. Season to taste with salt and pepper.

• In small bowl, combine cottage cheese and egg; mix well.

• Set 1 cup (250 mL) sauce aside. Spread 3/4 cup (175 mL) of the remaining sauce over bottom of 13- x 9-inch (3 L) baking or lasagne dish. Arrange layer of 4 lasagne noodles over sauce. Spread half of the remaining sauce over noodles, then half of the cottage cheese mixture and half of the mozzarella cheese. Cover with second layer of 4 noodles. Repeat sauce and cheese layers. Top with remaining noodles. Cover completely with reserved sauce. Sprinkle with Parmesan cheese.

• Bake in 350°F (180°C) oven for about 40 minutes or until noodles are tender. Let stand for 10 minutes before serving.

Makes 8 servings.

LAYERED PASTA AND BEAN BAKE

This casserole can be assembled, covered and refrigerated for up to two days before baking. Substitute rice vermicelli for the spaghetti to make it gluten-free Ⓖ*.*

1/2 lb	spaghetti, noodles OR macaroni	250 g
1/2 cup	light sour cream	125 mL
1/2 cup	1% cottage cheese	125 mL
1/2 cup	shredded mozzarella cheese	125 mL
1 tsp	canola oil	5 mL
1	onion, finely chopped	1
1	clove garlic, minced	1
1/3 cup	chopped walnuts OR pecans	75 mL
1/2 lb	mushrooms, chopped	250 g
1	can (14 oz/398 mL) tomato sauce	1
2 cups	cooked red kidney or black beans	500 mL
1/2 cup	chopped green sweet pepper	125 mL
1 tsp	ground thyme	5 mL
1/2 tsp	ground oregano	2 mL
1/4 tsp	freshly ground black pepper	1 mL
1/3 cup	grated Parmesan cheese	75 mL

• In large saucepan, cook spaghetti in lightly salted boiling water for about 12 minutes or until al dente. Drain well. Stir in light sour cream, cottage cheese and mozzarella until cheese melts. Set aside.

• Meanwhile, in large nonstick skillet, heat oil over medium heat. Cook onion, garlic and walnuts for about 5 minutes or until onion is translucent. Stir in mushrooms. Cook for about 6 minutes or until liquid from mushrooms evaporates. Stir in tomato sauce, beans, green pepper, thyme, oregano and pepper. Bring to boil.

• Spoon half of the pasta mixture into 10 cup (2.5 L) casserole. Cover with half of the bean mixture. Repeat layers. Sprinkle Parmesan over top.

• Bake in 350°F (180°C) oven for 30 minutes or until bubbly around edges and Parmesan begins to look golden.

Makes 8 servings.

Each serving: 1/8 of recipe

2	☐	Starchy
1/2	◩	Fruits & Vegetables
1 1/2	⬯	Protein
1	▲	Fats & Oils
1	➕	Extras

310	calories
1298	kilojoules
9 g	total fat
3 g	saturated fat
43 mg	cholesterol
15 g	protein
41 g	carbohydrate
652 mg	sodium
604 mg	potassium

GOOD: Calcium, Zinc, Thiamin, Vitamin B₁₂

EXCELLENT: Phosphorus, Iron, Magnesium, Riboflavin, Niacin, Folate

VERY HIGH: Fibre

Each serving: 1/6 of recipe

1 1/2 ▭ Starchy
1/2 ◪ Fruits & Vegetables
1 1/2 ⊘ Protein
1/2 ▲ Fats & Oils
1 ✚✚ Extras

263 calories
1101 kilojoules
7 g total fat
2 g saturated fat
12 mg cholesterol
15 g protein
36 g carbohydrate
828 mg sodium
616 mg potassium

GOOD: Calcium, Zinc, Riboflavin, Niacin, Vitamin B$_6$
EXCELLENT: Phosphorus, Iron, Magnesium, Folate
VERY HIGH: Fibre

BEAN & RICE CAKES PARMIGIANA

Here is another great bean and rice vegetarian dish. Its rich cheesy taste comes from the Parmesan cheese garnish.

1 tbsp	canola oil	15 mL
1	onion, minced	1
1	clove garlic, minced	1
1/4 lb	mushrooms, finely chopped	125 g
1 tsp	each dried thyme and ground cumin	5 mL
1/4 tsp	freshly ground black pepper	1 mL
1 tbsp	soy sauce	15 mL
2 tsp	Worcestershire sauce	10 mL
2 cups	cooked Romano or Dutch brown beans, mashed	500 mL
1 cup	cooked brown OR white short-grain rice	250 mL
2 tbsp	cornstarch	25 mL
2	egg whites	2
1/4 cup	cornmeal	50 mL
SAUCE:		
1	can (14 oz/398 mL) tomato sauce	1
1/2 tsp	each ground oregano and thyme	2 mL
1/2 cup	shredded skim milk mozzarella cheese	125 mL
1/2 cup	grated Parmesan cheese	125 mL

• In nonstick skillet, heat 1 tsp (5 mL) of the oil over medium heat; cook onion and garlic, stirring occasionally, for about 5 minutes or until onion is translucent. Stir in mushrooms; cook for 4 minutes or until liquid evaporates and mushrooms begin to brown. Stir in thyme, cumin, pepper, soy sauce and Worcestershire sauce. Transfer to bowl. Stir in beans, rice and cornstarch until well blended.

• With fork, beat egg whites; stir into bean mixture until well blended. Refrigerate for about 30 minutes or until mixture becomes firmer. Form about 1/4 cup (50 mL) at a time into patties about 1/2 inch (1 cm) thick. Coat each one with corn meal.

• Heat remaining oil in large nonstick skillet over medium heat; cook patties for 3 minutes on each side or until golden brown. Arrange in overlapping single layer in shallow casserole.

• Sauce: Combine tomato sauce, oregano and thyme; pour over patties. Sprinkle with mozzarella and Parmesan cheeses.

• Bake in 350°F (180°C) oven for 30 minutes or until heated through and cheese melts.

Makes 6 servings.

BEAN BURGERS

The satisfying toasted flavor of these vegetarian patties is fortified by the nuts and yeast extract (Marmite). Serve them with a plate of vegetables or in buns with all the trimmings as meatless hamburgers.

1 cup	cooked kidney beans, mashed	250 mL
2 tbsp	each cornstarch and cornmeal	25 mL
2 tbsp	chopped cashews OR walnuts	25 mL
1	onion, minced	1
1	carrot, grated	1
1	clove garlic, minced	1
2 tbsp	chopped fresh parsley OR cilantro OR 2 tsp (10 mL) dried	25 mL
1/4 tsp	freshly ground black pepper	1 mL
1	egg	1
1 tsp	soy sauce	5 mL
1 tsp	yeast extract	5 mL

• In bowl, stir together beans, cornstarch, cornmeal, cashews, onion, carrot, garlic, parsley and pepper. Beat in egg, soy sauce and yeast extract until well blended.

• Spray nonstick skillet with nonstick coating; heat over medium heat. Drop bean mixture by heaping tablespoonfuls (15 mL) about 2 inches (5 cm) apart onto skillet. With spoon, spread each one into a flat patty.

• Cook for 4 to 5 minutes on each side or until golden brown.

Makes 8 patties, 4 servings.

Each serving: 1/4 of recipe

1	☐ Starchy
1/2	▨ Protein
1/2	△ Fats & Oils

137	calories
572	kilojoules
3 g	total fat
0 g	saturated fat
53 mg	cholesterol
6 g	protein
20 g	carbohydrate
58 mg	sodium
287 mg	potassium

EXCELLENT: Vitamin A, Folate
MODERATE: Fibre

Each serving: 1/8 of recipe

1 ☐ Starchy
1 ⊘ Protein

145 calories
606 kilojoules
3 g total fat
0.5 g saturated fat
53 mg cholesterol
8 g protein
21 g carbohydrate
134 mg sodium
412 mg potassium

GOOD: Iron, Magnesium
EXCELLENT: Folate
HIGH: Fibre

VEGETABLE BEAN LOAF

There is a choice of herb and spice combinations just to show how the bean mixture adapts to different flavorings. The first exudes a taste of the Middle East; the other one, French country cuisine.

1 tsp	canola oil	5 mL
1	onion, finely chopped	1
1	clove garlic, minced	1
6	mushrooms, finely chopped	6
1	zucchini, shredded	1
3 cups	cooked red or white kidney, Romano or Dutch brown beans, mashed	750 mL
2 tbsp	chopped cashews, walnuts OR peanuts	25 mL
2 tbsp	each cornmeal and millet	25 mL
1 tbsp	tomato paste	15 mL
1 tbsp	soy sauce	15 mL
2 tsp	yeast extract	10 mL
1/2 tsp	each ground cumin, oregano and paprika OR 1/2 tsp (2 mL) each ground marjoram, thyme and basil	2 mL
1/4 tsp	freshly ground black pepper	1 mL
2	eggs, beaten	2

• Lightly spray 8- x 4-inch (1.5 L) loaf pan with nonstick coating; dust with cornmeal, coating bottom and sides. Set aside.

• In nonstick skillet, heat oil over medium heat; cook onion, garlic, mushrooms and zucchini, stirring occasionally, for 5 minutes or until moisture from mushrooms evaporates. Transfer to bowl.

• Stir in mashed beans, cashews, cornmeal, millet, tomato paste, soy sauce, yeast extract, cumin, oregano, paprika and pepper until well mixed. Beat in eggs until well blended. Spoon into prepared pan.

• Bake in 350°F (180°C) oven for 45 minutes or until tester inserted in centre comes out clean. Let stand for 5 minutes. Invert onto serving platter.

Makes 8 servings.

BAKED BEANS AND FRUIT

Prepare this a day ahead. The flavours seem to mingle and mellow as the casserole rests and then is reheated (at 300° F /150° C).

4 cups	cooked red kidney, or Dutch brown beans	1 L
1	large onion, coarsely chopped	1
2	apples, peeled and chopped	2
2	navel oranges, peeled and sliced	2
1/3 cup	molasses OR packed brown sugar	75 mL
1 tbsp	cider vinegar	15 mL
1 tbsp	minced fresh gingerroot OR 1 tsp (5 mL) ground ginger	15 mL
2 tsp	Dijon mustard	10 mL
1/2 tsp	salt	2 mL
1/4 tsp	freshly ground black pepper	1 mL
4	drops hot pepper sauce Hot water	4

• In 8 cup (2 L) casserole, layer cooked beans, then onion, then apples; top with orange slices.

• In 2 cup (500 mL) measure, combine molasses, cider vinegar, gingerroot, mustard, salt, pepper and hot pepper sauce. Add enough hot water to make 2 cups (500 mL) liquid; mix well. Pour over bean mixture.

• Cover and bake in 300°F (150°C) oven for about 1 hour or until beans and fruit are tender. Uncover and stir; bake, uncovered, for about 30 minutes longer or until some of the liquid has evaporated.

Makes 6 servings.

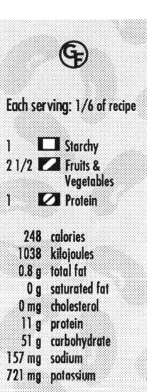

Each serving: 1/6 of recipe

1	Starchy
2 1/2	Fruits & Vegetables
1	Protein

248	calories
1038	kilojoules
0.8 g	total fat
0 g	saturated fat
0 mg	cholesterol
11 g	protein
51 g	carbohydrate
157 mg	sodium
721 mg	potassium

GOOD: Phosphorus, Zinc, Vitamin C

EXCELLENT: Iron, Magnesium, Folate

VERY HIGH: Fibre

CURRIED BEANS WITH RICE

To complete this meal add a crisp salad made with dark green greens, such as spinach or broccoli. There is no need for meat because the beans and rice combine to form complete protein.

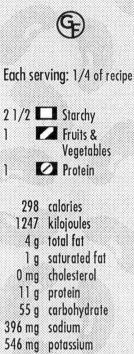

Each serving: 1/4 of recipe

2 1/2 ☐ Starchy
1 ◪ Fruits & Vegetables
1 ⊘ Protein

298 calories
1247 kilojoules
4 g total fat
1 g saturated fat
0 mg cholesterol
11 g protein
55 g carbohydrate
396 mg sodium
546 mg potassium

GOOD: Phosphorus, Iron, Zinc, Niacin
EXCELLENT: Magnesium, Folate
VERY HIGH: Fibre

1 tsp	canola oil	5 mL
1	onion, chopped	1
1	apple, unpeeled and chopped	1
1 1/2 tsp	curry powder	7 mL
1/2 tsp	salt	2 mL
Pinch	freshly ground black pepper	Pinch
2 cups	cooked red kidney or Romano beans	500 mL
1 cup	beef OR vegetable stock	250 mL
1 tbsp	raisins	15 mL
1 tbsp	chopped peanuts	15 mL
Half	small banana, chopped	Half
1 tbsp	unsweetened desiccated coconut	15 mL
1 tsp	lemon juice	5 mL
2 cups	hot cooked rice	500 mL
	Chopped fresh chives OR parsley	

• In nonstick skillet or saucepan, heat oil over medium heat. Cook onion, apple, curry powder, salt and pepper, stirring often, for 5 minutes or until onion is translucent.

• Add beans, crushing some with fork; add stock, raisins and peanuts, stirring well. Bring to boil; reduce heat and simmer, uncovered, and stirring occasionally, for 15 minutes or until thickened.

• In small bowl, combine banana, coconut and lemon juice.

• To serve, spoon bean mixture over rice. Serve banana mixture on the side. Garnish with chives.

Makes 4 servings.

Beans 'n' Rice

Here is a presentation that is centuries old – the co-starring of beans and rice – and found in many international cuisines. The added cheese comes from Mexican-style beans and rice.

1 tsp	canola oil	5 mL
1	onion, chopped	1
1	clove garlic, chopped	1
1 tsp	chili powder	5 mL
1/2 tsp	ground cumin	2 mL
1/4 tsp	celery seed	1 mL
1/4 tsp	freshly ground black pepper	1 mL
1	can (19 oz/540 mL) tomatoes	1
2 cups	cooked red kidney beans	500 mL
1 cup	cooked brown OR white long-grain rice	250 mL
1 tsp	Worcestershire sauce	5 mL
1	green sweet pepper, chopped	1
1/2 tsp	salt	2 mL
1/3 cup	shredded Cheddar cheese	75 mL
	Chopped fresh cilantro OR parsley	

• In large saucepan, heat oil over medium heat; cook onion and garlic, stirring occasionally, for 5 minutes or until onion is translucent. Stir in chili powder, cumin, celery seed and pepper; cook for 1 minute.

• Add tomatoes, beans, rice and Worcestershire sauce; stir well. Bring to boil, reduce heat and simmer for about 20 minutes or until most of the liquid evaporates.

• Stir in green pepper. Cook for about 2 minutes or until heated through. Season to taste with salt.

• Garnish each serving with cheese and cilantro.

Makes 6 servings.

VARIATION:
Cuban Beans & Rice
(sometimes called Moors & Christians)
• In place of kidney beans, use 2 cups (500 mL) cooked black beans.

Each serving: 1/6 of recipe

1	☐	Starchy
1/2	◪	Fruits & Vegetables
1	◪	Protein
1	+++	Extras

174	calories
727	kilojoules
3 g	total fat
1 g	saturated fat
6 mg	cholesterol
8 g	protein
28 g	carbohydrate
332 mg	sodium
494 mg	potassium

GOOD: Phosphorus, Iron, Magnesium, Vitamin C
EXCELLENT: Folate
VERY HIGH: Fibre

Calculations approximately the same as above.

Each serving: 1/6 of recipe

1 1/2 ☐ Starchy
1 ▨ Fruits &
Vegetables
1 1/2 ⊘ Protein
1 ➕ Extras

233 calories
958 kilojoules
3 g total fat
0 g saturated fat
0 mg cholesterol
13 g protein
42 g carbohydrate
796 mg sodium
982 mg potassium

GOOD: Phosphorus, Zinc,
Vitamin A, Niacin,
Vitamin B$_6$
EXCELLENT: Iron, Magnesium,
Folate
VERY HIGH: Fibre

Each serving: 1/6 of recipe

2 1/2 ☐ Starchy
1 ▨ Fruits &
Vegetables
1 ⊘ Protein
1 ➕ Extras

CHILI

There are probably as many versions of chili as there are homey bowls to serve it in. This affordable one is great to have on hand for a spur-of-the moment gathering. Keeps in the refrigerator for four days; in the freezer for up to three months.

2 tsp	canola oil	10 mL
2	onions, coarsely chopped	2
2	stalks celery, coarsely chopped	2
2	cloves garlic, minced	2
1	green sweet pepper, chopped	1
1	can (19 oz/540 mL) tomatoes	1
2 tbsp	chili powder	25 mL
1 tbsp	unsweetened cocoa powder	15 mL
2 tsp	ground cumin	10 mL
1/2 tsp	salt	2 mL
1 tsp	granulated sugar	5 mL
1/2 tsp	crushed red chili pepper	2 mL
1/4 tsp	cinnamon	1 mL
4 cups	cooked light or dark red kidney beans	1 L
1	can (14 oz/398 mL) tomato sauce	1

• In large nonstick skillet, heat oil over medium heat; cook onions, celery, garlic and green pepper, stirring occasionally, for 15 minutes or until onion is translucent.

• Stir in tomatoes, breaking up with fork, chili powder, cocoa, cumin, salt, sugar, red chili pepper and cinnamon. Cook for 5 minutes. Stir in beans then tomato sauce. Simmer, covered, for about 1 hour. Or transfer to 10 cup (2.5 L) casserole or two 6 cup (1.5 L) casseroles and bake in 350°F (180°C) oven for 40 minutes or until heated through and flavors have blended.

Makes 6 servings.

VARIATION:
CHILI WITH CORN

• Prepare Chili and add 1 can (7 oz/199 mL) kernel corn when adding tomato sauce.

Makes 6 servings

VARIATION:
CHILI WITH CORN (continued)

Continued from p.96

254	calories
1061	kilojoules
3g	total fat
0 g	saturated fat
0 mg	cholesterol
13g	protein
47g	carbohydrate
881mg	sodium
1018 mg	potassium

GOOD: Phosphorus, Zinc,
    Vitamin A, Niacin,
    Vitamin B_6, Vitamin C

EXCELLENT: Iron, Magnesium,
    Folate

VERY HIGH: Fibre

SPEEDY SANTA FE BEANS

It is prudent to keep canned beans on hand on the cupboard shelf for this quick-to-fix rush-hour meal.

1 tbsp	soft margarine OR canola oil	15 mL
1/4 cup	chopped onion	50 mL
1/4 cup	chopped green sweet pepper	50 mL
1/4 cup	chopped red or green sweet pepper	50 mL
1 cup	medium hot salsa	250 mL
2 tbsp	barbecuc sauce,	25 mL
2 tsp	prepared mustard	10 mL
1/2 tsp	salt	2 mL
1/4 tsp	freshly ground black pepper	1 mL
1	can (19 oz/540 mL) red kidney beans	1
1	can (19 oz/540 mL) white kidney beans	1

• In saucepan, melt margarine over medium heat; cook onion and sweet peppers for about 4 minutes or until onion is translucent. Stir in salsa, barbecue sauce and mustard. Season with salt and pepper.

• Drain and rinse red and white kidney beans; add to saucepan. Stir gently; bring to boil. Reduce heat and simmer, stirring once or twice, for 15 minutes or until heated.

Makes 8 servings, about 4 cups (1 L).

Each serving: 1/8 of recipe

1	▢	Starchy
1	⊘	Protein
1	➕	Extras

150	calories
627	kilojoules
1 g	total fat
0 g	saturated fat
0 mg	cholesterol
9 g	protein
25 g	carbohydrate
168 mg	sodium
561 mg	potassium

GOOD: Iron, Magnesium,
    Vitamin A

EXCELLENT: Folate

VERY HIGH: Fibre

POLENTA WITH BEANS

Here a Tomatoey bean sauce dresses up polenta – a staple for many Italian country cooks. The combination provides complete protein.

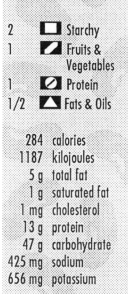

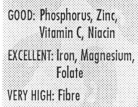
2/3 cup	cornmeal	150 mL
1/2 tsp	salt	2 mL
1 tsp	olive oil	5 mL
1	clove garlic, minced	1
4	regular tomatoes OR 8 Italian tomatoes (or use drained canned tomatoes)	4
1/2 tsp	each ground oregano and dried basil	2 mL
1/4 tsp	ground marjoram	1 mL
1/4 tsp	crushed red chili pepper	1 mL
2 cups	cooked Romano or red kidney beans	500 mL
8	pitted black olives, sliced	8
2 tbsp	chopped walnuts, toasted	25 mL
2 tsp	capers OR chopped dill pickle	10 mL
2 tsp	lemon juice	10 mL
2 tbsp	grated Parmesan cheese	25 mL
	Chopped fresh fennel OR parsley	

• In small bowl, stir 1 cup (250 mL) of water into cornmeal and set aside. In bottom of double boiler, bring about 2 inches (5 cm) water to simmer over medium heat.

• Pour 1 cup (250 mL) water into top of double boiler; bring to boil. Stir in cornmeal mixture and salt; cook, stirring constantly, until mixture begins to boil. Place over double boiler bottom; cover and cook, stirring occasionally, for 40 minutes.

• Meanwhile, in nonstick saucepan, heat oil over medium heat; cook garlic for 2 minutes.

• Coarsely chop tomatoes; add to saucepan. Stir in oregano, basil, marjoram and red chili pepper; bring to boil. Cover and cook, stirring occasionally, for 10 minutes. Stir in beans, olives, walnuts and capers. Cover and cook, stirring occasionally, for 20 minutes or until thickened. Stir in lemon juice.

• Stir 1 tbsp (15 mL) of the grated Parmesan into cooked cornmeal (the polenta). Mound in centre of serving plate. Sprinkle with remaining Parmesan.

• Stir fennel into bean mixture. Spoon around polenta.

Makes 4 servings.

Risotto with Beans

To achieve the creamy consistency characteristic of risotto the rice is continually stirred as it cooks in hot liquid that is always added in small amounts throughout the cooking.

2 tsp	canola oil	10 mL
1	onion, chopped	1
1	carrot, grated	1
3 cups	cooked yellow eye or red kidney beans	750 mL
1	can (7 1/2 oz/213 mL) tomato sauce	1
2 cups	vegetable OR chicken stock	500 mL
1 tbsp	olive oil	15 mL
1/2 tsp	each dried rosemary, sage and thyme	2 mL
3/4 cup	arborio rice	175 mL
1/4 cup	dry white wine	50 mL
2 tbsp	grated Parmesan cheese	25 mL
	Chopped fresh parsley	

• In saucepan, heat canola oil over medium heat; cook onion and carrot for about 5 minutes or until onion is translucent.

• Stir in beans, tomato sauce and stock; bring to boil. Reduce heat and simmer, uncovered, for 20 minutes or until slightly reduced.

• In another heavy saucepan, heat olive oil over medium heat. Stir in rosemary, sage and thyme. Add rice and stir for about 2 minutes or until rice is shiny. Add wine and cook, stirring constantly, until wine is absorbed.

• With ladle or measure, remove about 1/2 cup (125 mL) liquid from bean mixture. (Don't worry if a few beans get included in liquid.) Pour into rice and cook, stirring frequently, until liquid is absorbed. Repeat 3 more times until rice is creamy and tender. Stir in Parmesan cheese.

• Spoon into centre of large shallow serving bowl. Spoon bean mixture around rice. Garnish with parsley. Serve immediately.

Makes 8 servings.

Each serving: 1/8 of recipe

2		Starchy
1/2		Fruits & Vegetables
1/2		Protein

236	calories
986	kilojoules
3 g	total fat
0 g	saturated fat
0 mg	cholesterol
9 g	protein
40 g	carbohydrate
514 mg	sodium
544 mg	potassium

GOOD: Iron, Magnesium, Niacin
EXCELLENT: Vitamin A, Folate
HIGH: Fibre

ENCHILADAS WITH RED SAUCE

When tortillas are wrapped around a filling of beans, meat or chicken and baked in a spicy sauce they are called enchiladas. One caution, if you use canned refried beans rather than our homemade ones the total fat count will be higher.

2 cups	Refried Beans (p.144)	500 mL
6	8-inch (20 cm) Gluten-Free Tortillas (p.178) OR regular corn flour tortillas	6
1/2 cup	shredded part-skim mozzarella cheese	125 mL
3	green onions, thinly sliced	3
1/4 cup	chopped fresh cilantro OR parsley OR 1 tbsp (15 mL) dried	50 mL

RED SAUCE:

1	can (14 oz/398 mL) tomato sauce	1
1	clove garlic, minced	1
1/4 cup	finely chopped red sweet pepper	50 mL
1 tsp	chili powder	5 mL
1 tsp	finely chopped pickled jalapeño pepper	5 mL
1/4 tsp	ground cumin	1 mL
Pinch	granulated sugar	Pinch
	Freshly ground black pepper	
1/3 cup	light sour cream OR low-fat yogurt	75 mL
6	pitted black OR pimiento-stuffed olives, sliced	6

• Evenly divide refried beans among tortillas; spread evenly. Sprinkle with mozzarella, onions and cilantro. Roll up and place, seam side down, in shallow casserole.

• Red Sauce: In saucepan, stir together tomato sauce, garlic, red pepper, chili powder, jalapeño pepper, cumin, sugar and pepper to taste; bring to boil. Reduce heat and simmer for 5 minutes or until flavors are blended. Spoon over rolled tortillas.

• Bake in 350°F (180°C) oven for 15 minutes or until heated through.

• Serve immediately on individual serving plates. Garnish each serving with sour cream and olives.

Makes 6 servings.

GF

Each serving: 1/6 of recipe

1 1/2 ☐ Starchy
1/2 ▨ Fruits & Vegetables
1 1/2 ⊘ Protein
1/2 ◮ Fats & Oils

246 calories
1028 kilojoules
6 g total fat
1 g saturated fat
9 mg cholesterol
14 g protein
35 g carbohydrate
774 mg sodium
651 mg potassium

GOOD: Phosphorus, Zinc, Niacin
EXCELLENT: Iron, Magnesium, Folate
VERY HIGH: Fibre

Vegetable Shepherd's Pie

Some cooks may feel more comfortable calling this "gardener's pie" since it is meatless and chuck full of vegetables.

1 tsp	canola oil	5 mL
1	onion, chopped	1
1	clove garlic, minced	1
1/3 cup	chopped walnuts	75 mL
2 cups	cooked red kidney or Romano beans	500 mL
1	can (7 1/2 oz/213 mL) tomato sauce	1
1/2 cup	water	125 mL
1 tsp	each Worcestershire sauce and soy sauce	5 mL
1/2 tsp	each salt and dried basil	2 mL
1/4 tsp	ground marjoram	1 mL
1/4 tsp	freshly ground black pepper	1 mL
5	potatoes (about 1 1/4 lbs/625 g), peeled	5
1	bay leaf	1
4	carrots, diced	4
3	stalks celery, diced	3
1/4 cup	2 % milk	50 mL
1/2 cup	shredded Cheddar cheese	125 mL
1/4 cup	grated Parmesan cheese	50 mL

• In saucepan, heat oil over medium heat; cook onion, garlic and walnuts, stirring occasionally, for 5 minutes or until onion is translucent. Add beans, tomato sauce, water, Worcestershire sauce, soy sauce, salt, basil, marjoram and pepper; bring to boil. Reduce heat and simmer for 30 minutes.

• Meanwhile, cut potatoes into chunks. In saucepan of lightly salted water, bring potatoes and bay leaf to boil; cook over medium heat for 20 minutes or until tender. Drain well. Discard bay leaf. Mash with milk until smooth. Fold in half the Cheddar cheese. Season to taste with salt and pepper.

• Meanwhile, in saucepan of lightly salted water cook carrots and celery over medium heat for 5 minutes; drain. Spread on bottom of 8 cup (2 L) deep casserole. Top with bean mixture. Spread mashed potatoes over beans. Sprinkle with remaining Cheddar and Parmesan cheeses.

• Bake in 350°F (180°C) oven for 30 minutes or until top is lightly browned.

Makes 6 servings.

Each serving: 1/6 of recipe

2	☐	Starchy
1/2	▨	Fruits & Vegetables
1 1/2	⊘	Protein
1	◣	Fats & Oils

312 calories
1306 kilojoules
10 g total fat
3 g saturated fat
20 mg cholesterol
14 g protein
44 g carbohydrate
659 mg sodium
1120 mg potassium

GOOD: Calcium, Zinc, Vitamin C, Niacin

EXCELLENT: Folate, Vitamin B$_6$, Phosphorus, Iron, Magnesium, Vitamin A

VERY HIGH: Fibre

VEGETABLE BEAN AU GRATIN

It may be mixing cuisines but this calls for fried rice, rice pilaf or polenta as an accompaniment. The grains complement the beans and any of the combinations make a wonderful tasty meal for vegetarians, one with wholesome complete protein.

2 tsp	olive oil	10 mL
2	cloves garlic, minced	2
1	onion, chopped	1
1	zucchini, diced	1
1	red sweet pepper, diced	1
1 cup	broccoli florets	250 mL
1	can (19 oz/540 mL) plum tomatoes	1
1 1/2 cups	cooked Romano OR red kidney beans	375 mL
1/4 cup	white wine OR vegetable stock	50 mL
1 tsp	dried thyme	5 mL
1/2 tsp	fennel seeds, crushed	2 mL
1/4 tsp	salt	1 mL
1 tbsp	lemon juice	15 mL
2 tbsp	chopped fresh parsley OR 2 tsp (10 mL) dried	25 mL
1/4 cup	grated Parmesan cheese	50 mL
2 tbsp	shredded Cheddar cheese	25 mL
1	rice cake, crushed	1

• In saucepan, heat oil over medium heat; cook garlic and onion, stirring occasionally, for 5 minutes or until onion is translucent.

• Add zucchini, red pepper and broccoli; stir-fry for 2 minutes. Stir in tomatoes, breaking up with fork if whole, beans, wine, thyme, fennel seeds and salt; bring to boil. Cook for 5 minutes to slightly reduce liquid. Stir in lemon juice and parsley. Spoon into shallow casserole or gratin dish.

• Combine Parmesan and Cheddar cheeses and rice cake crumbs. Sprinkle over casserole.

• Bake in 350°F (180°C) for 30 minutes or until cheese melts and top begins to turn golden brown.

Makes 6 servings.

Tomatoey Macaroni, Cheese and Beans

You can forget about this quick-to-fix combination while it's in the oven. Or, for an even speedier version, cover and microwave casserole on High 100% power for 15 minutes then sprinkle with topping.

1 tsp	canola oil	5 mL
1	onion, finely chopped	1
1 1/2 cups	cooked kidney or Romano beans	375 mL
1 cup	elbow macaroni	250 mL
1 cup	diced Cheddar cheese	250 mL
1	can (19 oz/540 mL) tomatoes	1
1 cup	water	250 mL
1/2 tsp	salt	2 mL
1/4 tsp	freshly ground black pepper	1 mL
1	rice cake, crushed	1
1/4 cup	grated Parmesan cheese	50 mL

• In skillet, heat oil over medium heat; cook onion, stirring occasionally, for 4 minutes or until translucent. Transfer to 8 cup (2 L) casserole sprayed with nonstick coating.

• Add beans, macaroni, Cheddar cheese, tomatoes, water, salt and pepper. Stir well, breaking up tomatoes with fork if whole.

• Cover and bake in 350°F (180°C) oven for 35 minutes or until macaroni is nearly tender.

• In bowl, combine rice cake crumbs and Parmesan; sprinkle over casserole. Bake for about 10 minutes longer or until topping begins to turn golden brown.

Makes 6 servings.

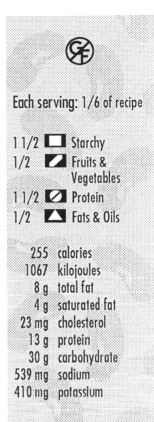

Each serving: 1/6 of recipe

1 1/2 ☐ Starchy
1/2 ◨ Fruits & Vegetables
1 1/2 ⊘ Protein
1/2 ◣ Fats & Oils

255 calories
1067 kilojoules
8 g total fat
4 g saturated fat
23 mg cholesterol
13 g protein
30 g carbohydrate
539 mg sodium
410 mg potassium

GOOD: Calcium, Phosphorus, Iron, Zinc, Magnesium, Niacin
EXCELLENT: Folate
HIGH: Fibre

TAMALE AND BEAN POT PIE

In place of the whole bean flour, all-purpose flour may be used but the pie will not be gluten-free ⊕.

1 tsp	canola oil	5 mL
1	medium onion, chopped	1
1	stalk celery, chopped	1
1	clove garlic, minced	1
2 cups	cooked beans, mashed	500 mL
1	can (7 1/2 oz/213 mL) tomato sauce	1
1/2 cup	water	125 mL
2 tsp	chili powder	10 mL
2 tsp	Worcestershire sauce	10 mL
1/2 tsp	salt	2 mL
1/4 tsp	freshly ground black pepper	1 mL
1	can (7 oz/199 mL) whole kernel corn, drained	1
1/2 cup	chopped green or red sweet pepper	125 mL

TOPPING:

1/2 cup	cornmeal	125 mL
2 tbsp	whole bean flour	25 mL
1 tbsp	sugar	15 mL
1 1/2 tsp	gluten-free baking powder	7 mL
1/2 tsp	salt	2 mL
1/2 cup	skim milk	125 mL
1	egg	1
1 tbsp	canola oil	15 mL

• In saucepan, heat oil over medium heat; cook onion, celery and garlic, stirring occasionally, for 6 minutes or until onion is translucent.

• Stir in beans, tomato sauce, water, chili powder, Worcestershire sauce, salt and pepper; bring to boil. Reduce heat and simmer for 10 minutes or until celery is almost tender. Stir in corn and green pepper. Spoon into 8 cup (2 L) casserole.

• Topping: In mixing bowl, combine cornmeal, flour, sugar, baking powder and salt.

• In small bowl, whisk together milk, egg and oil. Stir into dry ingredients until moistened. Spread evenly over bean mixture.

• Bake in 425°F (210°C) oven for 25 minutes or until golden brown.

Makes 6 servings.

MUSHROOMS AND BEANS

Two truly earthy flavors combine in this casserole, mushrooms and beans. The light rice noodles and sherry add a touch of sophistication.

2 tsp	soft margarine OR butter	10 mL
1/2 lb	mushrooms, sliced (about 3 cups/750 mL)	250 g
1 tbsp	minced onion	15 mL
1/4 tsp	minced garlic	1 mL
2 tbsp	cornstarch OR whole bean flour	25 mL
1 tbsp	cold water	15 mL
1/2 cup	strong chicken stock	125 mL
2 cups	cooked Romano, kidney or Dutch brown beans	500 mL
1 cup	frozen peas	250 mL
1/2 lb	rice vermicelli noodles	250 g
1/2 cup	10% cream	125 mL
2 tsp	soy sauce	10 mL
2 tbsp	sherry	25 mL
1 tsp	chopped fresh basil OR 1/4 tsp (1 mL) dried	2 mL

• In nonstick skillet, heat margarine over medium heat; cook mushrooms, onion and garlic, stirring occasionally, for about 5 minutes or until liquid evaporates.

• In small dish, stir cornstarch into water until smooth. Slowly add chicken stock. Stir into mushroom mixture. Cook, stirring until thickened.

• With fork, mash about one-third of the beans; add to skillet along with whole beans. Add peas; bring to boil. Cook, stirring, for about 5 minutes or until sauce thickens.

• Meanwhile, in bowl, pour boiling water over rice noodles. Let stand for about 4 minutes or until softened. Drain well.

• Stir cream and soy sauce into bean mixture and heat to just simmering.

• Just before serving, stir in sherry and basil. Serve over rice noodles.

Makes 4 servings.

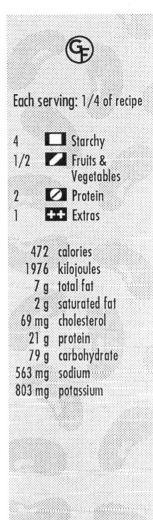

Each serving: 1/4 of recipe

4	▢	Starchy
1/2	◪	Fruits & Vegetables
2	◨	Protein
1	⊞	Extras

472	calories
1976	kilojoules
7 g	total fat
2 g	saturated fat
69 mg	cholesterol
21 g	protein
79 g	carbohydrate
563 mg	sodium
803 mg	potassium

GOOD: Thiamin, Vitamin B6, Vitamin B12

EXCELLENT: Phosphorus, Iron, Zinc, Magnesium, Vitamin D, Riboflavin, Niacin, Folate

VERY HIGH: Fibre

POTATO BEAN CAKES

Make these ahead and store, covered, at room temperature for 2 hours or in the refrigerator for up to 24 hours. Reheat them on nonstick skillet with no added fat. The cakes tend to be crisper and the flavor more intense when they are reheated.

1 cup	grated peeled raw potato	250 mL
1 cup	cooked red kidney or Dutch brown beans, roughly mashed	250 mL
2 tbsp	cornmeal	25 mL
1 tbsp	cornstarch	15 mL
2 tbsp	chopped celery leaves	25 mL
1 tbsp	chopped fresh parsley	15 mL
1	clove garlic, minced	1
1/2 tsp	curry powder	2 mL
1/2 tsp	salt	2 mL
1/4 tsp	freshly ground black pepper	1 mL
1	egg, beaten	1
2 tbsp	soft margarine OR butter	25 mL
1 cup	Mornay Sauce (p.112) OR Herb Sauce (p.112)	250 mL
1/2 cup	salsa	125 mL
1 tbsp	chopped fresh chives OR parsley	15 mL

• In bowl, stir together grated potato, beans, cornmeal, cornstarch, celery leaves, parsley, garlic, curry powder, salt and pepper. Stir in egg until well mixed.

• In nonstick skillet, heat half of the margarine over medium heat; in tablespoonfuls (15 mL), drop about one-eighth of the mixture at a time onto skillet to make 4 mounds. With spoon, spread into a flat cake.

• Cook for 5 minutes or until bottom is golden brown. Turn and cook for 4 minutes longer or until golden brown. Remove to plate and keep warm. Repeat with remaining potato mixture.

• For each serving, place 2 cakes, slightly overlapping, on plate. Spoon Mornay Sauce over top cake; spoon salsa over lower one. Sprinkle with chives.

Makes 4 servings.

RATATOUILLE

Leaving the skin on the vegetables and combining them with beans ensures a dish that is very high in dietary fibre. Serve it hot or cold with cooked brown or white rice for a meatless meal that supplies complete protein.

1/2 lb	eggplant (1 medium)	250 g
1/2 lb	zucchini (1 to 2)	250 g
1 tsp	salt	5 mL
2 tbsp	olive oil	25 mL
2	cloves garlic, minced	2
1	onion, chopped	1
1/4 lb	button mushrooms, quartered	125 g
1	small red sweet pepper, seeded and chopped	1
1	can (19 oz/540 mL) tomatoes OR 2 cups (500 mL) chopped fresh tomatoes	1
2 cups	cooked Romano or Dutch brown beans	500 mL
1 tbsp	chopped fresh basil OR 1 tsp (5 mL) dried	15 mL
1	bay leaf	1
1/2 tsp	granulated sugar	2 mL
1/4 tsp	freshly ground black pepper	1 mL
1 tbsp	capers, optional	15 mL
	Chopped fresh parsley	

• With sharp knife, cut eggplant and zucchini into 1 inch (2.5 cm) cubes. Place in sieve set over bowl; toss with salt to coat all pieces. Let stand for 15 minutes to draw bitterness and some liquid from eggplant.

• In large skillet, heat oil over medium heat; cook garlic, onion and mushrooms, stirring occasionally, for about 6 minutes or until liquid from mushrooms has nearly evaporated.

• Add drained zucchini and eggplant, red pepper, tomatoes, beans, basil, bay leaf, sugar and pepper; bring to boil. Reduce heat and simmer over medium-low heat, stirring occasionally, for about 45 minutes or until fairly thickened and eggplant is tender. Stir in capers, if desired. Discard bay leaf. Garnish with chopped parsley.

Makes 6 servings.

GF

Each serving: 1/6 of recipe

1	☐	Starchy
1/2	▨	Fruits & Vegetables
1	▨	Protein
1/2	▲	Fats & Oils

169 calories
708 kilojoules
5 g total fat
0 g saturated fat
0 mg cholesterol
7 g protein
25 g carbohydrate
671 mg sodium
678 mg potasssium

GOOD: Iron, Magnesium, Vitamin A, Niacin
EXCELLENT: Vitamin C, Folate
VERY HIGH: Fibre

Tomato Bean Pasta Sauce

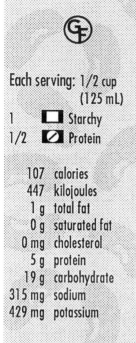

To keep the meal gluten-free *, serve over cooked rice, rice noodles or polenta for another of those beans and grain combinations that provides complete protein. Use for pizza, lasagne or over meatloaf.*

1 tsp	canola oil	5 mL
1	onion, chopped	1
2	cloves garlic, minced	2
6	mushrooms, chopped	6
1 tsp	each ground thyme and basil	5 mL
1 tsp	yeast extract	5 mL
1/2 tsp	ground oregano	2 mL
1/2 tsp	each granulated sugar and salt	2 mL
1/4 tsp	freshly ground black pepper	1 mL
1	can (5 1/2 oz/156 mL) tomato paste	1
2 cups	cooked red kidney or Romano beans, mashed	500 mL
2 cups	vegetable stock	500 mL

• In saucepan, heat oil over medium heat; cook onion, garlic and mushrooms, stirring occasionally, for 5 minutes or until onion is translucent. Stir in thyme, basil, yeast extract, oregano, sugar, salt and pepper. Cook, stirring, for 1 minute.

• Stir in tomato paste, beans and stock until well mixed; bring to boil. Reduce heat and simmer, uncovered and stirring occasionally, for about 45 minutes or until reduced by about one-third.

• Serve immediately or refrigerate in covered containers for up to 5 days or freeze for up to 2 months.

Makes 8 servings, 4 cups (1 L).

Each serving: 1/2 cup (125 mL)

1 ☐ Starchy
1/2 ☑ Protein

107	calories
447	kilojoules
1 g	total fat
0 g	saturated fat
0 mg	cholesterol
5 g	protein
19 g	carbohydrate
315 mg	sodium
429 mg	potassium

GOOD: Iron
EXCELLENT: Folate
HIGH: Fibre

Bean Stroganoff and Noodles

Substitute rice or polenta for the noodles for a gluten-free presentation. Steamed green beans or broccoli go nicely with this low-fat, high-fibre entrée.

1 tsp	canola oil	5 mL
1	onion, chopped	1
8	medium mushrooms, quartered	8
2 tsp	paprika	10 mL
1/2 tsp	ground thyme	2 mL
1 cup	beef OR vegetable stock	250 mL
2 tbsp	dry red wine	25 mL
2 tsp	Worcestershire sauce	10 mL
2 cups	cooked red kidney, Romano or Dutch brown beans	500 mL
1/2 cup	light sour cream	125 mL
1 tsp	red wine vinegar	5 mL
2 tsp	cornstarch	10 mL
	Freshly ground black pepper	
2 cups	cooked egg noodles	500 mL
2	green onions, thinly sliced	2

• In nonstick skillet, heat oil over medium heat; cook onion, stirring occasionally, for 4 minutes or until translucent. Add mushrooms and cook for 4 minutes or until mushrooms are softened.

• Sprinkle with paprika and thyme; cook, stirring, for 1 minute.

• Stir in stock, wine and Worcestershire sauce until well blended. With fork, crush about one-third of the beans; add to skillet along with remaining beans and bring to boil. Reduce heat and simmer, uncovered, for 10 minutes or until liquid is slightly reduced.

• In small bowl, combine sour cream, vinegar and cornstarch until smooth; stir into bean mixture. Cook, stirring, for 2 minutes or until thickened. Season to taste with pepper.

• Spoon over noodles. Garnish with green onions.

Makes 4 servings.

Each serving: 1/4 of recipe

2 1/2	■	Starchy
1 1/2	■	Protein
1/2	▲	Fats & Oils
1	++	Extras

309	calories
1293	kilojoules
7 g	total fat
3 g	saturated fat
37 mg	cholesterol
14 g	protein
46 g	carbohydrate
375 mg	sodium
544 mg	potassium

GOOD: Phosphorus, Zinc, Niacin

EXCELLENT: Iron, Magnesium, Folate

VERY HIGH: Fibre

THREE BEAN TERRINE

For a sit-down dinner or party buffet this is special. Both the color and flavor of each layer complement the others.

1 1/2 cups	each cooked Romano, white and red kidney beans	375 mL
1/2 cup	crumbled feta cheese	125 mL
1/4 cup	shredded Cheddar cheese	50 mL
3	egg whites	3
1/4 cup	light sour cream	50 mL
Half	pkg (300 g) frozen spinach leaves	Half
2 tsp	lemon juice OR white vinegar	10 mL
1/4 tsp	each salt, ground nutmeg and freshly ground black pepper	1 mL
2 tbsp	chopped sun-dried tomatoes	25 mL
2 tbsp	millet	25 mL
1 tbsp	chopped walnuts OR almonds	15 mL
1 1/2 tsp	yeast extract (Marmite)	7 mL
1	clove garlic	1
1/2 tsp	each dried basil and chili powder	2 mL
1/4 tsp	ground thyme	1 mL

• Spray 8 x 4 inch (1.5 L) loaf pan with nonstick coating; line bottom only with waxed paper cut to fit. Set aside.

• In food processor, combine white kidney beans, feta and Cheddar cheeses, 1 egg white and 1 tbsp (15 mL) sour cream. Process, scraping down sides of container frequently, for about 2 minutes or until puréed. Transfer to bowl. Set aside.

• Squeeze juice from spinach leaves. Add to food processor with Romano beans, lemon juice, salt, nutmeg, pepper, 1 egg white and 1 tbsp (15 mL) sour cream. Process, scraping down sides of container frequently, for about 2 minutes or until well blended. Spread evenly in prepared pan. Spread white bean mixture over top.

• In processor, combine red kidney beans, tomatoes, millet, nuts, yeast extract, garlic, basil, chili powder, thyme and the remaining egg white and sour cream. Process, scraping down sides of container frequently, for about 2 minutes or until well blended. Spread on top of white bean mixture.

• Bake in 350°F (180°C) oven in pan of water for 1 hour 15 minutes or until tester inserted in centre comes out clean.

• Cool on rack for 10 minutes. Turn out onto serving platter.

Makes 8 servings.

FRITTATA WITH ZUCCHINI AND BEANS

Whether served hot, warm or at room temperature, this makes a delicious, nutritious brunch or supper.

2 tbsp	soft margarine OR butter	25 mL
4	small mushrooms, quartered and sliced	4
1	medium onion, halved and thinly sliced	1
1	medium zucchini, halved and thinly sliced	1
1/4 tsp	freshly ground black pepper	1 mL
1 cup	cooked Romano, kidney or Dutch brown beans	250 mL
1/4 cup	chopped red sweet pepper	50 mL
2	eggs	2
1	egg white	1
1 tbsp	grated Romano OR Parmesan cheese	15 mL
1 tbsp	water	15 mL
1/2 tsp	salt	2 mL
1/4 tsp	ground nutmeg	1 mL

• In 10 inch (25 cm) nonstick skillet, melt margarine over medium-high heat; cook mushrooms, onion and zucchini, stirring occasionally, for 5 minutes or until onion is translucent. Season with pepper.

• Stir in beans and red pepper. Cook for 2 minutes or until heated through.

• In small bowl and using fork, beat together eggs, egg white, cheese, water, salt and nutmeg; pour over bean mixture. With spatula, lift vegetables to allow egg mixture to flow through to bottom of skillet.

• Reduce heat to low. Cover and cook for 10 minutes or until set. Invert onto serving plate.

Makes 4 servings.

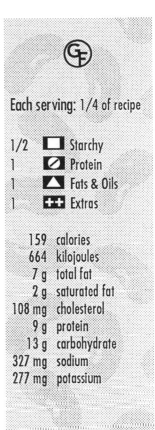

Each serving: 1/4 of recipe

1/2 ☐ Starchy
1 ∅ Protein
1 ▲ Fats & Oils
1 ✚ Extras

159 calories
664 kilojoules
7 g total fat
2 g saturated fat
108 mg cholesterol
9 g protein
13 g carbohydrate
327 mg sodium
277 mg potassium

GOOD: Vitamin D
EXCELLENT: Folate
MODERATE: Fibre

CREAM SAUCE

The bits of garlic and onion may be omitted resulting in a smoother sauce often listed in cookbooks as bechamel or white sauce. However, the flavor they exude makes this sauce more exciting.

1 tbsp	soft margarine OR butter	15 mL
1 tbsp	minced onion	15 mL
1/4 tsp	minced garlic	1 mL
2 tbsp	whole bean flour	25 mL
1/4 tsp	salt	1 mL
3/4 cup	skim milk	175 mL
1/2 tsp	Worcestershire sauce	2 mL
	White pepper	

• In saucepan, heat margarine over medium heat; cook onion and garlic for 3 minutes or until tender. Gradually whisk in bean flour and salt until well blended.

• Gradually whisk in milk; cook, whisking constantly, for about 2 minutes or until smooth and thickened. Whisk in Worcestershire sauce. Season to taste with pepper. (To thin, stir in additional milk or water, 1 tsp (5 mL) at a time.)

Makes 10 servings, 1 cup (250 mL).

VARIATIONS:
HERB SAUCE

• Whisk 1/4 cup (50 mL) chopped fresh parsley, 1/2 tsp (2 ml) ground marjoram and 1/4 tsp (1 mL) ground thyme into hot cooked sauce.

MORNAY SAUCE

Mornay sauce is simply cream sauce with cheese added.

• Whisk 1/4 cup (50 mL) grated Parmesan cheese into hot cooked sauce until cheese melts.

ENTREES

Spanish Rice with Pork and Beans

Old-Fashioned Baked Beans

Hawaiian Beans

Stampede Barbecued Beans

Bean Casserole

Country-Style Bean Stew

Lasagne

West Indian Bean Stew

Chili Con Carne

White Chili

Red Beans and Rice New Orleans Style

Jamaican Beans and Rice

Feijoada (Brazilian Bean Stew)

Chicken and Bean Ragout

Cassoulet

Jambalaya

Meat and Bean Loaf

Pot Roast with Turnips and Beans

Smoked Chops and Beans

Stir-Fry with Vegetables and Beans

Tourtière

Spinach and Black Bean Roll-Ups

SPANISH RICE WITH PORK AND BEANS

The flavor of this nutrient-dense casserole seems more intense the second time around. Make it ahead, cover and refrigerate it for one to two days then reheat it for a tasty quick meal when there is not the time to prepare it from scratch.

2 tsp	olive oil	10 mL
3/4 lb	lean boneless pork leg, loin or shoulder, cubes	375 g
4	cloves garlic (unpeeled)	4
1 cup	short grain rice (pearl or Arborio)	250 mL
1 tbsp	paprika	15 mL
1	can (19 oz/540 mL) tomatoes	1
2 cups	cooked Romano or kidney beans	500 mL
2 cups	chicken OR beef stock	500 mL

• In flameprooof casserole, heat oil over medium heat. Cook pork cubes and unpeeled garlic, stirring occasionally, for about 8 minutes or until pork is browned and garlic is golden brown.

• Stir in rice and paprika. Cook for 2 minutes or until rice is well coated. Pour in tomatoes, breaking up with fork if whole. Stir in beans.

• Meanwhile, in small saucepan, heat stock to boiling. Pour over bean mixture.

• Bake in 375°F (190°C) oven for 35 to 40 minutes or until rice is tender. Divide garlic among servings to be squeezed over each one or discarded.

Makes 4 servings.

OLD-FASHIONED BAKED BEANS

This dish is reminiscent of pioneer days when pots of beans slowly cooked all day long on or in the wood burning stoves. To reduce the fat we have substituted back bacon for the side pork called for in old-fashioned recipes.

3 cups	Dutch brown beans, soaked and drained	750 mL
1/3 cup	packed brown sugar	75 mL
1/4 cup	molasses	50 mL
1/4 cup	tomato paste	50 mL
1 tbsp	cider vinegar	15 mL
1	bay leaf	1
1 tbsp	dry mustard	15 mL
1 tsp	salt	5 mL
1/4 lb	chunk back bacon, cubed	125 g
6	whole cloves	6
1	large onion	1
	Salt and freshly ground pepper	

• In large saucepan, cover beans generously with water (about 8 cups/2 L); bring to boil. Reduce heat and simmer for 20 minutes or until nearly tender, but with a little crunch. Drain well. Pour into large 10 cup (2.5 L) bean pot, deep casserole or slow cooker.

• In small bowl, combine brown sugar, molasses, tomato paste, cider vinegar, dry mustard and salt. Stir into beans along with salt pork cubes.

• Stick whole cloves into onion; bury in middle of bean mixture. Pour on 2 cups (500 mL) hot water.

• Cover and bake in 275°F (140°C) oven, stirring occasionally, for 4 1/2 hours, adding more hot water , a little at a time, if mixture seems dry.

• Uncover and bake for 30 minute to 1 hour longer or until tender. Discard clove-studded onion and bay leaf. Season to taste with salt and pepper.

Makes 8 servings.

Hawaiian Beans

Traditionally, steamed brown bread was made to go with baked beans, especially Boston-baked beans. With this newer version serve rice cakes or our gluten-free Cornmeal Bread (p.156). That way the combination will be gluten-free. It still provides complete protein because the grain, in this case rice or corn, supplies the amino acid the beans lack.

1	Old-Fashioned Baked Beans (p.115)	1
1	can (14 oz/398 mL) pineapple chunks, drained	1
1/2 lb	gluten-free weiners	250 g
1/3 cup	toasted cashews or peanuts, coarsely chopped	75 mL

• Prepare Old-Fashioned Baked Beans following recipe directions, adding pineapple with salt pork cubes. Bake as directed.

• Cut weiners into bite-sized pieces. Stir into bean mixture along with cashews for last 30 minutes of cooking time or until weiners are thoroughly heated.

Makes 8 servings.

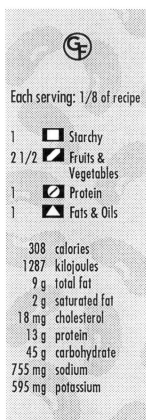

Each serving: 1/8 of recipe

1	☐	Starchy
2 1/2	▨	Fruits & Vegetables
1	⊘	Protein
1	▲	Fats & Oils

308	calories
1287	kilojoules
9 g	total fat
2 g	saturated fat
18 mg	cholesterol
13 g	protein
45 g	carbohydrate
755 mg	sodium
595 mg	potassium

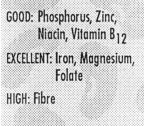

GOOD: Phosphorus, Zinc, Niacin, Vitamin B$_{12}$

EXCELLENT: Iron, Magnesium, Folate

HIGH: Fibre

STAMPEDE BARBECUED BEANS

Here's a great "pot o' beans" adapted from the one created by the home economists at the Calgary Co-Op. Susan Spicer is one of them and says, "Versions of these show up at stampede parties all over Alberta. They're wonderful on their own or as a side dish for barbecued chicken or ribs."

6	slices back bacon	6
1/2 lb	gluten-free kielbasa	250 g
2	cans (each 19 oz/540 mL) red kidney beans	2
2	cans (each 19 oz/540 mL) white kidney beans	2
1	can (19 oz/540 mL) pork and beans	1
1	can (14 oz/398 mL) tomato sauce	1
1	onion, chopped	1
1	clove garlic, minced	1
1 cup	shredded Cheddar cheese	250 mL
1/4 cup	molasses	50 mL
2 tbsp	brown sugar	25 mL
1/2 tsp	each paprika, dried oregano, thyme and dry mustard	2 mL
1/4 tsp	each cayenne and freshly ground black pepper	1 mL

• In skillet over medium heat, partly cook bacon. Remove and pat off excess fat with paper towels. Cut into 1/2 inch (1 cm) pieces.

• Remove casing from sausage; cut into bite-sized pieces.

• Drain and rinse red and white kidney beans. Transfer to large flameproof casserole or Dutch oven (no plastic handles). Add pork and beans, tomato sauce, onion, garlic, cheese, molasses, brown sugar, paprika, oregano, thyme, dry mustard, cayenne, pepper, bacon and sausage. Stir well.

• Cover with foil or lid. Set on barbecue grill over medium heat; close lid. Bake, stirring occasionally, for 1 hour or until flavors are well blended. Or bake in 350°F (180°C) oven.

Makes 10 servings.

Each serving: 1/10 of recipe

2	☐	Starchy
1 1/2	▨	Fruits & Vegetables
2 1/2	▨	Protein
1 1/2	◣	Fats & Oils

450	calories
1880	kilojoules
15 g	total fat
6 g	saturated fat
35 mg	cholesterol
23 g	protein
56 g	carbohydrate
650 mg	sodium
954 mg	potassium

GOOD: Calcium, Thiamin, Vitamin B$_6$, Vitamin B$_{12}$

EXCELLENT: Phosphorus, Iron, Zinc, Magnesium, Niacin, Folate

VERY HIGH: Fibre

Each serving: 1/12 of recipe

1 1/2 ▱ Starchy
1 1/2 ⊘ Protein
1　➕ Extras

223　Calories
917　kilojoules
5 g　total fat
1 g　saturated fat
13 mg　cholesterol
14 g　protein
29 g　carbohydrate
431 mg　sodium
577 mg　potassium

GOOD: Phosphorus, Iron,
　　　Zinc, Thiamin, Niacin,
　　　Vitamin B$_6$
EXCELLENT: Magnesium,
　　　　　Vitamin A, Folate
VERY HIGH: Fibre.

BEAN CASSEROLE

Any variety of dried beans may be used for this entree. If there is no time for the soaking and cooking use canned beans. Rinse and drain them before combining them with the other ingredients.

1 tsp	canola oil	5 mL
1 lb	boneless pork, cubed	500 g
1 tsp	paprika	5 mL
1/2 tsp	salt	2 mL
1/4 tsp	ground ginger	1 mL
1/4 tsp	freshly ground black pepper	1 mL
1	large onion, finely chopped	1
6 cups	cooked Romano or red kidney beans	1.5 L
1 cup	diced carrots	250 mL
1 cup	chopped celery	250 mL
1 cup	chopped green sweet pepper	250 mL
1 tbsp	packed brown sugar	15 mL
1	can (10 oz/284 mL) cream of mushroom soup	1
1/4 cup	finely chopped peanuts	50 mL

• In nonstick skillet, heat oil over medium heat. Add pork cubes; sprinkle with paprika, salt, ginger and pepper. Cook until lightly browned. Remove to paper towels to drain.

• Add onion to skillet; cook for about 4 minutes or until translucent. Add 1/2 cup (125 mL) water and deglaze skillet by stirring to scrape up any brown bits. Set aside.

• In large casserole, combine beans, carrots, celery and green pepper. Stir in onion mixture and pork cubes.

• Dissolve brown sugar in 1/2 cup (125 mL) water; stir into bean and pork mixture. Stir in cream of mushroom soup.

• Bake, covered, in 325°F (160°C) oven for about 35 minutes or until carrots are tender. Uncover and sprinkle with chopped peanuts; bake for 10 minutes longer.

Makes 12 servings.

COUNTRY-STYLE BEAN STEW

*Broccoli, steamed to tender-crisp and a crusty bread, such as
Seed Bread (p.155) to sop up the juices is all that this savory
stew needs to go with it.*

2 tsp	canola oil	10 mL
1 lb	lean ground beef	500 g
1/2 cup	chopped onion	125 mL
2	cloves garlic, minced	2
1/2 tsp	salt	2 mL
1/4 tsp	freshly ground black pepper	1 mL
1/4 tsp	ground thyme	1 mL
1 cup	diced carrots	250 mL
1 cup	diced rutabaga (yellow turnip)	250 mL
1/2 cup	sliced celery	125 mL
1/2 cup	chopped green sweet pepper	125 mL
1	can (19 oz/540 mL) tomatoes	1
3 cups	cooked red kidney or Dutch brown beans	750 mL

• In saucepan, heat oil over medium heat; cook ground beef,
onion, garlic, salt, pepper and thyme, stirring to break up
meat, for about 7 minutes or until meat is no longer pink.
Spoon off any excess fat.

• Add carrots, turnip, celery and green pepper. Stir in
tomatoes, breaking up with fork if whole; stir in beans.

• Bring to boil. Reduce heat and simmer, covered, for 20 minutes or until vegetables are tender.

Makes 8 servings.

EACH SERVING: 1/8 of recipe

1 1/2 ☐ Starchy
1/2 ◪ Fruits & Vegetables
2 1/2 ⊘ Protein
1/2 ▲ Fats & Oils
1 ✚ Extras

283	Calories
1185	kilojoules
10 g	total fat
3 g	saturated fat
31 mg	cholesterol
20 g	protein
29 g	carbohydrate
275 mg	sodium
892 mg	potassium

GOOD: Phosphorus, Vitamin C,
Riboflavin, Vitamin B₆
EXCELLENT: Iron, Zinc,
Magnesium,
Vitamin A, Niacin,
Folate,
Vitamin B₁₂
MODERATE: Fibre

LASAGNE

Replacing the pasta noodles with our Crepes (p.151) or Gluten-Free Tortillas (p.178) turns this into a gluten-free ⑤ lasagne. It can be frozen for up to three months and it is great to have on hand for a spur-of-the-moment après-ski party.

1/2 lb	lean ground beef	250 g
1	onion, chopped	1
1	clove garlic, minced	1
2 cups	cooked kidney beans, mashed	500 mL
1 1/4 cups	canned tomato paste	300 mL
2 cups	water	500 mL
2 tbsp	chopped fresh basil OR 2 tsp (10 mL) dried	25 mL
1 tsp	ground thyme	5 mL
1/2 tsp	ground oregano	2 mL
	Salt and freshly ground black pepper	
2 cups	1 % cottage cheese	500 mL
1	egg, lightly beaten	1
12	oven-ready lasagne noodles	12
2 cups	shredded mozzarella cheese (8 oz/250 g)	500 mL
1/2 cup	grated Parmesan cheese	125 mL

• In large nonstick skillet over medium heat, cook beef, onions and garlic, stirring to break up meat, for about 6 minutes or until beef is no longer pink and onion is translucent. Spoon off any excess fat. Stir in mashed beans, tomato paste, water, basil, thyme and oregano; bring to boil, reduce heat and simmer for 15 minutes or until slightly reduced. Season to taste with salt and pepper.

• In small bowl, combine cottage cheese and egg; mix well.

• Set 1 cup (250 mL) sauce aside. Spread 3/4 cup (175 mL) of the remaining sauce over bottom of 13 x 9 inch (3 L) baking or lasagne dish. Arrange layer of 4 lasagne noodles over sauce. Spread half remaining sauce over noodles, then half cottage cheese mixture and half mozzarella cheese. Cover with second layer of 4 noodles. Repeat sauce and cheese layers. Top with remaining noodles. Cover completely with reserved sauce. Sprinkle with Parmesan cheese.

• Bake in 350°F (180°C) oven for about 40 minutes or until noodles are tender. Let stand for 10 minutes before cutting.

Makes 8 servings.

West Indian Bean Stew

Traditionally, this stew calls for double or triple the amount of salt cod. We have used less here to cut down on the sodium. The flavor is still wonderful. If the mixture begins to look too dry and starts sticking to the pot during the long simmering stir in water, as it is required.

1/4 lb	boneless salt cod	125 g
2 cups	dried white or red kidney beans	500 mL
7 cups	water	1.75 L
1/2 tsp	ground allspice	2 mL
1	bay leaf	1
1/2 tsp	freshly ground black pepper	2 mL
1/4 tsp	crushed red chili pepper	1 mL
1/4 tsp	ground oregano	1 mL
4 cups	hot cooked rice	1 L
1	lemon, cut into 8 wedges	1

• Soak cod in water overnight; drain and rinse in fresh water. Drain again and cut into cubes; set aside.

• Rinse beans, place in large saucepan with 7 cups (1.75 L) water. Bring to boil; boil for 2 minutes. Add cod, allspice and bay leaf. Reduce heat and simmer, covered, for about 1 1/2 hours or until beans are tender.

• Stir in black and chili peppers and oregano; simmer for 10 minutes or until thickened. Discard bay leaf.

• Serve over rice. Garnish with lemon wedges.

Makes 8 servings.

Each serving: 1/8 of recipe

4	☐	Starchy
2	⊘	Protein

353	calories
1475	kilojoules
1 g	total fat
0 g	saturated fat
21 mg	cholesterol
23 g	protein
62 g	carbohydrate
1012 mg	sodium
1066 mg	potassium

GOOD: Calcium, Vitamin B_6
EXCELLENT: Phosphorus, Iron, Zinc, Magnesium, Niacin, Folate, Vitamin B_{12}
MODERATE: Fibre

CHILI CON CARNE

This chili with meat in it, that is what con carne means, is wonderful to have on hand. The beans help stretch the meat, making the dish cheaper than it would be if it were all meat. It can be refrigerated for up to four days or frozen for up to three months.

1 lb	lean ground beef	500 g
2	onions, coarsely chopped	2
2	stalks celery, coarsely chopped	2
2	cloves garlic, minced	2
1	green sweet pepper, chopped	1
1	can (19 oz/540 mL) tomatoes	1
1 tbsp	chili powder	15 mL
2 tsp	unsweetened cocoa powder	10 mL
2 tsp	ground cumin	10 mL
1 tsp	salt	5 mL
1/4 tsp	crushed red chili pepper	1 mL
1/4 tsp	cinnamon	1 mL
4 cups	cooked red kidney beans	1 L
1	can (14 oz/398 mL) tomato sauce	1

• In large nonstick skillet over medium heat, cook ground beef, stirring frequently, for 10 minutes. Add onions, celery, garlic and green pepper; cook for 15 minutes longer or until onion is translucent.

• Stir in tomatoes, breaking up with fork, chili powder, cocoa, cumin, salt, red chili pepper and cinnamon. Cook for 5 minutes for flavors to mingle.

• Stir in beans then tomato sauce.

• Simmer, covered, for about 1 hour. Or transfer to 10 cup (2.5 L) casserole or two 6 cup (1.5 L) casseroles and bake in 350°F (180°C) oven for 40 minutes or until heated through and flavors have blended.

Makes 8 servings.

Each serving: 1/8 of recipe

1	☐	Starchy
1/2	▨	Fruits & Vegetables
2 1/2	⊘	Protein
1/2	▲	Fats & Oils
1	⊞	Extras

282	calories
1181	kilojoules
9 g	total fat
3 g	saturated fat
31 mg	cholesterol
20 g	protein
30 g	carbohydrate
771 mg	sodium
866 mg	potassium

GOOD: Phosphorus, Riboflavin, Vitamin B_6

EXCELLENT: Iron, Zinc, Magnesium, Niacin, Folate, Vitamin B_{12}

VERY HIGH: Fibre

WHITE CHILI

This is a wonderful, make-ahead, one-pot meal to take to the ski cabin or summer cottage for a warming meal on a cold fall or winter week-end. Colorful marinated broccoli and carrots are wonderful with it and can also be prepared ahead.

2 tsp	canola oil	10 mL
1 lb	lean ground pork OR turkey OR chicken	500 g
2	stalks celery, chopped	2
2	cloves garlic, minced	2
1	onion, chopped	1
1 tbsp	chopped pickled jalapeño pepper	15 mL
1 tsp	ground cumin	5 mL
1 tsp	ground thyme	5 mL
1/2 tsp	chili powder	2 mL
1/2 tsp	salt	2 mL
Pinch	cayenne pepper	Pinch
1	bay leaf	1
2 cups	cooked white kidney beans	500 mL
1 cup	chicken stock	250 mL
1/2 cup	diced raw potato	125 mL
1 tbsp	fresh lime OR lemon juice	15 mL
2	green onions, thinly sliced	2

• In large saucepan, heat oil over medium heat. Cook pork, celery, garlic and onion, stirring to break up pork, for about 10 minutes or until pork is no longer pink.

• Stir in jalapeño pepper, cumin, thyme, chili powder, salt, cayenne and bay leaf. Cook, stirring, for 1 minute.

• Add beans, stock and potato; bring to boil. Reduce heat and simmer, partly covered, for 30 minutes. Discard bay leaf.

• Just before serving, stir in lime juice. Garnish with green onions.

Makes 4 servings.

Each serving: 1/4 of recipe

1 1/2 ☐ Starchy
5 1/2 ⊘ Protein

396	calories
1655	kilojoules
12 g	total fat
3 g	saturated fat
80 mg	cholesterol
44 g	protein
26 g	carbohydrate
525 mg	sodium
996 mg	potassium

EXCELLENT: Phosphorus, Iron, Zinc, Magnesium, Thiamin, Riboflavin, Niacin, Folate, Vitamin B₆ Vitamin B₁₂

VERY HIGH: Fibre

Red Beans and Rice New Orleans Style

For generations this has been the wash-day Monday bean pot that cooks have prepared in New Orleans. Now, it is also restaurant fare. It is similiar to other bean and rice dishes that appear in the cuisine of the Americas and West Indies. Hoppin' John, Cuban Moors and Christians, Limpin' Susan, to name a few. They range from mild to hot and spicy and use red, black or white beans.

1 tsp	canola oil	5 mL
3	cloves garlic, minced	3
2	onions, chopped	2
1	green sweet pepper, chopped	1
1	stalk celery, chopped	1
1 tsp	dried thyme	5 mL
1/2 tsp	dried oregano	2 mL
1/2 tsp	salt	2 mL
1/4 tsp	crushed red chili pepper	1 mL
1 cup	beef OR vegetable stock	250 mL
2 cups	cooked red kidney beans	500 mL
1/4 lb	lean ham, cubed	125 g
2 cups	hot cooked brown rice	500 mL
	Chopped fresh parsley OR cilantro	

• In nonstick skillet, heat oil over medium heat; cook garlic, onions, green pepper and celery, stirring often, for about 5 minutes or until onion is translucent.

• Stir in thyme, oregano, salt and red chili pepper. Pour in stock.

• With fork, crush about one-third of the beans. Add to skillet along with ham; stir well. Bring to boil, reduce heat and simmer, stirring occasionally, for about 20 minutes or until thickened.

• Spoon over rice. Garnish with parsley.

Makes 4 servings.

Each serving: 1/4 of recipe

2 1/2 ☐ Starchy
1 1/2 ◪ Protein
1 ➕ Extras

302 calories
1264 kilojoules
5 g total fat
1 g saturated fat
16 mg cholesterol
15 g protein
48 g carbohydrate
583 mg sodium
582 mg potassium

GOOD: Zinc, Vitamin C, Thiamin, Vitamin B₆
EXCELLENT: Phosphorus, Iron, Magnesium, Niacin, Folate
VERY HIGH: Fibre

Jamaican Beans and Rice

Coconut milk adds such a wonderful sweet, nutty flavor to this bean and rice combination that it is worth the added fat it also contributes.

1 tsp	canola oil	5 mL
1	onion, chopped	1
1	clove garlic, minced	1
2 cups	cooked kidney or black beans	500 mL
1 cup	coconut milk*	250 mL
1 cup	cubed cooked ham (4 oz/125 g)	250 mL
1/2 tsp	dried thyme	2 mL
1/2 tsp	chili powder	2 mL
1/2 tsp	each salt and freshly ground black pepper	2 mL
1/4 tsp	crumbled dried sage	1 mL
1/4 tsp	dried savory	1 mL
1 cup	long-grain rice	250 mL
1 cup	chopped tomato or red sweet pepper Chopped parsley	250 mL

• In saucepan, heat oil over medium heat. Cook onion and garlic for about 5 minutes or until translucent.

• Add beans, coconut milk, ham, thyme, chili powder, salt, pepper, sage and savory. Bring to boil, cook for 1 minute. Add rice and 2 cups (500 mL) water, bring back to boil, reduce heat, cover and simmer for 25 minutes or until rice is tender and liquid absorbed.

• Serve immediately or leave to cool. Cover and refrigerate for up to 3 days. Reheat when needed.

• Garnish with tomatoes and parsley.

Makes 6 servings.

GF

Each serving: 1/6 of recipe

2 1/2 ⬜ Starchy
1 ⧄ Protein
1 1/2 △ Fats & Oils
1 ⊞ Extras

318	Calories
1329	kilojoules
10 g	total fat
7 g	saturated fat
12 mg	cholesterol
13 g	protein
42 g	carbohydrate
497 mg	sodium
517 mg	potassium

GOOD: Phosphorus, Zinc, Thiamin, Niacin, Vitamin B$_6$
EXCELLENT: Iron, Magnesium, Folate

HIGH: Fibre

* To make coconut milk pour 1 1/2 cups (375 mL) boiling water over 1 cup (250 mL) unsweetened dessicated coconut and let stand for 30 minutes. Strain the liquid through cheesecloth, squeezing to extract the coconut milk.

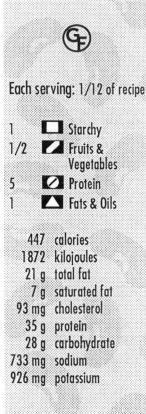

Each serving: 1/12 of recipe

1   ▢ Starchy
1/2 ◪ Fruits &
       Vegetables
5   ◉ Protein
1   ▲ Fats & Oils

  447 calories
1872 kilojoules
   21 g total fat
    7 g saturated fat
  93 mg cholesterol
  35 g protein
  28 g carbohydrate
733 mg sodium
926 mg potassium

GOOD: Riboflavin,

EXCELLENT: Phosphorus, Iron,
        Zinc, Magnesium,
        Thiamin, Niacin,
        Folate,
        Vitamin B_6,
        Vitamin B_{12}

VERY HIGH: Fibre

Feijoada (Brazilian Bean Stew)

In Brazil where beans are an important item at meal time, this is a party dish. Traditionally it is made there with assorted meats and black beans. Other dried beans are also good in this hearty dish for a large crowd. Refrigerate leftovers for a last minute meal a few days later.

2 1/2 cups	dried red kidney or black beans	625 mL
3/4 lb	stewing beef	375 g
3/4 lb	boneless pork shoulder, cut into 3/4 inch (2 cm) cubes	375 g
1/2 lb	corned beef	250 g
1/2 lb	gluten-free hot Italian sausage	250 g
1/2 lb	gluten-free kielbasa	250 g
6	cloves garlic, finely chopped	6
1	onion, coarsely chopped	1
1	can (19 oz/540 mL) tomatoes	1
1 tsp	red chili pepper flakes	5 mL
1 tsp	grated orange rind	5 mL
1	orange, thinly sliced	1

• Soak beans (p.12). Rinse well.

• In saucepan, cover stewing beef, pork and corned beef with water. Cut sausages into 1 inch (2.5 cm) slices. Add to saucepan; bring to boil. Reduce heat and simmer for 20 minutes. Drain and rinse meat.

• In large Dutch oven, combine beans, garlic, onion, tomatoes, red pepper flakes and orange rind. Add 4 cups (1L) water. Stir in meat, burying corned beef in bean mixture; bring to boil. Cover and transfer to oven.

• Bake in 350°F (180°C) oven for 1 1/2 hours. Uncover and bake, stirring occasionally, for another 1/2 hour or until beans are tender and most of the liquid has evaporated.

• Serve immediately. Or cool slightly, cover and refrigerate for up to 3 days; or freeze for up to 2 months. Reheat slowly in 325°F (160°C) oven, stirring once or twice, until heated through.

• Remove corned beef; slice and arrange over bean mixture. Garnish with orange slices.

Makes 12 servings.

CHICKEN AND BEAN RAGOUT

Here is a truly homey dish that ranks among the best when it comes to one-pot meals.

1/3 cup	whole bean flour	75 mL
	Salt and freshly ground pepper	
8	skinless chicken thighs, fat removed (about 2 1/2 lbs/1 kg)	8
1 tbsp	canola oil	15 mL
8	fresh gluten-free breakfast sausages	8
1	onion, coarsely chopped	1
1	clove garlic, minced	1
1	can (7 1/2 oz/213 mL) tomato sauce	1
1/2 cup	strong chicken stock	125 mL
4 cups	shredded cabbage or chopped kale	1 L
2 cups	cooked Dutch brown or kidney beans	500 mL
1 cup	cooked fresh, thawed or canned kernel corn	250 mL
1 tsp	dried rosemary	5 mL
1/2 tsp	dried sweet basil	2 mL
1/4 cup	chopped fresh parsley OR 1 tbsp (15 mL) dried	50 mL

• Season flour with salt and pepper; dredge chicken in mixture, reserving any remaining flour.

• In large nonstick skillet, heat oil over medium heat. In two batches, brown chicken; remove to 10 cup (2.5 L) casserole.

• Add sausages to skillet; cook for 7 minutes or until golden brown. Drain on paper towels. Cut each sausage in half; add to casserole. Pour all but 1 tsp (5 mL) drippings from skillet.

• Add onion and garlic to skillet; cook, stirring occasionally, for about 5 minutes or until onion is translucent. Stir in remaining flour mixture. Add tomato sauce and chicken stock. Bring to boil; cook for 1 minute, stirring to scrape up any brown bits from bottom of skillet.

• Stir in cabbage, beans and corn. Bring to boil; cook for 2 minutes. Season with rosemary and basil. Spoon over chicken mixture in casserole. Stir to mix well.

• Cover and bake in 350°F (180°C) oven for 40 minutes or until juices run clear when chicken is pierced. Stir in parsley.

Makes 8 servings.

Each serving: 1/8 of recipe

1	☐ Starchy
1/2	◪ Fruits & Vegetables
3 1/2	◙ Protein
1	◭ Fats & Oils

345	calories
1441	kilojoules
15 g	total fat
4 g	saturated fat
82 mg	cholesterol
28 g	protein
24 g	carbohydrate
570 mg	sodium
606 mg	potassium

GOOD: Phosphorus, Iron, Magnesium, Riboflavin, Vitamin B$_6$
EXCELLENT: Zinc, Niacin, Folate
HIGH: Fibre

CASSOULET

Dedicated gourmands call variations of this meat and bean dish, from classic French cooking, bistro-style beans. It is smart to prepare parts of it, such as the roast duck, the day before assembling the casserole.

2 1/2 cups	dried yellow eye OR white kidney beans, soaked (p.12)	625 mL
6	unpeeled cloves garlic, roasted	6
1	duck, 5 lb (2 kg), roasted	1
1/4 lb	back bacon, diced	125 g
2	carrots, sliced	2
2	bay leaves	2
1	onion, stuck with 4 cloves	1
1	onion, chopped	1
1 tsp	dried thyme	5 mL
1/2 tsp	each dried oregano, rosemary and ground cloves	2 mL
3/4 lb	boneless lean pork shoulder	375 g
3/4 lb	boneless lamb shoulder	375 g
1/2 lb	gluten-free kielbasa	250 g
1 tbsp	canola oil	15 mL
1	can (14 oz/398 mL) tomato sauce	1
1 cup	beef stock	250 mL
1/2 cup	dry red OR white wine	125 mL
1 1/2 cups	rice cake crumbs	375 mL
1/4 cup	chopped fresh parsley	50 mL
1 tbsp	margarine OR butter, melted	15 mL

• In small nonstick pan, roast garlic cloves in 350°F (180°C) oven for 10 minutes or until pulp is tender. Set aside.

• Place duck on rack in shallow roasting pan. Prick skin all over. Reduce oven temperature to 325°F (160°C). Roast duck for 2 1/2 hours or until meat is no longer pink and most of fat has rendered away. Remove meat from bones and cut into bite-sized pieces. Set aside.

• In saucepan, cover bacon with water; bring to boil. Reduce heat and simmer for 3 minutes. Drain and rinse with cold water.

• In large saucepan, combine beans, bacon, carrots, bay leaves, clove-studded onion, chopped onion thyme, oregano, rosemary and cloves. Squeeze pulp from the roasted garlic cloves; discard skins. Stir garlic pulp into bean mixture. Cover with 6 cups (1.5 L) water; bring to boil. Reduce heat, partly cover and simmer for about 55 minutes or until beans are tender. Drain well. Remove and discard bay leaves and cloves.

• Meanwhile, cut pork, lamb and kielbasa into bite-sized cubes. In saucepan, heat oil over medium heat. Cook meat cubes, in batches, until browned on all sides. Remove to plate.

• Add tomato sauce, beef stock and wine to sauce pan, scraping up any brown bits from bottom of pan; bring to boil. Reduce heat and simmer for 5 minutes to reduce slightly.

• Return meat to saucepan. Cover and simmer for about 1 hour or until tender.

• To assemble, spread one-third of the bean mixture in large casserole; layer with half the cooked duck then half the meat mixture. Repeat layers; top with remaining bean mixture.

• Combine rice cake crumbs and parsley. With fingers, rub in melted butter. Sprinkle over cassoulet.

• Bake, uncovered, in 350°F (180°C) oven for about 30 minutes or until crust in golden brown. With wooden spoon, break crust and push it down into cassoulet. (Add a little boiling water if cassoulet gets too dry.) Repeat once more; bake for 20 minutes or until crust is golden.

• To serve, spoon directly from casserole.

Makes 12 servings.

JAMBALAYA

Jambalaya which derives its name from the French word "jambon", meaning ham, comes from creole cooking. In it rice, tomatoes, peppers, onion, meats, poultry and shellfish are cooked together. The added beans soak up the rich flavor as it develops and raises the fibre content in this low-fat meal.

1 tsp	canola oil	5 mL
1	onion, coarsely chopped	1
1	clove garlic, minced	1
1	stalk celery, thinly sliced	1
1/2 cup	long-grain rice	125 mL
1/4 lb	cooked ham, cubed	125 g
1	can (19 oz/540 mL) tomatoes	1
1 cup	low-sodium chicken stock	250 mL
1 cup	cooked kidney beans	250 mL
1/2 tsp	ground thyme	2 mL
1/4 tsp	ground oregano	1 mL
1/4 tsp	freshly ground black pepper	1 mL
Pinch	crushed red chili pepper	Pinch
1/4 lb	cleaned fresh or defrosted raw shrimp	125 g
1	green sweet pepper, chopped	1
2 tbsp	chopped fresh parsley	25 mL

• In large saucepan or Dutch oven, heat oil over medium heat; cook onion, garlic and celery, stirring occasionally, for 5 minutes or until onion is translucent.

• Stir in rice; cook for 3 minutes or until rice is opaque.

• Add ham, tomatoes, stock, beans, thyme, oregano, pepper and red chili pepper; bring to a boil. Transfer to 6 cup (1.5 L) casserole.

• Cover and bake in 350°F (180°C) oven for 20 minutes. Stir in shrimp and green pepper. Bake, uncovered, for 20 minutes longer or until liquid is absorbed and shrimp are opaque and pink. Garnish with parsley.

Makes 4 servings.

Each serving: 1/4 of recipe

2 ▢ Starchy
1/2 ◨ Fruits & Vegetables
2 ⊘ Protein

277 calories
1157 kilojoules
4 g total fat
0 g saturated fat
58 mg cholesterol
20 g protein
39 g carbohydrate
849 mg sodium
748 mg potassium

GOOD: Phosphorus, Zinc, Vitamin D, Vitamin C, Thiamin
EXCELLENT: Iron, Magnesium, Niacin, Folate, Vitamin B$_6$, Vitamin B$_{12}$
HIGH: Fibre

MEAT AND BEAN LOAF

The beans not only extend the beef to make a less expensive meaty loaf but also add substantial dietary fibre, something a meat-only meatloaf does not provide.

4 cups	cooked Romano, Dutch brown or red kidney beans	1 L
3/4 lb	lean ground beef	375 g
1	onion, finely chopped	1
1	clove garlic, minced	1
1	carrot, shredded	1
1	rice cake, crumbled	1
1 tsp	Dijon mustard	5 mL
1 tsp	salt	5 mL
1/2 tsp	chili powder	2 mL
1/4 tsp	freshly ground black pepper	1 mL
1/2 cup	evaporated skim milk OR 2% milk	125 mL
1	egg	1

TOMATO CELERY SAUCE:

1	can (14 oz/398 mL) tomato sauce	1
2	stalks celery, finely chopped	2
1 tsp	dried basil	5 mL
1/2 tsp	dried thyme	2 mL
	Freshly ground black pepper	

• In flat-bottomed dish, mash beans with potato masher or fork. Add ground beef, onion, garlic, carrot, crumbled rice cake, mustard, salt, chili powder and pepper. Mash until thoroughly combined.

• In small bowl, beat together milk and egg. Stir into bean mixture until thoroughly blended.

• Lightly pack into 8- x 4-inch (1.5 L) loaf pan sprayed with nonstick coating; smooth top. Or shape into a mound on sprayed nonstick baking pan.

• Bake in 350°F (180°C) oven for 45 to 50 minutes or until meat thermometer registers 170°F (75°C) and meat is no longer pink. Let stand for 10 minutes before serving.

• Tomato Celery Sauce: Meanwhile, in small saucepan, combine tomato sauce, 1 cup (250 mL) water, celery, basil and thyme; bring to boil, cook for about 5 minutes or until slightly reduced and celery is tender-crisp. Spoon over individual servings of Meat and Bean Loaf.

Makes 8 servings.

Each serving: 1/8 of recipe

1	☐	Starchy
1	▨	Fruits & Vegetables
2 1/2	⊘	Protein

283 calories
1185 kilojoules
8 g total fat
3 g saturated fat
54 mg cholesterol
20 g protein
31 g carbohydrate
753 mg sodium
754 mg potassium

GOOD: Phosphorus, Riboflavin, Vitamin B$_6$

EXCELLENT: Iron, Zinc, Magnesium, Vitamin A, Niacin, Folate, Vitamin B$_{12}$

VERY HIGH: Fibre

Each serving: 1/6 of recipe

1 ☐ Starchy
4 ∅ Protein
1 ⊞ Extra

311	calories
1299	kilojoules
10 g	total fat
3 g	saturated fat
69 mg	cholesterol
32 g	protein
21 g	carbohydrate
389 mg	sodium
664 mg	potassium

GOOD: Magnesium,
Riboflavin, Vitamin B₆

EXCELLENT: Phosphorus, Iron,
Zinc, Niacin,
Folate,
Vitamin B₁₂

HIGH: Fibre

POT ROAST WITH TURNIPS AND BEANS

The turnip used to develop this recipe was the rutabaga. Smaller white turnips also work in it but you will need three or four. When the pot roast is cooked on top of the stove add a little water now and then to keep all the ingredients moist. The same evaporation is less likely to occur when it is baked in the oven.

1	beef cross-cut rib or chuck roast OR lamb OR pork shoulder butt roast (2 1/2 to 3 lb/1 to 1.3 kg)	1
1 tsp	ground marjoram	5 mL
1/2 tsp	crushed dried rosemary	2 mL
1 tsp	canola oil	5 mL
2	onions, halved lengthwise and sliced	2
2	stalks celery, sliced	2
1	clove garlic, minced	1
1/4 lb	mushrooms, quartered	125 g
1	rutabaga (turnip) OR butternut squash, peeled and cubed	1
2 cups	cooked Romano or white kidney beans	500 mL
Half	can (10 oz/284 mL) low sodium beef broth	Half
1/2 cup	water	125 mL
	Freshly ground black pepper	

• Wipe roast. Rub all over with marjoram and rosemary.

• In Dutch oven or deep flameproof casserole, heat oil over medium heat. Brown roast on all sides. Transfer to plate.

• Discard all but 1 tsp (5 mL) drippings from pan. Cook onions, celery, garlic and mushrooms for about 8 minutes or until onions are translucent and moisture from mushrooms has nearly evaporated.

• Stir in turnip and beans. Place roast on top. Pour broth and water over all. Season generously with pepper.

• Cover and simmer, turning roast over once, for 2 hours or until meat is tender. (OR, cover and roast in 325°F (160°C) oven, turning once, for 2 hours.)

• Slice meat. Serve with vegetables.

Makes 6 servings.

SMOKED CHOPS AND BEANS

Make this combination the focus of a great dinner for two. It takes only minutes to prepare with your own precooked dried beans or canned beans leaving time to relax before your meal while the chops and beans are cooking slowly in the oven. Add rice pilaf and Waldorf salad to the meal. Both of them can also be made earlier in the day. Reheat the pilaf in the oven.

1 1/2 cups	cooked red kidney or Romano beans	375 mL
1	onion, finely chopped	1
2 tbsp	ketchup	25 mL
1 tbsp	water	15 mL
1 tbsp	molasses	15 mL
2 tsp	prepared mustard	10 mL
1/2 tsp	salt	2 mL
1/4 tsp	freshly ground black pepper	1 mL
2	small smoked pork loin chops (total 200 g), well trimmed	2

• In small shallow casserole, combine beans, onion, ketchup, water, molasses, mustard, salt and pepper. Arrange chops on top.

• Cover and bake in 350°F (180°C) oven for 35 minutes. Uncover and bake for 10 minutes longer or until chops are golden brown.

Makes 2 servings.

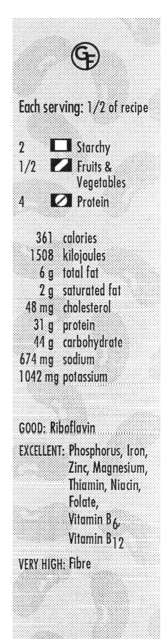

Each serving: 1/2 of recipe

2	Starchy
1/2	Fruits & Vegetables
4	Protein

361	calories
1508	kilojoules
6 g	total fat
2 g	saturated fat
48 mg	cholesterol
31 g	protein
44 g	carbohydrate
674 mg	sodium
1042 mg	potassium

GOOD: Riboflavin

EXCELLENT: Phosphorus, Iron, Zinc, Magnesium, Thiamin, Niacin, Folate, Vitamin B$_6$, Vitamin B$_{12}$

VERY HIGH: Fibre

Each serving: 1/6 of stir-fry

2 ☐ Starchy
1/2 ◪ Fruits &
      Vegetables
2 1/2 ⊘ Protein
1 ➕ Extra

305 calories
1274 kilojoules
6 g total fat
1 g saturated fat
36 mg cholesterol
21 g protein
40 g carbohydrate
504 mg sodium
718 mg potassium

GOOD: Phosphorus, Iron,
        Magnesium,
        Riboflavin, Vitamin B$_6$
Excellent: Zinc, Vitamin A,
        Thiamin, Niacin,
        Folate,
        Vitamin B$_{12}$
High: Fibre

STIR-FRY WITH VEGETABLES AND BEANS

Like all stir-fry dishes, this one is quick and easy to cook. The trick is to have all the ingredients ready beside the stove before you start. Time the cooking of the rice so that it will be done as soon as the stir-fry is cooked. The rice can wait but the stir-fry loses its freshness if it has to wait for the rice.

3/4 lb	lean boneless pork, beef OR chicken	375 g
1 tbsp	canola oil	15 mL
1	clove garlic, minced	1
1 cup	diagonally sliced celery	250 mL
1 cup	thinly sliced carrot	250 mL
1/2 cup	coarsely chopped onion	125 mL
2 tbsp	shredded fresh gingerroot	25 mL
1 1/2 cups	cooked red kidney or Romano beans	375 mL
1 cup	broccoli florets	250 mL
1 cup	chicken stock	250 mL
4 tsp	soy sauce	20 mL
1 tbsp	cornstarch	15 mL
1/4 cup	cold water	50 mL
3 cups	hot cooked rice	750 mL

• Cut pork across the grain into very thin strips about 2 inches (5 cm) long.

• In large heavy skillet or Chinese wok, heat oil over medium-high heat. Stir-fry garlic for 1 minute. Add pork; stir-fry for about 4 minutes or until no longer pink.

• Add celery, carrot, onion and gingerroot; stir-fry for 3 minutes. Add beans and broccoli; stir-fry for about 4 minutes or until vegetables are tender-crisp.

• Stir in chicken stock and soy sauce; bring to boil.

• Mix cornstarch with cold water until smooth. Push vegetable mixture to one side of skillet. Stir cornstarch mixture into stock in pan; cook, stirring, for about 1 minute or until thickened and clear. Stir to coat vegetable mixture.

• Serve immediately with rice.

Makes 6 servings.

Tourtière

Using beans in the filling of this French Canadian savory to replace more than half the meat in the usual all-meat pie reduces its fat content substantially and turns each serving into an impressive source of dietary fibre.

1 lb	lean ground pork	500 g
2	cloves garlic, minced	2
1	onion, finely chopped	1
1 tsp	salt	5 mL
1 tsp	crumbled sage	5 mL
1/2 tsp	ground allspice	2 mL
1/4 tsp	ground nutmeg	1 mL
1/4 tsp	freshly ground black pepper	1 mL
Pinch	ground cloves	Pinch
1 cup	chicken stock	250 mL
1 1/2 cups	cooked red kidney beans, mashed	375 mL
	Gluten-Free Pastry (p.177) for double-crust 9-inch (1 L) pie	

• In large heavy saucepan over low heat, stir together pork, garlic, onion, salt, sage, allspice, nutmeg, pepper and cloves; stir in stock. Cook, stirring and breaking up meat, for about 15 minutes or until meat is no longer pink.

• Stir in beans until well mixed. Simmer for 15 minutes or until liquid is just evaporated. Cool for about 30 minutes.

• On surface dusted with cornstarch (or between sheets of plastic wrap or waxed paper, roll out half of the pastry and line 9 inch (23 cm/1 L) pie plate; trim at edge of pie plate. Spoon in meat mixture, pressing firmly in place.

• Roll out remaining pastry and fit over top, allowing 1/2-inch (1 cm) overhang. Tuck overhang under edge of bottom crust; seal, form rim around pie and flute edges. Slash steam vents in top. (Tourtière may be frozen unbaked; add 10 minutes to baking time.)

• Bake in 425°F (225°C) oven for 10 minutes. Reduce heat to 350°F (180°C); bake for about 35 minutes longer or until golden brown.

• Serve immediately, or cool, wrap and refrigerate for up to 3 days; freeze for up to 3 months.

Makes 8 servings.

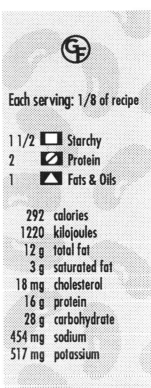

Each serving: 1/8 of recipe

1 1/2 □ Starchy
2 ▨ Protein
1 ▲ Fats & Oils

292 calories
1220 kilojoules
12 g total fat
3 g saturated fat
18 mg cholesterol
16 g protein
28 g carbohydrate
454 mg sodium
517 mg potassium

GOOD: Iron, Zinc, Thiamin, Niacin, Folate
VERY HIGH: Fibre

SPINACH AND BLACK BEAN FISH ROLL-UPS

Once rolls are assembled they can be wrapped and refrigerated for up to six hours. Bake them just before serving. They are nice for a small dinner party when you know your guests will appreciate low-fat cooking. Bake Parmesan cheese-sprinkled tomato halves in the oven with them for a colorful sweet-tart accompaniment.

1 cup	cooked black beans, mashed	250 mL
Half	pkg (300 g) frozen chopped spinach, squeezed as dry as possible	Half
1 tsp	lemon juice	5 mL
1/2 tsp	salt	2 mL
1/4 tsp	freshly ground black pepper	1 mL
1/2 cup	puréed cooked black beans	125 mL
1/2 cup	light sour cream	125 mL
1 tbsp	chopped fresh dill OR 1 tsp (5 mL) dried dillweed	15 mL
4	sole fillets (about 4 oz/125 g each) Lemon zest or grated lemon peel	4

• In bowl, combine mashed beans, chopped spinach, lemon juice, salt and pepper.

• In another bowl, stir together puréed beans, sour cream and dill; stir one-third into spinach mixture. Cover and refrigerate remaining sour cream mixture.

• Divide spinach mixture evenly into four and spread across centre of each fish fillet. Roll fillet loosely around filling and secure with toothpick.

• Place seam side down in shallow baking dish sprayed with nonstick coating. Spray roll-ups lightly with nonstick coating.

• Bake, uncovered, in 400°F (200°C) oven for about 15 minutes or until fish just flakes when tested with fork.

• In small saucepan, bring reserved sour cream sauce just to simmering. Pour over fish roll-ups to serve. Garnish with lemon zest.

Makes 4 servings.

SIDE DISHES

Bean, Zucchini and Tomato Medley

Lots o' Tomatoes and Beans

Corn and Bean Pudding

Tex-Mex Corn and Bean Pudding

Bean-Fried Rice

Pasta and Beans with Pesto

Puréed Carrots and Beans

Refried Beans

Mexican Beans

Scalloped Potatoes and Beans

Cows in the Grass

Bean Dal

Bean Soufflé

BEANS, ZUCCHINI AND TOMATO MEDLEY

This is a glorious, low-fat, high-fibre melange of different colors and shapes that knows no season now that zucchini are available throughout the year. When fresh tomatoes are plentiful and reasonably priced substitute about six of them for the canned ones.

2 tsp	olive oil	10 mL
1	onion, coarsely chopped	1
1	clove garlic, minced	1
6	mushrooms	6
2	medium zucchini	2
1	can (19 oz/540 mL) tomatoes	1
2 cups	cooked Dutch brown beans or Romano beans	500 mL
1 cup	small gluten-free pasta shapes	250 mL
1 tsp	ground thyme	5 mL
1/2 tsp	salt	2 mL
1/2 tsp	ground oregano	2 mL
	Freshly ground black pepper	
1/4 cup	grated Parmesan cheese	50 mL
2 tbsp	chopped fresh parsley OR 2 tsp (10 mL) dried	25 mL

• In nonstick skillet, heat olive oil over medium heat; cook onion and garlic, stirring occasionally, for about 4 minutes or until onion is translucent.

• Cut mushrooms into quarters. Cut zucchini lengthwise in half, then into 1 inch (2.5 cm) thick slices. Add mushrooms and zucchini to skillet; cook for 2 minutes.

• Stir in tomatoes, breaking up with fork, 1/2 cup (125 mL) water, beans, pasta, thyme, salt and oregano; season to taste with pepper.

• Bring to boil; reduce heat and simmer for 15 minutes or until pasta is *al dente*, tender but still firm.

• Sprinkle each serving with Parmesan cheese and parsley.

Makes 4 servings.

LOTS O' TOMATOES AND BEANS

When fresh tomatoes are too expensive replace them with a can of tomatoes (19 oz/540 mL). At first this mixture is very juicy but the long cooking reduces the liquid and creates a unique fruity but savory flavor.

1 tsp	canola oil	5 mL
2	onions, thinly sliced from top to bottom	2
6	tomatoes, peeled	6
1 1/2 cups	cooked kidney or black beans	375 mL
1 tsp	salt	5 mL
1/4 tsp	freshly ground black pepper	1 mL
1/2 cup	packed brown sugar	125 mL
1 tbsp	chopped fresh basil OR cilantro OR 1 tsp (5 mL) dried	15 mL

• In large heavy-bottomed skillet, heat oil over medium heat. Arrange onions evenly over pan.

• Cut each tomato into 6 wedges; layer on top of onions. Spoon beans over top. Sprinkle with salt and pepper. Then sprinkle brown sugar over all.

• Cook over medium-low heat, shaking pan occasionally to prevent sticking, for 45 minutes or until nearly all liquid has evaporated. (Stir once or twice only if mixture seems to be sticking to bottom of skillet.)

• Sprinkle with basil. Simmer for 2 minutes longer.

Makes 6 servings.

Each serving: 1/6 of recipe

1/2 ☐ Starchy
2 1/2 ◩ Fruits & Vegetables

167	Calories
699	kilojoules
1 g	total fat
0 g	saturated fat
0 mg	cholesterol
5 g	protein
36 g	carbohydrate
406 mg	sodium
518 mg	potassium

GOOD: Iron, Magnesium, Vitamin C
EXCELLENT: Folate
HIGH: Fibre

CORN AND BEAN PUDDING

Our tasters came back for seconds when they sampled this comforting casserole. For those who go for the flavors of the southwest, add a new twist to this family favorite and make the Tex-Mex variation.

1 tsp	canola oil	5 mL
1	small onion, finely chopped	1
2	eggs	2
1 cup	milk	250 mL
1/2 tsp	salt	2 mL
4	drops hot pepper sauce	4
2 cups	cooked kidney or Dutch brown beans	500 mL
1	can (14 oz/398 mL) cream-style corn	1

• In small nonstick skillet, heat oil over medium heat; cook onion, stirring occasionally, for about 4 minutes or until translucent.

• In 6 cup (1.5 L) casserole sprayed with nonstick coating, beat eggs, milk, salt and hot pepper sauce until smooth. Stir in beans, corn and cooked onion; mix well.

• Place casserole in larger pan; pour enough hot water into larger pan to come 2 inches (5 cm) up sides.

• Bake in 350°F (180°C) oven for 20 minutes. Stir mixture; bake for 20 minutes longer or until tester inserted near centre comes out clean.

Makes 6 servings.

VARIATION:
TEX-MEX CORN & BEAN PUDDING

• Add 1/3 cup (75 mL) chopped red or green sweet pepper or combination and 2 tsp (10 mL) chopped pickled jalapeno pepper.

Bean-Fried Rice

Chinese-style fried rice is one of those versatile international dishes that accommodates all sorts of added ingredients. Either serve this version with its added beans on a bed of lettuce, or spoon it onto one side of each lettuce leaf and roll up to be eaten by hand.

2 tbsp	canola oil	25 mL
3 cups	cooked short-grain rice	750 mL
1 1/2 cups	cooked kidney or Black beans	375 mL
4	green onions, minced	4
3	eggs, lightly beaten	3
2 tbsp	soy sauce	25 mL
1 tbsp	minced fresh cilantro OR	15 mL
	1 tsp (5 mL) dried	
1/4 tsp	freshly ground black pepper	1 mL
6	lettuce leaves	6

• In large nonstick skillet, heat oil over medium heat. Stir-fry rice for about 4 minutes or until golden. Add beans and green onions; mix well.

• Push rice mixture to sides of skillet. Pour eggs into centre and scramble until semi-cooked. Stir into rice mixture. Sprinkle with soy sauce, cilantro and pepper; mix well.

• Serve on a bed of lettuce.

Makes 6 servings.

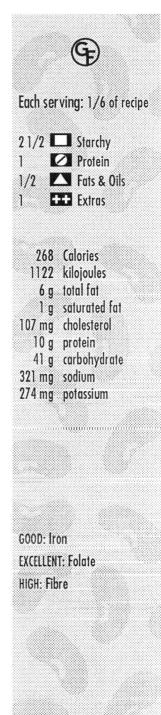

Each serving: 1/6 of recipe

2 1/2 ☐ Starchy
1 ⊘ Protein
1/2 ▲ Fats & Oils
1 ✚✚ Extras

268 Calories
1122 kilojoules
6 g total fat
1 g saturated fat
107 mg cholesterol
10 g protein
41 g carbohydrate
321 mg sodium
274 mg potassium

GOOD: Iron
EXCELLENT: Folate
HIGH: Fibre

PASTA & BEANS WITH PESTO

This flavorful pasta tossed with high-fibre beans is one to make over and over again when basil goes wild in the herb garden. The fresh basil mixture (pesto) can be prepared ahead. It keeps in the refrigerator for four days, in the freezer for three months.

1 cup	fresh basil leaves	250 mL
2	cloves garlic	2
2 tbsp	walnuts OR pine nuts	25 mL
2 tbsp	olive oil	25 mL
1 cup	grated Parmesan cheese	250 mL
1 cup	2% milk	250 mL
	Salt and freshly ground black pepper	
2 cups	cooked red kidney beans	500 mL
1/2 lb	gluten-free penne OR spiral pasta, cooked	250 g

• In food processor, chop basil, garlic and walnuts. Gradually add oil, processing until nearly smooth. Stir in 1/2 cup (125 mL) grated Parmesan.

• In heavy medium saucepan over medium heat, bring milk to boil. Whisk in pesto (basil mixture). Season to taste with salt and pepper. Stir in beans; cook for 2 minutes to thoroughly heat beans.

• In large bowl, combine pasta, bean mixture and remaining 1/2 cup (125 mL) Parmesan cheese. Toss to coat pasta evenly.

Makes 4 servings.

Each serving: 1/4 of recipe

3 1/2 ☐ Starchy
3 ▨ Protein
2 ▲ Fats & Oils

538 Calories
2252 kilojoules
20 g total fat
7 g saturated fat
69 mg cholesterol
28 g protein
63 g carbohydrate
714 mg sodium
751 mg potassium

GOOD: Thiamine, Riboflavin
EXCELLENT: Calcium,
Phosphorus, Iron,
Zinc, Magnesium,
Niacin, Folate,
Vitamin B$_{12}$
VERY HIGH: Fibre

Puréed Carrots with Beans

Here is a wonderful make-ahead side dish to reheat gently in a pretty casserole dish in the oven. Try other vegetables puréed with beans, especially root vegetables such as rutabaga, parsnip and beets.

3/4 lb	carrots (about 5 medium)	375 g
1 cup	cooked Romano or Dutch brown beans	250 mL
1 tbsp	grated fresh gingerroot OR 1/2 tsp (2 mL) ground ginger	15 mL
1 tsp	brown sugar	5 mL
Pinch	nutmeg	Pinch
	Freshly ground black pepper	

• Peel carrots; cut into thick slices. Cook in saucepan of lightly salted boiling water for 15 minutes or until tender. Drain well.

• In food processor or blender, combine hot carrots, beans, gingerroot, brown sugar and nutmeg. Process until smoothly puréed. Season to taste with pepper.

Makes 4 servings, about 2 cups (500 mL).

Each serving: 1/4 of recipe

1/2 ☐ Starchy
1 ▧ Fruits & Vegetables
1 ▨ Protein

110 calories
461 kilojoules
0 g total fat
0 g saturated fat
0 mg cholesterol
5 g protein
22 g carbohydrate
36 mg sodium
458 mg potassium

GOOD: Magnesium
EXCELLENT: Vitamin A, Folate
HIGH: Fibre

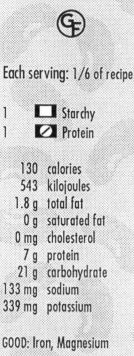

Each serving: 1/6 of recipe

| 1 | ☐ Starchy |
| 1 | ⊘ Protein |

130	calories
543	kilojoules
1.8 g	total fat
0 g	saturated fat
0 mg	cholesterol
7 g	protein
21 g	carbohydrate
133 mg	sodium
339 mg	potassium

GOOD: Iron, Magnesium

EXCELLENT: Folate

HIGH: Fibre

Each serving: 1/6 of recipe

1	☐ Starchy
1	⊘ Protein
1/2	▲ Fats & Oils

169	calories
706	kilojoules
5 g	total fat
2 g	saturated fat
9 mg	cholesterol
10 g	protein
21 g	carbohydrate
194 mg	sodium
319 mg	potassium

GOOD: Phosphorus, Iron, Magnesium

EXCELLENT: Folate

HIGH: Fibre

REFRIED BEANS

In Mexico refried beans are called "frijoles refritos" and almost appear at every meal, even at breakfast with eggs. Any variety of beans can be refried which is simply recooking mashed beans to flavor them and reduce the moisture in them.

2 tsp	bacon fat OR canola oil	10 mL
1	small onion, minced	1
1	clove garlic, minced	1
3 cups	cooked kidney or black beans	750 mL
3	drops hot pepper sauce	3
	Salt and freshly ground black pepper	

• In nonstick skillet, heat bacon fat over medium heat. Cook onion and garlic for 5 minutes or until onion is translucent.

• Gradually add beans mashing with the back of a spoon. Cook, stirring often, until thickened. Add hot pepper sauce. Season to taste with salt and pepper.

• With spatula and tilting skillet, shape mixture into oblong roll. Roll onto a plate or platter or spoon into container with cover.

Makes 6 servings, 2 cups (500 mL).

VARIATION:
MEXICAN BEANS

• Stir 1/2 cup (125 mL) shredded Cheddar OR Monterey Jack cheese and 1 tsp (5 mL) chili powder into the hot bean mixture until cheese melts.

SCALLOPED POTATOES & BEANS

The addition of beans to old-fashioned scalloped potatoes turns them into an exciting, trendy high-fibre casserole.

4	medium potatoes	4
1	yellow onion, thinly sliced	1
1 1/2 cups	cooked kidney or Dutch brown beans	375 mL
1 tbsp	butter	15 mL
2 tbsp	whole bean OR all-purpose flour	25 mL
	Salt and freshly ground black pepper	
Pinch	ground nutmeg	Pinch
2 cups	2% milk (approximately)	500 mL

• Peel potatoes and cut crosswise into thin slices. Reserve about one-quarter for top layer. Spread one-third of remaining potatoes evenly in 8 cup (2 L) baking dish or casserole sprayed with nonstick coating. Cover with one-third of the onions then one-third of the beans. Dot with one-third of the butter cut into tiny bits; sprinkle with one-third of the flour and salt and pepper to taste.

• Repeat layering twice. Sprinkle with nutmeg. Top with reserved potatoes. Add milk until it can be seen between potato slices.

• Cover and bake in 350°F (180°C) oven for 45 minutes. Uncover and bake for about 45 minutes longer or until potatoes are tender and top is golden brown.

Makes 6 servings.

NOTE: When all-purpose flour is used in the recipe, Scalloped Potatoes and Beans are no longer gluten-free 🌾.

Each serving: 1/6 of recipe

1 1/2	☐	Starchy
1	⊘	Protein
1	++	Extras

187	Calories
783	kilojoules
3 g	total fat
2 g	saturated fat
11 mg	cholesterol
8 g	protein
30 g	carbohydrate
195 mg	sodium
661 mg	potassium

GOOD: Phosphorus, Magnesium, Vitamin D, Vitamin B₆

EXCELLENT: Folate

HIGH: Fibre

Each serving: 1/4 of recipe

1 1/2 ☐ Starchy
1 ⊘ Protein
1 ✚✚ Extras

186 Calories
779 kilojoules
3 g total fat
0.5 g saturated fat
0 mg cholesterol
10 g protein
31 g carbohydrate
237 mg sodium
587 mg potassium

GOOD: Phosphorus
EXCELLENT: Iron, Magnesium,
Folate
VERY HIGH: Fibre

COWS IN THE GRASS

One of our testers at Centralia College named this tasty, colorful combination of green and brown or red beans. In the preparation, blanching the fresh beans is important because it helps preserve their bright green color. Frozen beans can be used instead of the fresh ones and when they are omit the blanching step.

1 lb	fresh green beans	500 g
2 cups	cooked Dutch brown or kidney beans	500 mL
1/2 tsp	salt	2 mL
1 tbsp	soft margarine OR butter	15 mL
1/4 tsp	granulated sugar	1 mL

• Cut green beans into 1 inch (2.5 cm) pieces. Blanch beans in boiling water for 1 minute. Drain and rinse under cold running water until chilled.

• In saucepan, combine green beans, Dutch brown beans and salt. Pour in enough water to cover; bring to boil. Reduce heat and simmer, uncovered, for 10 minutes or until green beans are tender but still bright green.

• Drain well. Stir in margarine and sugar.

Makes 4 servings.

Bean Dal

This adaptation of an East Indian dish has the consistency of spaghetti sauce. It's great with rice and the same side dishes that are served with curries; peanuts, coconut, sliced bananas, raisins, chutney.

1 tsp	canola oil	5 mL
1	onion, chopped	1
1	clove garlic, minced	1
1 tsp	ground cumin	5 mL
1/2 tsp	chopped pickled jalapeño pepper	2 mL
1/2 tsp	salt	2 mL
1/2 tsp	turmeric	2 mL
1/4 tsp	ground cardamom	1 mL
Pinch	ground ginger	Pinch
2 cups	cooked Romano, white kidney or Dutch brown beans	500 mL
3/4 cup	water	175 mL
2 cups	cooked brown rice	500 mL

• In nonstick skillet, heat oil over medium heat; cook onion and garlic, stirring occasionally, for about 5 minutes or until onion is translucent. Stir in cumin, jalapeño pepper, salt, turmeric, cardamom and ginger. Cook for 1 minute longer.

• Stir in beans and water. Bring to boil, reduce heat and simmer for 5 minutes.

• Transfer to food processor or blender. Process, scraping down bowl once or twice, for about 2 minutes or until puréed and sauce-like in consistency, adding a little water if desired.

• To serve, spoon over cooked rice.

Makes 4 servings, 2 cups (500 mL).

Each serving: 1/4 of recipe

2 1/2 ☐ Starchy
1 ⊘ Protein

239	Calories
1000	kilojoules
2 g	total fat
0 g	saturated fat
0 mg	cholesterol
10 g	protein
45 g	carbohydrate
203	mg sodium
446	mg potassium

GOOD: Phosphorus, Zinc, Niacin

EXCELLENT: Iron, Magnesium, Folate

VERY HIGH: Fibre

Each serving: 1/4 of recipe

1 1/2 ▭ Starchy
1 1/2 ⊘ Protein

177 calories
741 kilojoules
1 g total fat
0 g saturated fat
3 mg cholesterol
14 g protein
27 g carbohydrate
301 mg sodium
501 mg potassium

GOOD Phosphorus, Iron,
      Zinc, Magnesium,
      Riboflavin,
      Vitamin B12

EXCELLENT: Folate
HIGH: Fibre

BEAN SOUFFLÉ

The timing is as crucial for this high-fibre, low-fat soufflé as it is with any other one. It will deflate as it cools. Still, the texture is soft and fluffy as long as it is served while it is fresh and warm.

1 tsp	soft margarine OR butter	5 mL
1 tbsp	cornmeal	15 mL
2 cups	cooked kidney, Romano or black beans	500 mL
2 tsp	grated lemon rind	10 mL
1/4 tsp	ground nutmeg	1 mL
4	egg whites	4
1/2 tsp	salt	2 mL
Sauce:		
1 cup	low-fat yogurt	250 mL
1 tsp	lemon juice	5 mL
1/2 tsp	granulated sugar	2 mL

• Rub margarine on bottom and sides of 4 cup (1 L) soufflé dish. Sprinkle with cornmeal to coat bottom and sides.

• In food processor or blender, combine beans, 1 tsp (5 mL) of the lemon rind and nutmeg; purée, scraping down sides of container once or twice, for 1 to 2 minutes or until smooth.

• In mixer bowl, beat egg whites and salt until stiff peaks form. Stir about 1 cup (250 mL) into pureed beans to lighten them. Gently fold in remaining egg whites until evenly coloured. Spoon into prepared soufflé dish.

• Bake in 350°F (180°C) oven for 35 to 40 minutes or until lightly browned and puffed. Serve immediately.

• Sauce: Meanwhile, in small bowl, combine yogurt, lemon juice and sugar. Spoon over each serving of soufflé. Garnish with remaining lemon rind.

Makes 4 servings.

GLUTEN-FREE

Pancakes ◆ Blueberry Pancakes
Crêpes (Thin Pancakes)
Tea Biscuits ◆ Chili Cheese Biscuits
Cheesey Crackers ◆ Seed and Nut Crackers
Gluten-Free Bread ◆ Seed Bread
Herb Bread ◆ Foccacia
Gluten-Free Pizza Crust
Cornmeal Bread ◆ Peppery Corn Bread
Bean, Cornmeal & Millet Loaf
Spicy Muffins ◆ Spicy Raisin Nut Muffins
Honey Carrot Date Muffins
Chocolate Mocha Cake
Jelly Roll
Chocolate Cake
Creamy Chocolate Frosting
Creamy White Chocolate Frosting
Fluffy Frosting
Orange Cake
Banana Cake
Spicy Carrot Cake
Brownies
Fudgy Almond Brownies
Gingersnaps ◆ Cinnamon Hearts
Chocolate Chip Cookies
Chocolate Pecan Raisin Hermits
Chocolate Pecan Ginger Hermits
Lemon Wafers
Peanut Butter Cookies
Chocolate Marshmallow Nut Squares
Coconut Crisps
Cream Puffs
Gluten-Free Pastry
Gluten-Free Tortillas
Crisp Corn and Bean Chips

Pancakes

If thinner pancakes are desired, stir a little more milk into the batter.

1/3 cup	whole bean flour	75 mL
1/3 cup	cornmeal	75 mL
1/3 cup	cornstarch, OR rice flour	75 mL
2 tsp	granulated sugar	10 mL
2 tsp	gluten-free baking powder	10 mL
1/2 tsp	salt	2 mL
2	eggs	2
1 1/2 cups	1 % milk	375 mL
2 tbsp	soft margarine OR butter, melted	25 mL

• In mixing bowl, combine whole bean flour, cornmeal, cornstarch, sugar, baking powder and salt.

• In another bowl, beat together eggs and milk; quickly stir into dry ingredients until just mixed (batter will be lumpy). Fold in margarine.

• Using about 1/4 cup (50 mL) for each pancake, pour batter onto hot, lightly oiled, nonstick griddle or skillet; cook until puffy and bubbles begin to break on top. Turn and cook until golden brown on both sides.

Makes 12 pancakes, 6 servings.

VARIATION
Blueberry Pancakes

• Fold 1 cup (250 mL) blueberries into batter.

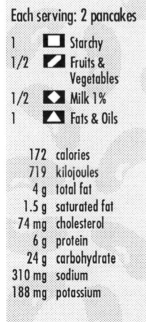

Each serving: 2 pancakes

1	□ Starchy
1/2	◆ Milk 1%
1	▲ Fats & Oils

160	calories
669	kilojoules
4 g	total fat
1.5 g	saturated fat
74 mg	cholesterol
4 g	protein
20 g	carbohydrate
310 mg	sodium
194 mg	potassium

Each serving: 2 pancakes

1	□ Starchy
1/2	▰ Fruits & Vegetables
1/2	◆ Milk 1%
1	▲ Fats & Oils

172	calories
719	kilojoules
4 g	total fat
1.5 g	saturated fat
74 mg	cholesterol
6 g	protein
24 g	carbohydrate
310 mg	sodium
188 mg	potassium

CRÊPES (THIN PANCAKES)

The thinness of crepes makes them more elegant than pancakes. For convenience, make them ahead to have on hand to be rolled around appetizer, main course or dessert fillings. Stack cooled crepes with waxed paper between them. Wrap and refrigerate for up to 2 days or freeze no longer than 3 months. A stack takes about 3 hours to thaw at room temperature.

1/2 cup	whole bean flour	125 mL
1/4 cup	cornstarch OR rice flour	50 mL
1 tsp	granulated sugar	5 mL
1/4 tsp	salt	1 mL
2	eggs	2
2	egg whites	2
1 cup	1 % milk	250 mL
1 tbsp	soft margarine OR butter	15 mL

• In mixing bowl, combine whole bean flour, cornstarch, sugar and salt.

• In another bowl, beat together eggs, egg whites and milk. Stir in dry ingredients and beat until smooth. Or, place flour, cornstarch, sugar, salt, eggs and milk in container of blender or food processor and process until smooth.

• Cover; refrigerate for 1 hour to allow batter to rest.

• Melt butter, 1 tsp (5 mL) at a time, in 8-inch (20 cm) nonstick crêpe or omelet pan. Add more butter to pan as required.

• Using about 1/4 cup (50 mL) batter for each crêpe, pour batter onto hot pan; swirl to coat bottom of pan with thin layer; cook for about 1 minute or until top looks dry and bottom is faintly golden. Loosen edges with spatula, slip on to tea towel.

• Let cool, then stack between layers of waxed paper.

Makes 12 crêpes.

Each serving: 2 crêpes

1	☐ Starchy
1/2	◪ Protein
1/2	▲ Fats & Oils

120 calories
501 kilojoules
3 g total fat
1 g saturated fat
73 mg cholesterol
6 g protein
14 g carbohydrate
149 mg sodium
209 mg potassium

GOOD: Vitamin D,
Vitamin B$_{12}$

MODERATE: Fibre

TEA BISCUITS

Like any baking powder biscuit dough this one is just as versatile. Here are two ideas for this one. Make it, especially the Chili Cheese variation below, to top a meat pie. Or for a sweet treat that is gluten-free, substitute it for the dough in Quick Cinnamon Pinwheels (p.181).

1 1/2 cups	whole bean flour	375 mL
1/4 cup	cornstarch OR rice flour	50 mL
1/4 cup	cornmeal	50 mL
2 tbsp	gluten-free baking powder	25 mL
2 tsp	granulated sugar	10 mL
1/2 tsp	salt	2 mL
1/3 cup	soft margarine OR butter	75 mL
1 cup	2% milk	250 mL

• In mixing bowl, stir together bean flour, cornstarch, cornmeal, baking powder, sugar and salt.

• With pastry blender or two knives, cut in margarine until mixture resembles a combination of coarse and fine crumbs.

• Quickly stir in milk to make soft dough. Turn out onto surface lightly sprinkled with cornstarch. With hands lightly dusted with cornstarch, knead 8 to 10 times or for about 20 seconds until dough feels smooth.

• Roll out or pat, to 1/2 to 3/4 inch (1 to 2 cm) thickness. With floured 2 to 2 1/2 inch (5 to 6 cm) round cookie cutter, cut out rounds. (or with sharp serrated knife, cut dough into squares, triangles or rectangles.) Place on nonstick baking sheets 1 inch (2.5 cm) apart.

• Bake in 400°F (200°C) oven for 12 to 15 minutes or until golden brown.

Makes 24 biscuits.

VARIATION
CHILI CHEESE BISCUITS

• Stir 1/4 cup (50 mL) grated Parmesan cheese and 1 tsp (5 mL) chili powder into crumbly mixture before adding milk.

CHEESY CRACKERS

These whole bean flour crackers have that satisfying crispy crunchy texture that makes appetizer and soup crackers so appealing. They store well in a dry place in a covered container for as long as two months. Recrisp them, if necessary, by warming them for a few minutes in a hot oven.

3/4 cup	whole bean flour	175 mL
1/4 cup	grated Parmesan cheese	50 mL
2 tbsp	each cornstarch and cornmeal	25 mL
1 tsp	baking soda	5 mL
1/2 tsp	chili powder	2 mL
1/2 tsp	salt	2 mL
1/4 cup	soft margarine OR butter	50 mL
1/2 cup	low-fat yogurt	125 mL

• In bowl, stir together bean flour, Parmesan cheese, cornstarch, cornmeal, baking soda, chili powder and salt.

• With pastry blender or two knives, cut in margarine until mixture is crumbly. Stir in yogurt until blended. Let stand for 5 minutes. Turn out onto surface lightly dusted with cornstarch; knead 5 to 6 times to form smooth ball.

• With stockinette-covered rolling pin or with plastic wrap between rolling pin and dough, roll out to 1/8 inch (3 mm) thickness. With 2 inch (5 cm) round cookie cutter, cut into crackers. Arrange close together on nonstick baking sheets.

• Bake in 350°F (180°C) oven for 10 to 12 minutes or until golden brown.

Makes 72 crackers.

VARIATION
SEED AND NUT CRACKERS

• Omit Parmesan cheese and chili powder. Add 1 tbsp (15 mL) each poppy seeds, ground nuts and sesame seeds to dry ingredients.

Each serving: 8 crackers
1/2 ☐ Starchy
1/2 ⬭ Protein
1/2 ▲ Fats & Oils

108 calories
451 kilojoules
5 g total fat
1 g saturated fat
2 mg cholesterol
3 g protein
10 g carbohydrate
337 mg sodium
156 mg potassium

GOOD: Vitamin D
MODERATE: Fibre

Each serving: 8 crackers
1/2 ☐ Starchy
1/2 ⬭ Protein
1 ▲ Fats & Oils

111 calories
464 kilojoules
6 g total fat
1 g saturated fat
0 mg cholesterol
3 g protein
10 g carbohydrate
285 mg sodium
164 mg potassium

GOOD: Vitamin D
MODERATE: Fibre

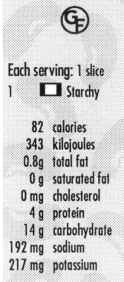

Gluten-Free Bread

Dense and delicious, that is a fair description for this bread. Because there is no gluten in whole bean flour the dough made from it is not as strong and elastic as dough made from wheat flour. However, in this bread the tapioca and egg white join forces to help hold the cell structure of the air bubbles created by the action of yeast and gluten-free baking powder. The bread is lightest when both leavening agents are used.

1 tsp	granulated sugar	5 mL
1/2 cup	warm water	125 mL
1	envelope active dry yeast	1
1 cup	water	250 mL
2 tbsp	minute tapioca	25 mL
2 cups	whole bean flour	500 mL
1/4 cup	cornmeal	50 mL
2 tbsp	cornstarch	25 mL
2 tsp	gluten-free baking powder	10 mL
1 tsp	salt	5 mL
2	egg whites	2
1/2 cup	skim milk	125 mL
1 tsp	poppy seeds	5 mL

• Spray 8 x 4 inch (1.5 L) loaf pan with nonstick coating; coat inside with cornmeal. Set aside.

• In small bowl, dissolve sugar in warm water. Sprinkle yeast over top; set aside for 10 minutes or until frothy. Stir well.

• In saucepan, combine water and minute tapioca; bring to boil. Cook for 1 to 2 minutes or until thickened and clear.

• In mixing bowl, stir together bean flour, cornmeal, cornstarch, baking powder and salt.

• In separate bowl, whisk together egg whites and milk; whisk in yeast and tapioca mixture. Stir into dry ingredients, beating until smooth. Set aside for 10 minutes.

• Turn out onto surface generously dusted with cornstarch. Dust hands with cornstarch and sprinkle a little over dough. Knead for 4 to 5 times; form into oblong. Fit into prepared pan. Brush top with milk; sprinkle with poppy seeds.

• Bake in 400°F (200°C) oven for 45 minutes or until browned and loaf sounds hollow when tapped.

Makes 1 loaf, 16 slices.

VARIATIONS:

SEED BREAD

• Add 1 tbsp (15 mL) each sesame seeds, poppy seeds and millet to dry ingredients.

HERB BREAD

• Add 1 tsp (5 mL) dried basil and 1/2 tsp (2 mL) each dried rosemary, thyme and dillweed to dry ingredients of Gluten-Free Bread or Seed Bread. (For a more fragrant fresher herb taste use finely chopped fresh herbs when you can. Increase the amount to three times the amount of dried herb called for in the recipe.)

FOCCACIA

• On nonstick baking sheet, pat dough into a round or square about 1 1/2 inches (4 cm) thick. Sprinkle with dried or fresh rosemary, pressing it lightly to adhere to crust. Let stand for 10 minutes.

• Bake in 400°F (200°C) oven for 35 minutes or until crust is golden brown.

GLUTEN-FREE PIZZA CRUST

• Spray two pizza pans with nonstick coating. Set aside.

• Divide Gluten-Free, Seed or Herb Bread dough in half. With hands dusted with cornstarch, flatten each half into disc; place one in centre of each pizza pan. With cornstarch-dusted hands, press out to edges of pans. (Crust can be wrapped and frozen for up to 4 weeks; thaw for 15 minutes before proceeding.) Spread, as desired, with tomato paste and toppings.

• Bake in 400°F (200°C) oven for 25 minutes or until crust is golden and topping cooked.

Makes 2 pizza crusts, 8 servings each.

Each serving: 1/16 of recipe

Calculations approximately the same as Gluten-Free Bread

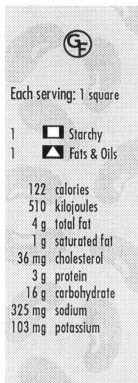

CORNMEAL BREAD

When you use this hot from the oven drizzled with puréed fruit or syrup for dessert, call it johnnycake. Cornmeal bread sounds right when it accompanies soups and stews. It is also great used in place of regular bread for the stuffing of roast turkey or chicken.

1 cup	cornmeal	250 mL
3/4 cup	boiling water	175 mL
1/4 cup	soft margarine	50 mL
2	eggs, separated	2
1/2 cup	skim OR 1% milk	125 mL
1 tbsp	granulated sugar	15 mL
1/2 cup	whole bean flour	125 mL
1/4 cup	cornstarch OR potato flour	50 mL
1 tbsp	gluten-free baking powder	15 mL
1 tsp	salt	5 mL

• Lightly grease 8-inch (2 L) cake pan with soft margarine. Sprinkle lightly with a little of the cornmeal. Set aside.

• In small bowl, combine cornmeal and boiling water; let stand for 10 minutes to soften. Beat in margarine, egg yolks and milk until smooth.

• In mixing bowl, combine whole bean flour, cornstarch, gluten-free baking powder and salt.

• In small bowl, beat egg whites until foamy. Gradually beat in sugar until stiff peaks form.

• In mixing bowl, combine whole bean flour, cornstarch, gluten-free baking powder and salt. Stir in cornmeal mixture until well blended. Fold in egg whites until well blended.

• Spoon into prepared pan; spread to corners and smooth top.

• Bake in 375°F (190°C) oven for 35 minutes or until lightly browned and tester inserted into centre comes out clean.

• Let cool in pan. Cut into squares and serve warm or at room temperature.

Makes 16 squares.

VARIATION:
PEPPERY CORN BREAD

• To dry ingredients, add 1/4 tsp (1 mL) freshly ground black pepper.

• After folding in egg whites, fold in 1/2 cup (125 mL) finely chopped red sweet pepper and 2 tbsp (25 mL) chopped pickled jalapeño peppers.

BEAN, CORNMEAL & MILLET LOAF

Both the millet and cornmeal add grainy flavor and crunchy texture to this quick bread. It seems to taste best when it is a day old, so wrap the loaf and let stand for 24 hours at room temperature before slicing it.

1 1/2 cups	buttermilk	375 mL
1 cup	cooked white kidney beans, puréed	250 mL
1/2 cup	cornmeal	125 mL
1/4 cup	millet	50 mL
1/4 cup	molasses	50 mL
1 cup	whole bean flour	250 mL
2 tsp	gluten-free baking powder	10 mL
1 tsp	baking soda	5 mL
1 tsp	salt	5 mL
2	eggs, separated	2
1 tsp	granulated sugar	5 mL
2 tbsp	soft margarine OR butter, melted	25 mL
1/4 cup	raisins	50 mL

• Line bottom only of 8 x 4 inch (1.5 L) nonstick loaf pan with waxed paper cut to fit. Set aside.

• In bowl, stir together buttermilk, beans, cornmeal, millet and molasses; let stand for 5 minutes.

• In mixing bowl, stir together flour, baking powder, baking soda and salt.

• In separate bowl, beat egg whites until foamy; beat in sugar until stiff peaks form.

• With whisk, beat egg yolks and margarine into bean mixture. Add to dry ingredients all at once; stir until blended. Fold in stiffly beaten egg whites and raisins until well mixed.

• Pour into prepared pan; smooth top.

• Bake in 350°F (180°C) oven for 50 minutes or until tester inserted in centre comes out clean.

• Let cool for 5 minutes. With knife, loosen sides and ends. Remove from pan to wire rack to cool completely.

Makes 1 loaf, 16 slices.

SPICY MUFFINS

Once you have tried these nice 'n' spicy muffins you may vary the spiciness to suit your own taste. Enjoy them fresh, then wrap and freeze the ones that are left for later. It takes only minutes to warm one or two for breakfast and they are great for the lunch bag.

1 cup	whole bean flour	250 mL
1/3 cup	cornmeal	75 mL
1 tsp	gluten-free baking powder	5 mL
1 tsp	baking soda	5 mL
1 tsp	ground cinnamon	5 mL
1/4 tsp	salt	1 mL
Pinch	each ground cloves, nutmeg and cardamom	Pinch
1/2 cup	packed brown sugar	125 mL
1/4 cup	soft margarine OR butter	50 mL
1	egg OR 2 egg whites	1
1 cup	buttermilk OR sour milk	250 mL

• In mixing bowl, stir together flour, cornmeal, baking powder, baking soda, cinnamom, salt, cloves, nutmeg and cardamom.

• In small bowl, cream together sugar and margarine. Whisk in egg and milk until well blended. Add to dry ingredients all at once; stir just until moistened. Do not overmix.

• Spoon into nonstick or paper-lined 2 1/2 inch (6 cm) muffin cups, filling three-quarters full.

• Bake in 375°F (190°C) oven for 20 minutes or until tops are firm to the touch.

Makes 12 medium muffins.

VARIATION:
SPICY RAISIN NUT MUFFINS
• Add 1/3 cup (75 mL) raisins and 2 tbsp (25 mL) chopped walnuts or pecans to dry ingredients of Spicy Muffins.

Honey Carrot Date Muffins

The muffins are marvelous with the sweetness from the honey and dates ringing through them.

1 cup	whole bean flour	250 mL
1/4 cup	cornmeal	50 mL
1/4 cup	cornstarch	50 mL
1 tbsp	gluten-free baking powder	15 mL
1/2 tsp	ground cinnamon	2 mL
1/2 tsp	salt	2 mL
1/4 tsp	ground allspice	1 mL
Pinch	ground cloves	Pinch
1/2 cup	grated carrots	125 mL
1/2 cup	chopped pitted dates	125 mL
1/2 cup	honey	125 mL
1/4 cup	soft margarine OR butter	50 mL
2	eggs	2
1/2 cup	skim milk	125 mL

• In mixing bowl, stir together flour, cornmeal, cornstarch, baking powder, cinnamom, salt, allspice and cloves. Stir in carrots and dates.

• In separate bowl, cream together honey and margarine. Whisk in eggs and milk until well blended. Add to dry ingredients all at once; stir just until moistened.

• Spoon into nonstick or paper-lined 2 1/2 inch (6 cm) muffin cups, filling three-quarters full.

• Bake in 375°F (190°C) oven for 20 minutes or until tops are firm to the touch.

Makes 12 medium muffins.

Each serving: 1 muffin

1/2 ▢ Starchy
1 1/2 ◨ Fruits & Vegetables
1 ◭ Fats & Oils

166 calories
694 kilojoules
4 g total fat
0.9 g saturated fat
36 mg cholesterol
3 g protein
28 g carbohydrate
200 mg sodium
214 mg potassium

GOOD: Vitamin D, Vitamin A
MODERATE: Fibre

Each serving: 1/16 of recipe

Cake only:

1/2 ☐ Starchy

1 1/2 ◪ Fruits & Vegetables

109	calories
455	kilojoules
0 g	total fat
0 g	saturated fat
0 mg	cholesterol
2 g	protein
24 g	carbohydrate
189 mg	sodium
127 mg	potassium

MODERATE: Fibre

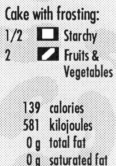

Cake with frosting:

1/2 ☐ Starchy

2 ◪ Fruits & Vegetables

139	calories
581	kilojoules
0 g	total fat
0 g	saturated fat
0 mg	cholesterol
2 g	protein
31 g	carbohydrate
202 mg	sodium
132 mg	potassium

MODERATE: Fibre

CHOCOLATE MOCHA CAKE

This is it! A completely fat-free cake with the rich flavor of chocolate but none of the fat. Also, the fluffy frosting recommended has no fat in it.

1 cup	whole bean flour	250 mL
3/4 cup	granulated sugar	175 mL
1/2 cup	cornstarch	125 mL
1/2 cup	unsweetened cocoa powder	125 mL
2 tsp	gluten-free baking powder	10 mL
1 tsp	baking soda	5 mL
1/2 tsp	salt	2 mL
4	egg whites	4
1 1/2 cups	strong coffee, cooled	375 mL
1/3 cup	corn syrup	75 mL
	Fluffy Frosting (p.163)	

• Spray bottom only of nonstick 9-inch (2.5 L) square cake pan with nonstick coating. Set aside.

• In mixing bowl, stir together bean flour, 1/2 cup (125 mL) of the sugar, cornstarch, cocoa, baking powder, baking soda and salt.

• In separate bowl, beat egg whites until foamy. Gradually beat in remaining sugar until stiff peaks form.

• In small bowl, whisk together coffee and corn syrup; whisk into dry ingredients until smooth. Fold in egg whites until blended. Pour into prepared pan; spread to corners, smoothing top.

• Bake in 350°F (180°C) oven for 40 minutes or until tester inserted into centre comes out clean. Cool in pan, or cool for 5 minutes in pan before turning out onto wire rack to cool completely. Spread Fluffy Frosting over cake.

Makes 1 cake, 16 servings.

Photograph courtesy of *Best Foods Canada Inc.*

JELLY ROLL

Slices of jelly roll filled with dietetic spread or light jam are as wonderful for the lunch box as they are at home with a cup of tea. The roll also makes a scrumptious base for pretty tantillizing desserts such as our Strawberry Cream Roll (p.204).

3/4 cup	whole bean flour	175 mL
1/4 cup	cornstarch	50 mL
3/4 cup	granulated sugar	175 mL
2 tsp	gluten-free baking powder	2 mL
1/2 tsp	salt	2 mL
3/4 cup	water	175 mL
2 tbsp	canola oil	25 mL
2	egg yolks	2
4	egg whites	4
1/4 tsp	cream of tartar	1 mL
2 tsp	almond extract	10 mL

• Line bottom only of 18 x 12-inch (3 L) jelly roll pan with waxed paper. Set aside.

• In bowl, stir together flour, cornstarch, 1/3 cup (75 mL) of the sugar, baking powder and salt.

• Whisk together water, oil, egg yolks and almond extract.

• In large mixing bowl, beat egg whites and cream of tartar until soft peaks form. Gradually beat in remaining sugar until stiff shiny peaks form.

• Pour egg yolk mixture into dry ingredients. Beat for 1 minute or until very smooth and blended. Beat in half the egg whites. Fold in remaining egg whites until well blended. Pour into prepared pan. With spatula, smooth top.

• Bake in 325°F (160°C) oven for 15 minutes or until cake springs back when touched in centre. Let cool for 5 minutes.

• Spread tea towel on flat surface. Loosen edges of jelly roll. Invert onto tea towel; peel off paper. With sharp knife, cut about 1/4 inch (5 mm) strip from each edge. Roll up with tea towel. Transfer to rack to cool.

• Unroll; remove tea towel. Spread with filling of choice. Roll up; wrap with waxed paper or plastic wrap. Refrigerate for 1 hour before slicing.

Makes 1 jelly roll cake, 16 servings.

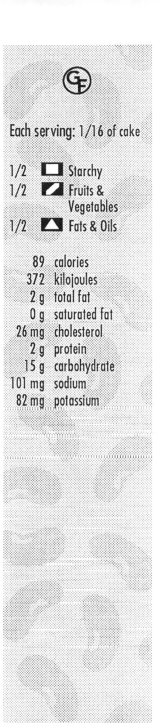

GF

Each serving: 1/16 of cake

1/2	☐	Starchy
1/2	◨	Fruits & Vegetables
1/2	◮	Fats & Oils

89	calories
372	kilojoules
2 g	total fat
0 g	saturated fat
26 mg	cholesterol
2 g	protein
15 g	carbohydrate
101 mg	sodium
82 mg	potassium

CHOCOLATE CAKE

When you have a whim for ice cream and cake, this is the cake to satisfy that desire. It stands nicely on its own without frosting. However, if you want icing on the cake use one of our low-fat, gluten-free frostings but remember to add on the additional Food Choice Values, especially when the dessert is for people with diabetes.

2/3 cup	whole bean flour	150 mL
1/3 cup	unsweetened cocoa powder	75 mL
1/4 cup	cornstarch	50 mL
2/3 cup	granulated sugar	150 mL
2 tsp	gluten-free baking powder	10 mL
1/2 tsp	salt	2 mL
2/3 cup	water	150 mL
1/4 cup	canola oil	50 mL
2	egg yolks	2
1 tsp	vanilla	5 mL
4	egg whites	4
1/4 tsp	cream of tartar	1 mL

• Very lightly brush oil on bottom of nonstick 8-inch (2 L) square or round cake pan. Set aside.

• In bowl, Stir together bean flour, cocoa, cornstarch, 1/3 cup (75 mL) of the sugar, baking powder and salt.

• In 2 cup (500 mL) measure, whisk together water, oil, egg yolks and vanilla.

• In large mixing bowl and using clean beaters, beat egg whites and cream of tartar until soft peaks form. Gradually beat in remaining sugar; beat for 1 to 2 minutes longer or until stiff shiny peaks form.

• Pour egg yolk mixture into dry ingredients. Beat for 1 minute or until very smooth and blended. Beat in half the egg whites. With wire whisk, fold in remaining egg whites until blended well.

• Pour into prepared pan. With knife, cut through batter to remove air bubbles. Smooth top.

• Bake in 325°F (160°C) oven for about 40 minutes or until cake tester inserted into centre comes out clean. Let cool for 5 minutes. With knife, loosen sides. Let cool completely on cake rack.

Makes 1 cake, 16 servings.

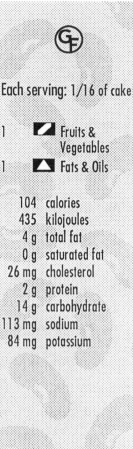

Each serving: 1/16 of cake

1		Fruits & Vegetables
1		Fats & Oils

104	calories
435	kilojoules
4 g	total fat
0 g	saturated fat
26 mg	cholesterol
2 g	protein
14 g	carbohydrate
113 mg	sodium
84 mg	potassium

CREAMY CHOCOLATE FROSTING

This is perfect to spread over a cool cake or brownie to make a thin layer of frosting.

1/2 cup	semisweet chocolate chips	125 mL
1/4 cup	light cream cheese	50 mL
2 tbsp	corn syrup	25 mL

• In small microwaveable bowl, microwave chocolate chips at Medium- High (70 %) power for 1 1/2 minutes. Or melt chocolate in top of double boiler over boiling water.

• Cool for 5 minutes. Beat in light cream cheese and syrup until smooth and creamy.

• Spread over cool cake or brownie to make a thin layer of frosting.

Makes about 2/3 cup (150 mL), enough to thinly frost 9 inch (2.5 L) square or round cake.

VARIATION:
CREAMY WHITE CHOCOLATE FROSTING

• Use white chocolate chips instead of the semisweet chocolate chips in the recipe.

FLUFFY FROSTING

Seven-minute and boiled frostings are the grandmothers of this airy frosting which is less sweet and much easier to make. This one uses boiling corn syrup; the others require cooking a sugar syrup to just the right temperature.

1/2 cup	corn syrup	125 mL
1	egg white	1
1/4	cream of tartar	1 mL
1 tsp	vanilla	5 mL

• In saucepan over medium heat, bring syrup to boil.

• In small mixing bowl, beat egg white and cream of tartar until soft peaks form. Beat in vanilla. Gradually beat in hot syrup for about 3 minutes or until stiff and shiny.

Makes about 2 cups (500 mL).

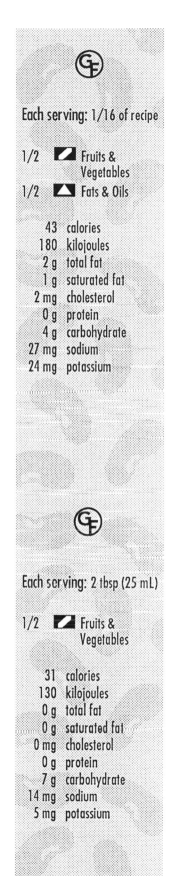

Each serving: 1/16 of recipe

1/2 Fruits & Vegetables
1/2 Fats & Oils

43	calories
180	kilojoules
2 g	total fat
1 g	saturated fat
2 mg	cholesterol
0 g	protein
4 g	carbohydrate
27 mg	sodium
24 mg	potassium

Each serving: 2 tbsp (25 mL)

1/2 Fruits & Vegetables

31	calories
130	kilojoules
0 g	total fat
0 g	saturated fat
0 mg	cholesterol
0 g	protein
7 g	carbohydrate
14 mg	sodium
5 mg	potassium

Each serving: 1/16 of cake

1 1/2 ◨ Fruits &
      Vegetables
1/2 ◩ Fats & Oils

 94 calories
393 kilojoules
  2 g total fat
  0 g saturated fat
 26 mg cholesterol
  2 g protein
 16 g carbohydrate
154 mg sodium
123 mg potassium

ORANGE CAKE

The centre of this light chiffon-style cake may collapse slightly if the cake is baked in a regular cake pan rather than a tube pan. For a special celebration, frost and decorate it. For a delicious dessert, serve slices of unfrosted cake with succulent fresh fruit sauces.

1 cup	whole bean flour	250 mL
1/4 cup	cornstarch	50 mL
2/3 cup	granulated sugar	150 mL
1 tsp	gluten-free baking powder	5 mL
1 tsp	baking soda	5 mL
1/2 tsp	salt	2 mL
2/3 cup	orange juice	150 mL
2 tbsp	canola oil	25 mL
2	egg yolks	2
2 tbsp	lemon or lime juice	25 mL
2 tsp	grated orange rind	10 mL
4	egg whites	4
1/4 tsp	cream of tartar	1 mL

• In bowl, stir together flour, cornstarch, 1/2 cup (125 mL) of the sugar, baking powder, baking soda and salt.

• Make a well in dry ingredients. Pour in orange juice, oil, egg yolks, lemon juice and orange rind. Beat for 1 minute or until very smooth and blended.

• In large mixing bowl and using clean beaters, beat egg whites and cream of tartar until soft peaks form. Gradually beat in remaining sugar; beat for 1 to 2 minutes longer or until stiff shiny peaks form.

• With wire whisk, gently fold egg yolk mixture into stiffly beaten egg whites until blended well.

• Pour into 10 -inch (4 L) tube pan. With knife, cut through batter to remove air bubbles. Smooth top.

• Bake in 325°F (160°C) oven for about 45 minutes or until cake tester inserted into centre comes out clean. Let cool for 5 minutes. Invert pan; allow to cool completely.

Makes 1 cake, 16 servings.

Banana Cake

The flavor of the banana and whole bean flour go together in this light cake. For a dazzling dinner party torte, cut it into layers then spread flavored whipped topping or whipped cream between them and reassemble the cake. Frost with more of the whipped mixture and garnish with fresh berries.

1 cup	whole bean flour	250 mL
1/4 cup	cornstarch	50 mL
3/4 cup	granulated sugar	175 mL
1 tsp	gluten-free baking powder	5 mL
1 tsp	baking soda	5 mL
1/2 tsp	salt	2 mL
2/3 cup	mashed banana (2 bananas)	150 mL
1/4 cup	canola oil	50 mL
2 tbsp	lemon juice	25 mL
2	egg yolks	2
2 tsp	vanilla	10 mL
4	egg whites	4
1/4 tsp	cream of tartar	1 mL

• Spray 10-inch (3 L) Bundt or tube pan with nonstick spray. Set aside.

• In bowl, stir together flour, cornstarch, 1/3 cup (75 mL) of the sugar, baking powder, baking soda and salt.

• In 2 cup (500 mL) measure, whisk together banana, oil, lemon juice, egg yolks and vanilla.

• In large mixing bowl and using clean beaters, beat egg whites and cream of tartar until soft peaks form. Gradually beat in remaining sugar; beat for 1 to 2 minutes longer or until stiff shiny peaks form.

• Pour banana mixture into dry ingredients. Beat for 1 minute or until very smooth and blended. Beat in half the egg whites. With wire whisk, fold in remaining egg whites until blended well.

• Pour into prepared pan. With knife, cut through batter to remove air bubbles. Smooth top.

• Bake in 325°F (160°C) oven for about 40 minutes or until cake tester inserted into centre comes out clean. Let cool for 5 minutes. With knife, loosen sides. Let cool completely on cake rack.

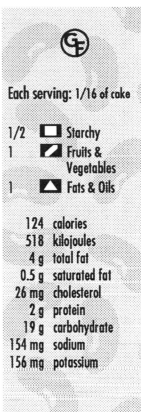

Each serving: 1/16 of cake

1/2	☐	Starchy
1	◪	Fruits & Vegetables
1	▲	Fats & Oils

124	calories
518	kilojoules
4 g	total fat
0.5 g	saturated fat
26 mg	cholesterol
2 g	protein
19 g	carbohydrate
154 mg	sodium
156 mg	potassium

MODERATE: Fibre

Each serving: 1/16 of recipe

Without frosting:

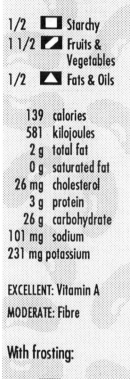

1/2 □ Starchy
1 1/2 ▨ Fruits &
        Vegetables
1/2 △ Fats & Oils

  139 calories
  581 kilojoules
    2 g total fat
    0 g saturated fat
  26 mg cholesterol
    3 g protein
  26 g carbohydrate
101 mg sodium
231 mg potassium

EXCELLENT: Vitamin A
MODERATE: Fibre

With frosting:

1/2 □ Starchy
2   ▨ Fruits &
        Vegetables
1/2 △ Fats & Oils

  182 calories
  760 kilojoules
    3 g total fat
    1 g saturated fat
  29 mg cholesterol
    3 g protein
  31 g carbohydrate
129 mg sodium
254 mg potassium

EXCELLENT: Vitamin A
MODERATE: Fibre

SPICY CARROT CAKE

This gluten-free version is just as moist and spicy as regular carrot cake using wheat flour. Take it frosted to a pot-luck supper for everyone to enjoy. Frosting adds not only glamour but sweetness and calories and changes the Food Choice Value of one piece of cake.

2	eggs, beaten	2
1/2 cup	packed brown sugar	125 mL
1/3 cup	granulated sugar	75 mL
1/4 cup	water	50 mL
2 tbsp	canola oil	25 mL
1 tsp	vanilla	5 mL
1 cup	whole bean flour	250 mL
1/2 cup	cornmeal	125 mL
2 tbsp	corn starch	25 mL
1 1/2 tsp	gluten-free baking powder	7 mL
1/2 tsp	baking soda	2 mL
1 tsp	ground cinnamon	5 mL
1/2 tsp	ground nutmeg	2 mL
1/2 tsp	salt	2 mL
1 1/2 cups	grated raw carrots	375 mL
1/3 cup	raisins	75 mL
1/4 cup	candied mixed fruit	50 mL
2 tbsp	finely chopped walnuts OR pecans	25 mL
	Creamy White Chocolate Frosting (p.163), optional	

• Spray bottom only of nonstick 9-inch (2.5 L) square cake pan with nonstick coating. Set aside.

• In mixing bowl, beat eggs. Gradually beat in sugars, beating until thick and light. Beat in water, oil and vanilla.

• In bowl, stir together bean flour, cornmeal, cornstarch, baking powder, baking soda, cinnamon, nutmeg and salt; stir into egg mixture. Stir in carrots, raisins, candied fruit and nuts. Pour into prepared pan; smooth top.

• Bake in 350°F (180°C) oven for about 30 minutes or until tester inserted in centre comes out clean. Cool in pan, or cool for 5 minutes before turning out onto rack to cool completely.

• Spread with Creamy White Chololate Frosting, if desired.

Makes 1 cake, 16 servings.

BROWNIES

These chocolatey whole bean flour brownies are a pleasure for the taste buds. They are doubly delicious topped with the Creamy Chocolate Frosting (p.163) but it does add calories.

1/2 cup	whole bean flour	125 mL
1/4 cup	cornstarch	50 mL
1/4 cup	unsweetened cocoa powder	50 mL
1 1/2 tsp	gluten-free baking powder	7 mL
1/2 tsp	baking soda	2 mL
1/2 tsp	salt	2 mL
1/3 cup	chopped walnuts	75 mL
1/3 cup	soft margarine OR butter	75 mL
3/4 cup	granulated sugar	175 mL
2	eggs OR 3 egg whites	2
1/4 cup	water	50 mL
1 tsp	vanilla	5 mL
	Creamy Chocolate Frosting (p.163), optional	

• Lightly spray bottom of 9-inch (2.5 L) square cake pan with nonstick coating. Set aside.

• In small bowl, combine flour, cornstarch, cocoa, baking powder, baking soda and salt until well blended. Stir in walnuts.

• In mixing bowl, cream together margarine and sugar. Beat in eggs one at a time. Stir in dry ingredients alternately with water until blended; beat well. Stir in vanilla until blended.

• Spoon into prepared pan; spread into corners and smooth top.

• Bake in 350°F (180°C) oven for 45 minutes or until tester inserted into centre comes out clean.

• Cool in pan. With knife, loosen sides. If desired, frost with Creamy Chocolate Frosting. Cut into squares.

Makes 20 brownies.

Each serving: 1 brownie

Without frosting:

1 Fruits & Vegetables
1 Fats & Oils

94	calories
393	kilojoules
4 g	total fat
0 g	saturated fat
21 mg	cholesterol
1 g	protein
11 g	carbohydrate
116 mg	sodium
57 mg	potassium

With frosting:

1 1/2 Fruits & Vegetables
1 Fats & Oils

129	calories
539	kilojoules
6 g	total fat
2 g	saturated fat
23 mg	cholesterol
2 g	protein
15 g	carbohydrate
138 mg	sodium
77 mg	potassium

FUDGY ALMOND BROWNIES

The texture of these brownies is so fudgy they are more like a confection than cake and never need a frosting.

1/3 cup	soft margarine OR butter	75 mL
2	squares unsweetened chocolate (2 oz/60 g)	2
1/2 cup	granulated sugar	125 mL
2	eggs, well beaten	2
1/3 cup	whole bean flour	75 mL
1/4 cup	cornstarch OR rice flour	50 mL
1/2 tsp	salt	2 mL
1 tsp	almond extract	5 mL
1/3 cup	sliced almonds	75 mL

• Lightly spray bottom only of nonstick 8-inch (2 L) square cake pan with nonstick coating. Set aside.

• In saucepan over low heat, combine margarine and chocolate; melt, stirring constantly. Remove from heat; stir in sugar and eggs.

• In bowl, stir together bean flour, cornstarch and salt; stir into chocolate mixture. Stir in almond extract; fold in sliced almonds. Pour into prepared pan; spread to corners, smoothing top.

• Bake in 350°F (180°C) oven for about 25 minutes or until firm and brownie begins to pull away from pan. Cool in pan on wire rack. Cut into squares.

Makes 16 brownies.

Gingersnaps

These cookies are another variation of old-fashioned favorites. And, this is the dough to roll out and use for Gingerbread Men or Houses and cut out cookies. Decorate the baked cookies with Fluffy Frosting (p.163). (Spoon it into a decorating bag fitted with a writing tip). The frosting hardens as it dries.

3/4 cup	whole bean flour	175 mL
1/4 cup	potato flour OR cornstarch	50 mL
2 tsp	gluten-free baking powder	10 mL
1 tsp	ground ginger	5 mL
1/2 tsp	each ground cinnamon and nutmeg	2 mL
Pinch	each ground cloves and allspice	Pinch
1/2 tsp	baking soda	2 mL
1/2 tsp	salt	2 mL
1/4 cup	soft margarine OR butter	50 mL
1/4 cup	packed brown sugar	50 mL
1/4 cup	molasses	50 mL
1/4 cup	water	50 mL
2 tsp	vanilla	10 mL

• In bowl, stir together bean and potato flours, baking powder, ginger, cinnamon, nutmeg, cloves, allspice, baking soda and salt.

• In mixing bowl, cream together margarine, brown sugar and molasses. Stir in dry ingredients alternately with water. Stir in vanilla until blended.

• Form into roll about 2 inches (5 cm) in diameter; wrap and chill for about 2 hours. With serrated knife, cut into thin slices. OR do not chill dough and roll out on surface lightly dusted with potato flour to 1/8 inch (3 mm) thickness. With cookie cutters, cut into desired shapes.

• Place 1 inch (2.5 cm) apart on nonstick baking sheets.

• Bake in 325°F (160°C) oven for 8 to 10 minutes or until edges are golden brown.

Makes 60 cookies.

VARIATION:
Cinnamon Hearts

• Increase ground cinnamon to 1 1/2 tsp (7 mL). Omit ground ginger. Roll out dough and cut out with heart-shaped cookie cutters.

GF

Each serving: 3 cookies

1 ◪ Fruits & Vegetables
1/2 ◮ Fats & Oils

64	calories
267	kilojoules
2 g	total fat
0 g	saturated fat
0 mg	cholesterol
0.9 g	protein
10 g	carbohydrate
110 mg	sodium
99 mg	potassium

Calculations approximately the same as above.

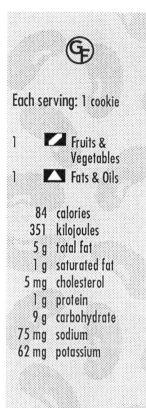

Each serving: 1 cookie

1   ◪ Fruits &
        Vegetables
1   ◭ Fats & Oils

  84   calories
 351   kilojoules
   5 g   total fat
   1 g   saturated fat
  5 mg   cholesterol
   1 g   protein
   9 g   carbohydrate
 75 mg   sodium
 62 mg   potassium

CHOCOLATE CHIP COOKIES

Forty thousand samples of these cookies were tasted at the 1992 Royal Winter Fair in Toronto. Everyone loved them.

1 cup	whole bean flour	250 mL
1/2 tsp	baking soda	2 mL
1/2 tsp	salt	2 mL
2/3 cup	soft margarine OR butter	150 mL
1/2 cup	granulated sugar	125 mL
1/4 cup	packed brown sugar	50 mL
1	egg	1
1 tsp	vanilla	5 mL
1 cup	chocolate chips (6 oz/170 g)	250 mL

• In bowl, stir together bean flour, baking soda and salt.

• In mixing bowl, cream together margarine, granulated and brown sugars. Beat in egg and vanilla until light and fluffy. Stir in dry ingredients until blended. Fold in chocolate chips.

• Drop by heaping teaspoonfuls (5 mL), about 2 inches (5 cm) apart onto nonstick baking sheets.

• Bake in 350°F (180°C) oven for 10 to 12 minutes or until golden brown.

Makes 36 cookies.

CHOCOLATE PECAN RAISIN HERMITS

These drop cookies are soft when freshly baked. As they age they become more crunchy. Candied ginger adds a snappy hot-sweet sensation to the variation.

2	squares unsweetened chocolate (2 oz/60 g)	2
1 1/2 cups	whole bean flour	375 mL
2 tbsp	cornstarch	25 mL
2 tsp	gluten-free baking powder	10 mL
1 tsp	baking soda	5 mL
1/4 tsp	salt	1 mL
1/3 cup	soft margarine OR butter	75 mL
2/3 cup	packed brown sugar	150 mL
2 tbsp	corn syrup	25 mL
1	egg	1
1 tsp	vanilla	5 mL
1/2 cup	light sour cream	125 mL
1/4 cup	water	50 mL
1/4 cup	chopped pecans	50 mL
1/4 cup	raisins	50 mL

• In small bowl over boiling water, melt chocolate. (Or melt it in microwave oven following manufacturer's directions.) Cool to room temperature.

• In bowl, stir together bean flour, cornstarch, baking powder, baking soda and salt.

• In mixing bowl, cream together margarine, brown sugar and corn syrup. Beat in egg and vanilla until light and fluffy. Stir in dry ingredients alternately with sour cream and water until blended. Fold in pecans and raisins.

• Drop by teaspoonfuls (5 mL), about 2 inches (5 cm) apart onto nonstick baking sheets.

• Bake in 350°F (180°C) oven for 12 to 15 minutes or until beginning to brown.

Makes 60 cookies.

VARIATION:
CHOCOLATE PECAN GINGER HERMITS

• Omit raisins and add 1/4 cup (50 mL) chopped rinsed preserved or candied ginger.

Each serving: 2 cookies

1   Fruits & Vegetables

1   Fats & Oils

89	calories
372	kilojoules
4 g	total fat
1 g	saturated fat
8 mg	cholesterol
1 g	protein
12 g	carbohydrate
100 mg	sodium
118 mg	potassium

Calculations approximately the same as above

LEMON WAFERS

The thinner these wafers are the crisper they are and the quicker they bake. Store in a dry place in a covered container.

1/4 cup	soft margarine OR butter	50 mL
1/3 cup	granulated sugar	75 mL
1/2 cup	whole bean flour	125 mL
1/4 cup	rice flour	50 mL
1/2 tsp	gluten-free baking powder	2 mL
1/2 tsp	baking soda	2 mL
1/4 tsp	salt	1 mL
	Grated rind and juice of 1 lemon	
1 tbsp	ground almonds	15 mL

• In mixing bowl, cream together margarine and sugar until smooth.

• Stir together whole bean and rice flours, baking powder, baking soda, salt and lemon rind.

• Add enough water to lemon juice to make 1/4 cup (50 mL).

• Alternately, stir dry ingredients and liquid into creamed mixture until soft dough forms. Divide dough in half.

• On surface dusted with rice flour, roll out, each portion under a sheet of plastic wrap, to thickness of 1/8 inch (3 mm). With crinkle-edged 2 inch (5 cm) round cutter, cut out cookies.

• With metal lifter, transfer to nonstick baking sheets, leaving 1 inch (2.5 cm) space between cookies. Lightly sprinkle with ground almonds; gently press in place.

• Bake in 350°F (180°C) for 10 minutes or until lightly browned around edges. Let cool on wire racks.

Makes 48 cookies.

Each serving: 3 cookies

1/2 ☐ Starchy
1/2 ▲ Fats & Oils

64	calories
267	kilojoules
2 g	total fat
0.5 g	saturated fat
0 mg	cholesterol
0.9 g	protein
8 g	carbohydrate
65 mg	sodium
52 mg	potassium

Peanut Butter Cookies

These are quick and easy to prepare and they are also quickly devoured.

3/4 cup	whole bean flour	175 mL
1/4 cup	cornstarch OR potato flour	50 mL
2 tsp	gluten-free baking powder	10 mL
1/2 tsp	baking soda	2 mL
1/2 tsp	salt	2 mL
1/2 cup	smooth gluten-free peanut butter	125 mL
2 tbsp	soft margarine OR butter	25 mL
1/2 cup	packed brown sugar	125 mL
2 tbsp	corn syrup	25 mL
1/4 cup	water	50 mL
1 tsp	vanilla	5 mL
1 tsp	almond extract	5 mL

• In bowl, stir together flour, cornstarch, baking powder, baking soda and salt.

• In mixing bowl, cream together peanut butter, margarine, brown sugar and syrup. Stir in dry ingredients alternately with water. Stir in vanilla and almond extracts until well blended.

• Form into 1 inch (2.5 cm) balls. Place 2 inches (5 cm) apart on nonstick baking sheets. Flatten balls by pressing with tines of fork dipped into cornstarch to prevent sticking.

• Bake in 350°F (180°C) oven for 10 to 12 minutes or until golden brown.

Makes 48 cookies.

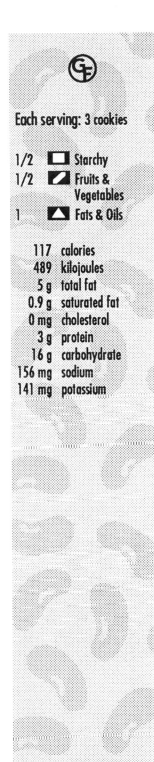

Each serving: 3 cookies

1/2 ☐ Starchy
1/2 ◪ Fruits & Vegetables
1 ▲ Fats & Oils

117 calories
489 kilojoules
5 g total fat
0.9 g saturated fat
0 mg cholesterol
3 g protein
16 g carbohydrate
156 mg sodium
141 mg potassium

CHOCOLATE MARSHMALLOW NUT SQUARES

These squares are like fudge but not as sweet. They are best made a day or two ahead and should be stored in the refrigerator.

1 cup	semisweet chocolate chips	250 mL
1/3 cup	smooth gluten-free peanut butter	75 mL
2 tbsp	corn syrup	25 mL
1 1/2 cups	cooked red kidney or Dutch brown beans	375 mL
1/2 tsp	ground cinnamon	2 mL
1 1/2 cups	miniature gluten-free marshmallows	375 mL
1/4 cup	chopped walnuts	50 mL

• Lightly spray bottom of 9-inch (2.5 L) square cake pan with nonstick coating. Set aside.

• In large saucepan over low heat, melt chocolate chips and peanut butter, stirring constantly until smooth. (Or in large microwaveable container, microwave at MEDIUM 50 % power for about 2 1/2 minutes or until mixture can be stirred smooth.) Stir in corn syrup. Remove from heat. Cool for 5 minutes.

• In food processor, puree beans and cinnamon. Stir into chocolate mixture until well blended. Stir in marshmallows and walnuts until coated.

• Press evenly into prepared pan. Chill for about 45 minutes or until firm.

• Cover and refrigerate for at least 8 hours or up to 6 days before serving. Cut into squares.

Makes 24 squares.

COCONUT CRISPS

Two egg whites may be used for these cookies instead of one egg.

3/4 cup	whole bean flour	175 mL
1 tsp	gluten-free baking powder	5 mL
1/2 tsp	salt	2 mL
1/2 cup	soft margarine OR butter	125 mL
1/2 cup	packed brown sugar	125 mL
1	egg	1
2 tsp	vanilla	10 mL
1/2 cup	unsweetened desiccated coconut	125 mL

• In bowl, stir together bean flour, baking powder and salt.

• In mixing bowl, cream together margarine and brown sugar. Beat in egg and vanilla until light and fluffy. Stir in dry ingredients and coconut.

• Drop by tablespoonfuls (15 mL) about 2 inches (5 cm) apart onto nonstick baking sheet.

• Bake in 350°F (180°C) oven for 10 to 12 minutes until golden brown.

Makes 36 cookies.

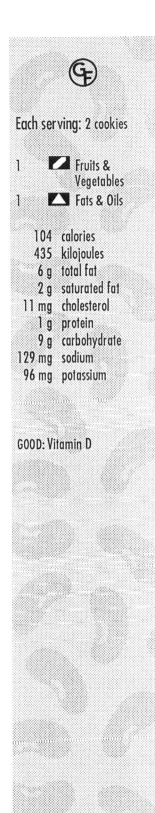

Each serving: 2 cookies

1 Fruits & Vegetables
1 Fats & Oils

104 calories
435 kilojoules
6 g total fat
2 g saturated fat
11 mg cholesterol
1 g protein
9 g carbohydrate
129 mg sodium
96 mg potassium

GOOD: Vitamin D

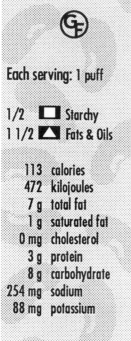

CREAM PUFFS

Split and fill these with flavored whipped topping or cream, iced milk or sherbet and drizzle a little chocolate syrup over top for a beautiful dessert. They are also good just as they are with soups and salads. Make smaller ones (12 instead of 6) to fill with savory fillings or salads to serve as appetizers or snacks.

1/4 cup	whole bean flour	50 mL
1/4 cup	rice flour	50 mL
1/2 tsp	salt	1 mL
1/2 cup	water	125 mL
1/4 cup	soft margarine OR butter	50 mL
3	egg whites	3

• In small dish, stir together bean flour, rice flour and salt.

• In saucepan over medium-high heat, bring water and margarine to a rolling boil. Stir in flour all at once and continue stirring for about 30 seconds or until mixture leaves side of pan and forms a ball. Remove from heat.

• Beat in egg whites, one at a time, beating until thoroughly blended and mixture is smooth and velvety.

• Drop by spoonfuls into 6 mounds about 2 inches (5 cm) apart on paper-lined baking sheet.

• Bake in 375°F (190°C) oven for 45 minutes or until puffed and golden brown. Remove from oven. Cut slash into side of each puff. Turn off oven; return puffs to cool in oven.

Makes 6 cream puffs.

Each serving: 1 puff

1/2 ▢ Starchy
1 1/2 ◣ Fats & Oils

113 calories
472 kilojoules
7 g total fat
1 g saturated fat
0 mg cholesterol
3 g protein
8 g carbohydrate
254 mg sodium
88 mg potassium

EXCELLENT: Vitamin D

Gluten-Free Pastry

Since whole bean flour makes a more tender pastry than wheat flour not as much fat is required as is needed for pastry using whole wheat flour.

1 1/2 cups	whole bean flour	375 mL
1/4 cup	cornstarch	50 mL
1 tbsp	cornmeal	15 mL
1 tsp	gluten-free baking powder	5 mL
1/2 tsp	salt	2 mL
6 tbsp	vegetable shortening	90 mL
1	egg white	1
3/4 cup	cold water	175 mL

• In mixing bowl, stir together bean flour, cornstarch, cornmeal, baking powder and salt. With pastry blender or two knives, cut in shortening until mixture is crumbly.

• Whisk together egg white and water. Stir into dry ingredients to make a soft dough. Press into ball. Divide in half; flatten each half into a patty.

• On cornstarch dusted surface with stockinette-covered rolling pin (or between sheets of plastic wrap or waxed paper) roll out dough to 1/8 inch (3 mm) thick circle shape.

• Carefully roll up onto rolling pin; unroll over pie plate. (Or remove plastic wrap from top of pastry; using remaining bottom sheet for support, carefully place pastry, plastic wrap up, into pie plate.) Press smoothly into pan. (If pieces break away, press them back in place.)

For pie shell or single-crust pie:

• Trim edge leaving 1/2 inch (1 cm) overhang. Tuck under to make double layer of pastry around rim; flute edge. (For straight-sided flan pan, fold the overhang to the inside.) Line inside of pastry shell with piece of foil.

• Bake in 400°F (200°C) oven for 15 to 18 minutes or until edges are golden brown. Remove foil.

For double-crust pie:

• Trim edge of pastry evenly. Fill as recipe directs. Roll out remaining pastry for top crust. Fit over filling; trim, leaving 1/2 inch (1 cm) overhang. Tuck overhang under edge of bottom crust; press firmly together. Flute edges to seal tightly. Cut steam vents in top crust. Bake as recipe directs.

Makes pastry for 1 double-crust 9-inch (23 cm) pie or two 9-inch (23 cm) pie shells or 24 medium tart shells.

Each serving: 1/8 of crust

SINGLE CRUST:

1/2	☐ Starchy
1	▲ Fats & Oils

92	calories
384	kilojoules
4 g	total fat
1 g	saturated fat
0 mg	cholesterol
2 g	protein
9 g	carbohydrate
22 mg	sodium
137 mg	potassium

MODERATE: Fibre

DOUBLE CRUST:

1	☐ Starchy
1 1/2	▲ Fats & Oils

184	calories
769	kilojoules
8 g	total fat
2 g	saturated fat
0 mg	cholesterol
4 g	protein
18 g	carbohydrate
44 mg	sodium
274 mg	potassium

HIGH: Fibre

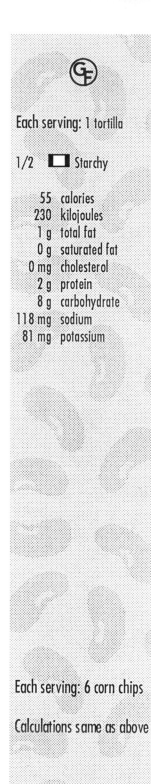

GLUTEN-FREE TORTILLAS

The combination of whole bean flour, cornmeal and cornstarch with egg whites and water makes very respectable tortillas to use in any recipe calling for them. They are best fresh but will keep, wrapped, in the refrigerator for 3 days.

1/3 cup	whole bean flour	75 mL
1/4 cup	cornmeal	50 mL
2 tbsp	cornstarch	25 mL
1/2 tsp	salt	2 mL
3	egg whites	3
1 1/2 cups	water	375 mL
	Canola oil	

• In small bowl, stir together bean flour, cornmeal, cornstarch and salt.

• In bowl, whisk together egg whites and water; gradually whisk in dry ingredients.Let stand at room temperature for 1 hour.

• Warm small nonstick skillet over medium heat; brush very lightly with oil.

• Stir batter. Pour 1/4 cup (50 mL) at a time into skillet; spread evenly over bottom. Cook until just dry on top. Turn carefully; cook until lightly brown on underside. Remove to plate.

• Use immediately. (Or stack, wrap and refrigerate for up to 4 days or freeze for up to 4 weeks.)

Makes 8 tortillas.

VARIATION:
CRISP CORN AND BEAN CHIPS

• Cut each tortilla into 6 wedges. Arrange wedges in single layer on nonstick baking sheets. Bake in 300°F (150°C) oven for about 20 to 25 minutes or until lightly browned, crisp and dry. (Some pieces may be damper than others and may require a few more minutes baking.) Cool and pack into airtight bags.

Makes 8 servings, 48 corn chips.

BREADS & MUFFINS

Bean Biscuits

Dropped Biscuits

Quick Cinnamon Pinwheels

Country-Style Pancakes

Blueberry Scones

Bean Bread

Cheese Bean Bread

Raisin Bean Bread

Beany Pizza Crust

Banana Loaf

Date Loaf

Apricot, Oat and Bean Muffins

Orange Muffins

Orange Date Loaf

BEAN BISCUITS

These biscuits are best when they are mixed and kneaded quickly. They will be soft but adding more flour will make them heavier.

2 1/2 cups	all-purpose flour	625 mL
1/2 cup	whole wheat flour	125 mL
4 tsp	baking powder	20 mL
1 tbsp	granulated sugar	15 mL
1/2 tsp	salt	2 mL
1/3 cup	butter OR soft margarine	75 mL
1 cup	cooked white or red kidney beans	250 mL
2/3 cup	2% milk	150 mL

• In mixing bowl, stir together all-purpose and whole wheat flours, baking powder, sugar and salt.

• With pastry blender or two knives, cut in butter until mixture resembles a combination of coarse and fine crumbs.

• In food processor or blender, puree beans with milk. (Or mash beans and stir in milk.) Stir into dry ingredients all at once to make light soft dough.

• Turn out onto lightly floured surface; sprinkle lightly with all-purpose flour. Knead 8 to 10 times or for about 20 seconds until dough feels puffy and surface is smooth.

• With floured rolling pin or with hands, roll or pat out to thickness of 1/2 to 3/4 inch (1 to 2 cm). With floured (2 to 2 1/2 inches/5 to 6 cm) cookie cutter, cut out rounds. Or with sharp serrated knife, cut into squares, triangles or rectangles. Place 1 inch (2.5 cm) apart on nonstick baking sheets.

• Bake in 400°F (200°C) oven for 12 to 15 minutes or until golden brown.

Makes 16 biscuits.

Each serving: 1 biscuit

1 1/2 ☐ Starchy
1 ▲ Fats & Oils

162 calories
677 kilojoules
4 g total fat
0.8 g saturated fat
0 mg cholesterol
5 g protein
26 g carbohydrate
169 mg sodium
204 mg potassium

GOOD: Folate
MODERATE: Fibre

VARIATIONS
DROPPED BISCUITS

• Increase milk to 1 cup (250 mL). Stir into crumbly mixture; omit kneading and rolling. Drop by heaping tablespoonfuls (15 mL) onto baking sheet.

Makes 16 biscuits.

QUICK CINNAMON PINWHEELS

• On lightly floured surface, roll or pat out dough into rectangle about 1/3 inch (8 mm) thick. Spread with 1 tbsp (15 mL) soft margarine. Sprinkle evenly with 1/2 cup (125 mL) packed brown sugar and 1 1/2 tsp (7 mL) ground cinnamon. Starting at wide side, roll up jelly-roll style into long cylinder. With sharp knife, cut into 16 slices. Place 2 inches (5 cm) apart on nonstick baking sheets. Bake as directed for biscuits.

Makes 16 pinwheels.

Each serving: 1 biscuit

Calculations approximately the same as Bean Biscuits

Each serving: 1 pinwheel

1 1/2 ☐ Starchy
1/2 ◩ Fruits & Vegetables
1 ▲ Fats & Oils

194	calories
811	kilojoules
4 g	total fat
1 g	saturated fat
1 mg	cholesterol
5 g	protein
32 g	carbohydrate
179 mg	sodium
226 mg	potassium

GOOD: Iron, Vitamin D, Folate
MODERATE: Fibre

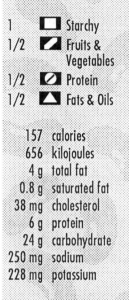
COUNTRY-STYLE PANCAKES

The whole bean flour and natural bran give these light pancakes a great boost of dietary fibre, both the soluble and insoluble types. For a thinner pancake stir in additional water or milk.

3/4 cup	all-purpose flour	175 mL
1/2 cup	whole bean flour	125 mL
1/4 cup	natural bran	50 mL
1 tbsp	granulated sugar	15 mL
2 tsp	baking powder	10 mL
1/2 tsp	salt	2 mL
1	egg	1
1 cup	2% milk	250 mL
1 tbsp	canola oil OR melted margarine	15 mL

• In mixing bowl, combine all-purpose and bean flours, bran, sugar, baking powder and salt.

• In separate bowl, beat together egg, milk and oil; quickly stir into dry ingredients until just mixed.

• Using about 1/3 cup (75 mL) for each pancake, pour batter onto hot, lightly oiled, preferably nonstick, griddle or skillet.

• Cook until puffy and bubbles begin to break on top. Turn and continue to cook until golden brown on underside.

Makes 6 servings, 12 pancakes.

BLUEBERRY SCONES

The addition of mashed beans enhances the texture, flavor and nutitional quality of these scones. They are great for breakfast or tea time.

1 cup	all-purpose flour	250 mL
1/2 cup	whole wheat flour	125 mL
2 tbsp	granulated sugar	25 mL
1 tbsp	baking powder	15 mL
1/2 tsp	salt	2 mL
1/2 cup	mashed red or white kidney beans	125 mL
1/3 cup	chilled soft margarine OR butter	75 mL
1	egg	1
1/2 cup	skim milk	125 mL
1/2 cup	fresh blueberries OR chopped cranberries	125 mL
	Milk and granulated sugar	

• In mixing bowl, stir together all-purpose and whole wheat flours, sugar, baking powder and salt. With pastry blender or two knives, cut in mashed beans until mixture resembles fine crumbs. Cut in margarine until mixture is a combination of coarse and fine crumbs.

• In small bowl, whisk together egg and milk. Add all at once to crumbly mixture, stirring to make a sticky dough. Stir in blueberries.

• Turn out onto lightly floured surface. Sprinkle lightly with flour. Knead about 8 times until dough feels puffy and surface is smooth.

• With floured rolling pin or hands, roll or pat out to thickness of 1 inch (2.5 cm). Cut into triangles or rounds. Place about 2 inches (5 cm) apart onto nonstick baking sheets. Brush with milk and sprinkle lightly with granulated sugar.

• Bake in 425°F (220°C) oven for 12 to 15 minutes or until golden and firm to the touch.

Makes 16 scones.

Each serving: 1 scone

1	☐	Starchy
1	◣	Fats & Oils

101	calories
422	kilojoules
4 g	total fat
0.8 g	saturated fat
13 mg	cholesterol
2 g	protein
13 g	carbohydrate
155 mg	sodium
63 mg	potassium

GOOD: Vitamin D

BEAN BREAD

What a superb bread! It is more robust than plain white bread with an exciting new taste, particularly when it is toasted.

1 tsp	granulated sugar	5 mL
1/2 cup	lukewarm water	125 mL
1	pkg active dry yeast	1
2 1/2 cups	all-purpose flour	625 mL
1 1/2 cups	cooked red kidney or Dutch brown beans, puréed	375 mL
1 tsp	salt	5 mL
1/4 cup	canola oil	50 mL
1	egg	1

• Spray 8- x 4-inch (1.5 L) nonstick loaf pan with nonstick coating. Set aside.

• In mixing bowl, dissolve sugar in warm water. Sprinkle yeast into water and let stand for 10 minutes or until foamy.

• In separate bowl, stir together flour, puréed beans and salt.

• Beat oil and egg into yeast mixture. Stir in about half of the flour mixture. Gradually mix in remaining flour mixture to make slightly sticky ball of dough.

• On lightly floured surface, knead dough for about 5 minutes or until elastic and smooth. Form into ball; place in lightly oiled bowl, rotating ball to lightly coat surface. Cover with waxed paper and damp cloth. Let rise in warm place for about 1 hour or until doubled in bulk. Punch down.

• Shape into loaf; place in prepared pan. Cover; let rise in warm place for about 1 hour or until doubled in bulk.

• Bake in 375°F (190°C) oven for 35 to 40 minutes or until loaf sounds hollow when tapped.

Makes 1 loaf, 16 slices.

Each serving: 1 slice

1   ▢ Starchy
1/2 ▲ Fats & Oils

125	calories
522	kilojoules
3 g	total fat
0 g	saturated fat
13 mg	cholesterol
3 g	protein
18 g	carbohydrate
150 mg	sodium
102 mg	potassium

GOOD: Folate

CHEESE BEAN BREAD

To make attractive loaves to present on a buffet table with bread board and knife, shape the dough into two ovals, place on nonstick baking sheet, slash tops in several places, brush with milk and sprinkle with poppy seeds. Then, let rise and bake.

1 tsp	granulated sugar	5 mL
1/2 cup	lukewarm water	125 mL
1	pkg active dry yeast	1
2 1/4 cups	all-purpose flour	550 mL
1 1/2 cups	cooked Romano or white or red kidney beans, puréed	375 mL
1 cup	shredded old Cheddar cheese	250 mL
1/4 cup	grated Parmesan cheese	50 mL
1 tsp	salt	5 mL
1/4 cup	canola oil	50 mL
1	egg	1

• Spray 8- x 4-inch (1.5 L) nonstick loaf pan with nonstick coating. Set aside.

• In mixing bowl, dissolve sugar in warm water. Sprinkle yeast into water and let stand for 10 minutes or until foamy.

• In separate bowl, stir together flour, puréed beans, Cheddar and Parmesan cheeses and salt.

• Beat oil and egg into yeast mixture. Stir in about half the flour mixture. Gradually mix in remaining flour mixture to make a slightly sticky ball of dough.

• On lightly floured surface, knead dough for about 5 minutes or until elastic and smooth. Form into ball; place in lightly oiled bowl, rotating ball to lightly coat surface. Cover with waxed paper and damp cloth. Let rise in warm place for about 1 hour or until doubled in bulk. Punch down.

• Shape into loaf; place in prepared pan. Cover; let rise in warm place for about 1 hour or until doubled in bulk.

• Bake in 375°F (190°C) oven for 35 to 40 minutes or until loaf sounds hollow when tapped.

Makes 1 loaf, 16 slices.

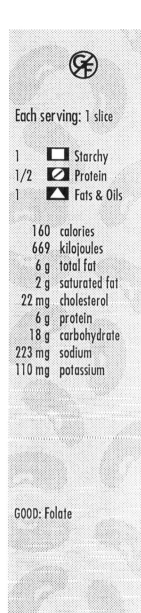

Each serving: 1 slice

1		Starchy
1/2		Protein
1		Fats & Oils

160	calories
669	kilojoules
6 g	total fat
2 g	saturated fat
22 mg	cholesterol
6 g	protein
18 g	carbohydrate
223 mg	sodium
110 mg	potassium

GOOD: Folate

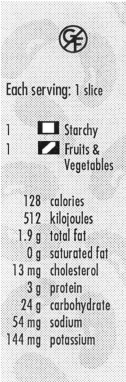

Each serving: 1 slice

1   ☐ Starchy
1   ▨ Fruits &
      Vegetables

128 calories
512 kilojoules
1.9 g total fat
0 g saturated fat
13 mg cholesterol
3 g protein
24 g carbohydrate
54 mg sodium
144 mg potassium

GOOD: Folate

RAISIN BEAN BREAD

Try this scrumptious bread toasted and spread sparingly with light cream cheese with a cup of tea. For the lunch box, make sandwiches from thin slices with light cream cheese as the filling.

1 tsp	granulated sugar	5 mL
1/2 cup	lukewarm water	125 mL
1	envelope active dry yeast	1
2 1/4 cups	all-purpose flour	550 mL
1 cup	cooked white or red kidney beans, puréed	250 mL
1/2 tsp	salt	2 mL
2 tbsp	canola oil	25 mL
1	egg, beaten	1
1 cup	seedless raisins	250 mL

• Spray 8- x 4-inch (1.5 L) nonstick loaf pan with nonstick coating. Set aside.

• In mixing bowl, dissolve sugar in water. Sprinkle yeast over water and let stand for 10 minutes or until foamy.

• In separate bowl, stir together flour, puréed beans and salt.

• Beat oil and egg into yeast mixture. Stir in about half the flour mixture. Gradually mix in remaining flour mixture and raisins to make slightly sticky ball of dough.

• On lightly floured surface, knead dough for about 5 minutes or until elastic and smooth. Form into ball; place in lightly oiled bowl, rotating to lightly coat surface. Cover with waxed paper and damp cloth. Let rise in a warm place for about 1 hour or until doubled in bulk. Punch down.

• Shape into loaf; place in prepared pan. Cover; let rise for about 1 hour or until doubled in bulk.

• Bake in 375°F (190°C) oven for 35 to 40 minutes or until loaf sounds hollow when tapped. Remove from pan. Let cool on wire rack.

Makes 1 loaf, 16 slices.

BEANY PIZZA CRUST

*Use your favorite pizza toppings on this crust with character.
If you are counting nutrients and calories and/or choices
remember to add the values of the additional foods. Unbaked
crusts can be kept frozen until they are needed.*

1 tsp	granulated sugar	5 mL
3/4 cup	warm water	175 mL
1	pkg active dry yeast	1
2 1/4 cups	all-purpose flour	550 mL
1 1/2 cups	cooked red or white kidney or Romano beans, puréed	375 mL
1 tsp	salt	5 mL
1/4 cup	canola oil	50 mL

• In mixing bowl, dissolve sugar in warm water. Sprinkle yeast
into water and let stand for 10 minutes or until foamy.

• In separate bowl, stir together flour, puréed beans and salt.

• Stir oil into yeast mixture. Stir in about half the flour
mixture. Gradually mix in remaining flour mixture to make
slightly sticky ball of dough.

• On lightly floured surface, knead dough for about 5 minutes
or until elastic and smooth. Cut in half; cover with clean tea
towel or waxed paper. Let rest for 10 minutes.

• On lightly floured surface, roll out each half of dough into
circle about 12 inches (30 cm) in diameter. Transfer to two
lightly oiled nonstick pizza pans or baking sheets. Stretch
dough to fit round pans or make large circle on baking sheets.
Let rest 10 minutes before adding toppings. (For thicker crust,
let dough rise for about 30 minutes.)

• Add toppings just before baking in 375°F (190°C) oven for
about 25 minutes or until crust is lightly golden.

Makes 2 pizza crusts, 8 pieces each.

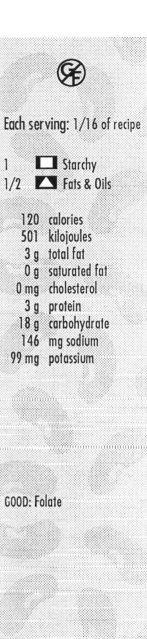

Each serving: 1/16 of recipe

1　□ Starchy
1/2　▲ Fats & Oils

120　calories
501　kilojoules
3 g　total fat
0 g　saturated fat
0 mg　cholesterol
3 g　protein
18 g　carbohydrate
146　mg sodium
99 mg　potassium

GOOD: Folate

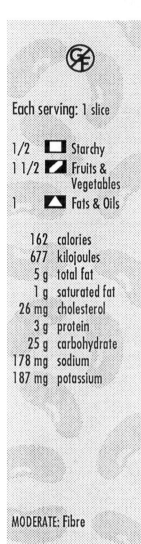

1/2 ▢ Starchy
1 1/2 ◪ Fruits &
　　　 Vegetables
1 　 ▲ Fats & Oils

162 calories
677 kilojoules
5 g total fat
1 g saturated fat
26 mg cholesterol
3 g protein
25 g carbohydrate
178 mg sodium
187 mg potassium

MODERATE: Fibre

BANANA LOAF

This is a quick bread that improves in both flavor and texture if it is allowed to mellow for a day. Simply wrap the cooled loaf in plastic wrap and set aside for 24 hours in the refrigerator or at room temperature before cutting.

1/3 cup	soft margarine OR butter	75 mL
3/4 cup	granulated sugar	175 mL
2	eggs	2
1 1/2 cups	mashed ripe bananas (3 large)	375 mL
1 cup	all-purpose flour	250 mL
1 cup	whole bean flour	250 mL
1 tsp	baking soda	5 mL
1/2 tsp	baking powder	2 mL
1/2 tsp	salt	2 mL
1/4 cup	chopped pecans	50 mL

• Line bottom only of 8- x 4-inch (1.5 L) nonstick loaf pan with waxed paper cut to fit. Set aside.

• In bowl, cream together margarine and sugar. Beat in eggs one at a time. Add banana; beat well.

• Combine all-purpose and whole bean flours, baking soda, baking powder and salt. Stir into creamed mixture. Stir in pecans. Pour into prepared pan; smooth top.

• Bake in 350°F (180°C) oven for about 55 minutes or until tester inserted into centre comes out clean.

• Let cool for 5 minutes. With knife, loosen sides and ends. Invert onto wire rack; remove paper. Let cool completely.

Makes 1 loaf, 16 slices.

Date Loaf

Few quick breads have as little fat in them as this one. It is the dates and whole bean flour that help keep the loaf moist and they also add to its fibre content.

1/2 lb	dates, finely chopped	250 g
1 cup	boiling water	250 mL
3/4 cup	all-purpose flour	175 mL
3/4 cup	whole bean flour	175 mL
3/4 cup	packed brown sugar	175 mL
1 tsp	baking soda	5 mL
1/2 tsp	baking powder	2 mL
1/2 tsp	salt	2 mL
1	egg	1
1 tbsp	soft margarine	15 mL
1 tsp	vanilla	5 mL

• Line bottom only of 8 x 4 inch (1.5 L) nonstick loaf pan with waxed paper cut to fit. Set aside.

• In small bowl, combine dates and water; set aside for 10 minutes to cool.

• In mixing bowl, stir together all-purpose and whole bean flours, brown sugar, baking soda, baking powder and salt.

• In small bowl, beat together egg, margarine and vanilla. Stir into date mixture. Add to dry ingredients all at once; stir just until moistened. Pour into prepared pan; smooth top.

• Bake in 350°F (180°C) oven for about 55 minutes or until tester inserted into centre comes out clean.

• Let cool for 5 minutes. With knife, loosen sides and ends. Invert onto wire rack; remove paper. Let cool completely.

Makes 1 loaf, 16 slices.

Each serving: 1 slice

1/2 ☐ Starchy
1 1/2 ◣ Fruits & Vegetables

114	calories
476	kilojoules
1 g	total fat
0 g	saturated fat
13 mg	cholesterol
2 g	protein
24 g	carbohydrate
138 mg	sodium
159 mg	potassium

MODERATE: Fibre

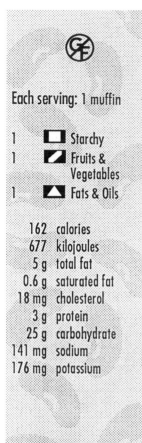

Each serving: 1 muffin

1   ☐ Starchy
1   ◪ Fruits &
     Vegetables
1   ◮ Fats & Oils

162 calories
677 kilojoules
5 g total fat
0.6 g saturated fat
18 mg cholesterol
3 g protein
25 g carbohydrate
141 mg sodium
176 mg potassium

APRICOT, OAT & BEAN MUFFINS

These are marvelous fruity muffins designed especially for those who don't like their muffins too sweet. For a lighter version with a little less fat use two egg whites in place of the whole egg.

1 cup	all-purpose flour	250 mL
1/2 cup	rolled oats	125 mL
1/4 cup	100% Bran cereal	50 mL
1/2 cup	packed brown sugar	125 mL
1 1/2 tsps	baking powder	7 mL
1 tsp	ground cinnamon	5 mL
1/2 tsp	baking soda	2 mL
1/2 tsp	salt	2 mL
1	egg, beaten	1
1/2 cup	cooked red kidney or Dutch brown beans, mashed	125 mL
1/2 cup	2% milk	125 mL
1/4 cup	canola oil	50 mL
1/2 cup	snipped dried apricots	125 mL

• In mixing bowl, stir together flour, rolled oats, bran cereal, sugar, baking powder, cinnamon, baking soda and salt.

• In small bowl, beat egg; beat in beans, milk and oil. Stir in apricots. Add to dry ingredients all at once; stir just until moistened.

• Spoon into nonstick or paper-lined medium 2 1/2 inch (6.5 cm) muffin cups, filling three-quarters full.

• Bake in 375°F (190°C) oven for 20 minutes or until tops are firm to the touch.

Makes 12 muffins.

ORANGE MUFFINS

Both the orange juice and marmalade contribute to the sweetness and unique flavor of these mouth-watering muffins. They are wonderful plain or with spreadable light cream cheese.

1 1/2 cups	all-purpose flour	375 mL
1/4 cup	granulated sugar	50 mL
1 1/2 tsp	baking powder	7 mL
1 tsp	baking soda	5 mL
1/2 tsp	ground cardamom	2 mL
1/2 tsp	salt	2 mL
1 cup	cooked white or red kidney beans, puréed	250 mL
1	egg, beaten OR 2 egg whites	1
1/4 cup	canola oil	50 mL
	Grated rind of 1 orange	
1/2 cup	orange juice	125 mL
1/3 cup	orange marmalade	75 mL
1/3 cup	chopped walnuts	75 mL

• In mixing bowl, stir together flour, sugar, baking powder, baking soda, cardamom and salt.

• In small bowl, stir together beans, egg, oil, orange rind, juice and marmalade; stir in walnuts. Add to dry ingredients all at once; stir just until moistened. Do not overmix.

• Spoon into nonstick or paper-lined 2 1/2 inch (6.5 cm) muffin cups, filling three-quarters full.

• Bake in 375°F (190°C) oven for 20 minutes or until tops are firm to the touch.

Makes 12 muffins.

Each serving: 1 muffin

1   ▭ Starchy
1   ◪ Fruits & Vegetables
1   ▲ Fats & Oils

181	calories
756	kilojoules
6 g	total fat
0 g	saturated fat
0 mg	cholesterol
3 g	protein
27 g	carbohydrate
190 mg	sodium
104 mg	potassium

MODERATE: Fibre

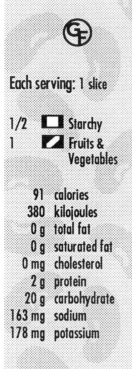

Each serving: 1 slice

1/2 ⬜ Starchy
1 🔳 Fruits &
Vegetables

91	calories
380	kilojoules
0 g	total fat
0 g	saturated fat
0 mg	cholesterol
2 g	protein
20 g	carbohydrate
163 mg	sodium
178 mg	potassium

MODERATE: Fibre

ORANGE DATE LOAF

This may be a surprise. Here is a completely fat-free date loaf. The corn syrup helps to keep it moist.

3/4 cup	chopped pitted dates (6 oz/175 g)	175 mL
1/2 cup	boiling water	125 mL
1 1/4 cups	whole bean flour	300 mL
1/4 cup	cornstarch	50 mL
2 tsp	gluten-free baking powder	10 mL
1 tsp	baking soda	5 mL
1/2 tsp	salt	2 mL
2	eggs whites	2
2 tbsp	granulated sugar	25 mL
3/4 cup	orange juice	175 mL
1/3 cup	corn syrup	75 mL
1 tbsp	grated orange rind	15 mL

• Line bottom only of 8 x 4-inch (1.5 L) nonstick loaf pan with waxed paper cut to fit. Set aside.

• In small bowl, combine dates and boiling water. Let cool for 10 minutes.

• In mixing bowl, stir together bean flour, cornstarch, baking powder, baking soda and salt.

• In separate bowl, beat egg whites until foamy; gradually beat in sugar until stiff peaks form.

• Stir orange juice, corn syrup and orange rind into date mixture. Add all at once to dry ingredients, stirring just until moistened. Fold in egg whites. Spread in prepared pan, smoothing top.

• Bake in 325°F (160°C) oven for 1 hour or until tester inserted into centre comes out clean. Cool on rack for 5 minutes.

• With knife, loosen sides and ends. Invert on rack; remove paper. Let cool completely.

Makes l loaf, 16 slices.

Photograph courtesy of *Best Foods Canada Inc.*

Cakes & Cookies

Jelly Cookie Gems

Oatmeal Bean Cookies

Double Chocolate Almond Cookies

Party Cake

Bean Brownies

Each serving: 1 cookie

1/2 ▰ Fruits &
        Vegetables

   30 calories
  125 kilojoules
  0.5 g total fat
    0 g saturated fat
    0 mg cholesterol
  0.6 g protein
    6 g carbohydrate
   43 mg sodium
   30 mg potassium

JELLY COOKIE GEMS

Many cookbooks call these thumbprint or thimble cookies depending, it seems, on what is used to make the hollow that holds the jelly.

1/2 cup	whole bean flour	125 mL
2 tbsp	cornstarch OR rice flour	25 mL
2 tbsp	cornmeal	25 mL
2 tsp	gluten-free baking powder	10 mL
1/2 tsp	ground cinnamon	2 mL
1/2 tsp	salt	2 mL
1/4 tsp	ground nutmeg	1 mL
2 tbsp	soft margarine OR butter	25 mL
2/3 cup	granulated sugar	150 mL
1/2 cup	cooked kidney or Romano beans, puréed	125 mL
1 tsp	vanilla	5 mL
1 tsp	almond extract	5 mL
7 tsp	raspberry jelly OR dietetic spread	35 mL

• In bowl, stir together bean flour, cornstarch, cornmeal, baking powder, cinnamon, salt and nutmeg.

• In mixing bowl, cream together margarine and sugar. Beat in puréed beans, vanilla and almond extract. Stir in dry ingedients until well blended.

• Form dough into 3/4 inch (2 cm) balls; place about 2 inches (5 cm) apart on very lightly greased nonstick baking sheets. With back of spoon or bottom of glass, press to 1/3-inch (8 mm) thickness. With end of wooden spoon or thumb, press a round indentation into centre of each cookie.

• Bake in 350°F (180°C) oven for 10 to 12 minutes or until golden brown. Cool for 5 minutes. While still warm, place about 1/4 tsp (1 mL) jelly into indentation in each cookie.

Makes 36 cookies.

OATMEAL BEAN COOKIES

Two of these sandwiched together with date filling make a great "dessert" to pack in the lunch box.

1/2 cup	all-purpose flour	125 mL
1/2 cup	rolled oats	125 mL
2 tsp	baking powder	10 mL
1/2 tsp	ground cinnamon	2 mL
1/2 tsp	salt	2 mL
2 tbsp	soft margarine	25 mL
1/2 cup	granulated sugar	125 mL
1/2 cup	cooked kidney or Romano beans, puréed	125 mL
1 tsp	vanilla	5 mL
1 tsp	almond extract	5 mL

• In bowl, stir together flour, rolled oats, baking powder, cinnamon and salt.

• In mixing bowl, cream together margarine and sugar. Beat in puréed beans, vanilla and almond extract. Stir in dry ingredients until well blended.

• Form dough into firm roll about 2 inches (5 cm) in diameter; wrap and chill for at least 2 hours or up to 10. With serrated knife, cut roll into 1/8-inch (3 mm) thick slices. Place about 2 inches (5 cm) apart on nonstick baking sheets.

• Bake in 350°F (180°C) oven for 10 to 12 minutes or until golden brown.

Makes 36 cookies.

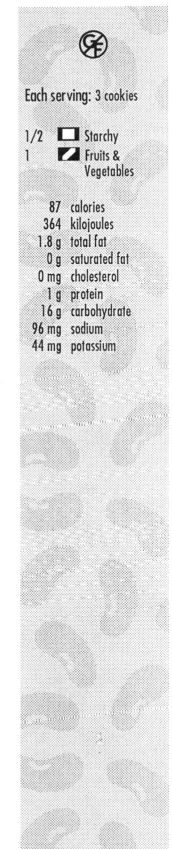

Each serving: 3 cookies

1/2	▢	Starchy
1	◪	Fruits & Vegetables

87 calories
364 kilojoules
1.8 g total fat
0 g saturated fat
0 mg cholesterol
1 g protein
16 g carbohydrate
96 mg sodium
44 mg potassium

Each serving: 2 cookies

1 1/2 ▨ Fruits &
Vegetables

1 ▲ Fats & Oils

126 calories
526 kilojoules
6 g total fat
2 g saturated fat
12 mg cholesterol
2 g protein
16 g carbohydrate
148 mg sodium
142 mg potassium

DOUBLE CHOCOLATE
ALMOND COOKIES

*Add this to the list of variations of the ever-popular chocolate
chip cookie. This one uses reduced amounts of fat and sugar
and whole bean flour, which is gluten-free.*

2	squares white chocolate (2 oz/60 g)	2
1 cup	whole bean flour	250 mL
1 tsp	gluten-free baking powder	5 mL
1 tsp	baking soda	5 mL
1/4 tsp	salt	1 mL
1/3 cup	soft margarine OR butter	75 mL
2/3 cup	packed brown sugar	150 mL
2 tbsp	corn syrup	25 mL
1	egg	1
1 tsp	almond extract	5 mL
1/2 cup	chocolate chips	125 mL
1/4 cup	chopped almonds	50 mL

• In small bowl over boiling water, melt white chocolate. (Or
melt it in microwave oven following manufacturer's
directions.) Cool to room temperature.

• In bowl, stir together bean flour, baking powder, baking
soda and salt.

• In mixing bowl, cream together margarine, brown sugar,
corn syrup and melted chocolate. Beat in egg and almond
extract until light and fluffy. Stir in dry ingredients until
blended. Fold in chocolate chips and almonds.

• Drop by heaping teaspoonfuls, about 2 inches (5 cm) apart,
onto nonstick baking sheets.

• Bake in 350°F (180°C) oven for 10 to 12 minutes or until
golden brown.

Makes 36 cookies.

PARTY CAKE

When you need a birthday or anniversary cake for a crowd our party cake is the answer. It stays moist for several days especially if it is frosted as soon as it cools.

1 cup	soft margarine OR butter	250 mL
2 cups	granulated sugar	500 mL
4	eggs	4
2 cups	cooked white or red kidney or Romano beans, puréed	500 mL
1 1/2 cups	all-purpose flour	375 mL
2 tsp	baking powder	10 mL
1/2 tsp	ground cinnamon	2 mL
1/2 tsp	salt	2 mL
1/4 tsp	each ground nutmeg and allspice	1 mL
Pinch	ground cloves	Pinch
1/2 cup	seedless raisins	125 mL

Almond Frosting:

1/4 cup	soft margarine OR butter	50 mL
1/4 tsp	almond extract	1 mL
2 cups	icing sugar, sifted	500 mL
2 tbsp	milk	25 mL

• Spray bottom only of nonstick 13- x 9-inch (3.5 L) cake pan with nonstick coating. Set aside.

• In mixing bowl, cream together margarine and sugar. Beat in eggs, one at a time. Beat in beans until well mixed.

• In separate bowl, stir together flour, baking powder, cinnamon, salt, nutmeg, allspice and cloves; add raisins. Stir into bean mixture until well mixed.

• Pour into prepared pan. Spread into corners and smooth top.

• Bake in 350°F (180°C) oven for 50 to 60 minutes or until tester inserted into centre comes out clean and top of cake springs back when touched lightly with finger. Cool in pan for 5 minutes before turning out onto rack to cool completely. (Or cool completely in pan.)

• Almond Frosting: In bowl, cream margarine; beat in almond extract. Blend in icing sugar alternately with milk, beating until smooth and adding a few drops more milk if thinner consistency is desired. Spread evenly over cooled cake.

Makes 24 servings, 1 large cake.

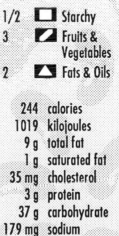

Each serving: 1/24 of recipe

Cake only

1/2 ☐ Starchy
2 ◪ Fruits & Vegetables
1 1/2 ◮ Fats & Oils

199 calories
831 kilojoules
8 g total fat
1 g saturated fat
35 mg cholesterol
3 g protein
28 g carbohydrate
163 mg sodium
98 mg potassium

EXCELLENT: Vitamin D

Cake with frosting

1/2 ☐ Starchy
3 ◪ Fruits & Vegetables
2 ◮ Fats & Oils

244 calories
1019 kilojoules
9 g total fat
1 g saturated fat
35 mg cholesterol
3 g protein
37 g carbohydrate
179 mg sodium
100 mg potassium

EXCELLENT: Vitamin D

BEAN BROWNIES

This is one of those recipes that made the rounds when it was first introduced because it was such a novelty using beans in brownies. Now, it's rated as great and used over and over by many cooks because the resulting brownies are so good and moist.

1 cup	cooked kidney or Romano beans, puréed	250 mL
1 1/2 cup	granulated sugar	375 mL
3/4 cup	all-purpose flour	175 mL
1/2 cup	unsweetened cocoa powder	125 mL
1 tsp	salt	5 mL
1/2 cup	canola oil	125 mL
4	eggs	4
1 tsp	vanilla	5 mL
1/2 cup	chopped walnuts	125 mL

• Spray bottom only of 13- x 9-inch (3.5 L) baking pan with nonstick coating.

• In mixing bowl, combine beans, sugar, flour, cocoa and salt. Add oil, eggs and vanilla. Beat on low speed or by hand, scraping down sides of bowl, until smooth. Stir in walnuts.

• Pour batter in prepared pan; spread into corners and smooth top.

• Bake in 350°F (180°C) oven for 30 minutes or until tester inserted into centre comes out clean.

• Cool in pan on wire rack. Cut into squares.

Makes 24 brownies.

DESSERTS

Mock Pumpkin Pie

Pecan Pie

Maple Bean Tarts

Candied Fruit Bars

Hazelnut Meringue Torte

Strawberry Cream Roll

Pineapple Upside-Down Cake

Peach Upside-Down Cake

Lemon Berry Pudding Cake

Chocolate Soufflé

Cheese Blintzes with Peach Sauce

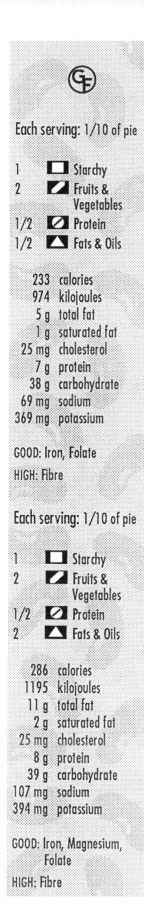

MOCK PUMPKIN PIE

Spruced up with sugar and spice the beans masquerade as pumpkin in this deep pie. It is filling and easily serves ten.

1	unbaked Gluten-Free (p.177) 9-inch (23 cm) single-crust pie shell	1
2 cups	cooked red kidney, Dutch brown or Romano beans	500 mL
1 cup	evaporated 2% milk	250 mL
1	egg	1
1	egg white	1
3/4 cup	brown sugar	175 mL
2 tbsp	corn syrup	25 mL
1 1/2 tsp	ground cinnamon	7 mL
1 tsp	vanilla	5 mL
1/2 tsp	ground ginger	2 mL
1/4 tsp	each ground nutmeg, allspice and cloves	1 mL
1/4 tsp	salt	1 mL
1 cup	whipped topping OR whipped cream	250 mL

• Line pie shell with foil. Bake in 425°F (220°C) oven for 7 minutes to partially bake. Remove foil; set aside.

• In food processor or blender, combine beans, evaporated milk, egg, egg white, brown sugar, cinnamon, vanilla, ginger, nutmeg, allspice, cloves and salt. Process with on/off motion for 2 to 3 minutes or until very smooth. Pour into pie shell.

• Bake in 425°F (220°C) oven for 5 minutes. Reduce oven temperature to 325°F (160°C); bake for 30 to 35 minutes longer or until tester inserted halfway between centre and edge comes out clean.

• Garnish each serving with 2 tbsp (25 mL) whipped topping.

Makes 1 pie, 10 servings.

VARIATIONS:
PECAN PIE

• Omit ginger, allspice, nutmeg and cloves. Add 1 tsp (5 mL) white vinegar to filling. Arrange 3/4 cup (175 mL) pecan halves on top of filling. Bake as directed.

Maple Bean Tarts

These are similiar to butter tarts but with a difference. The creamy texture of the puréed beans add character and the beans also add fibre.

24	Gluten-Free unbaked tart shells (p.177)	24

FILLING:

1 cup	cooked white kidney beans	250 mL
1/2 cup	maple syrup	125 mL
2	eggs	2
1/3 cup	packed brown suagr	75 mL
1/4 cup	butter OR soft margarine, melted	50 mL
1/2 cup	raisins	125 mL

• Filling: In food processor or blender, combine beans, maple syrup, eggs, brown sugar and butter. Process until puréed and blended.

• Divide raisins evenly among tart shells. Pour filling over raisins, filling tart shells three-quarters full.

• Bake in 350°F (180°C) oven for 20 minutes or until crust is golden brown and filling set.

Makes 24 tarts.

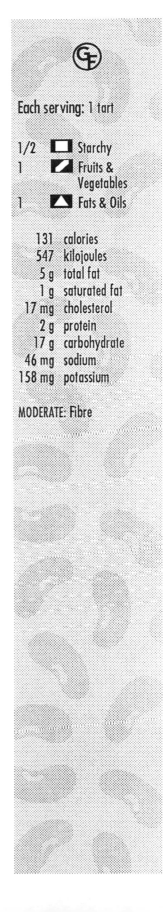

Each serving: 1 tart

1/2	Starchy
1	Fruits & Vegetables
1	Fats & Oils

131	calories
547	kilojoules
5 g	total fat
1 g	saturated fat
17 mg	cholesterol
2 g	protein
17 g	carbohydrate
46 mg	sodium
158 mg	potassium

MODERATE: Fibre

Candied Fruit Bars

Coconut and candied fruit make these squares not only chewy and delicious but also colorful and attractive.

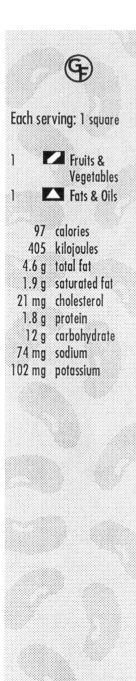
3/4 cup	whole bean flour	175 mL
1/4 cup	cornstarch	50 mL
2 tbsp	ground walnuts OR pecans	25 mL
1 tsp	gluten-free baking powder	5 mL
1/2 tsp	cinnamon	2 mL
Pinch	salt	Pinch
1/4 cup	soft margarine OR butter	50 mL
1	egg	1
1 tbsp	water	15 mL

Topping:

1/4 cup	packed brown sugar	50 mL
2 tbsp	corn syrup	25 mL
1	egg	1
1 tsp	vanilla	5 mL
1/2 cup	unsweetened desiccated or shredded coconut	125 mL
1/4 cup	chopped mixed candied fruit	50 mL

• In bowl, stir together bean flour, cornstarch, walnuts, baking powder, cinnamon and salt. With pastry blender or two knives, cut in margarine until crumbly.

• Beat together egg and water. Stir into crumbly mixture. Press into nonstick 8-inch (2 L) square cake pan.

• Bake in 325°F (160°C) oven for 15 minutes or until lightly browned and firm to the touch.

• Topping: In bowl, beat together brown sugar, corn syrup, egg and vanilla until well blended. Stir in coconut and candied fruit. Spread over warm base.

• Bake in 325°F (160°C) oven for 25 minutes or until top is golden.

• Cool on rack. Cut into squares.

Makes 20 squares.

Hazelnut Meringue Torte with Raspberry Cream

The meringue layers for this elegant finale for a meal can be made up to six days in advance. Wrap and store them in a dry place.

4	egg whites	4
Pinch	salt	Pinch
1/2 cup	granulated sugar	125 mL
1 tsp	vanilla	5 mL
1/2 cup	whole bean flour	125 mL
1/2 cup	toasted hazelnuts, finely chopped	125 mL
2 cups	whipped topping OR whipped cream	500 mL
3 cups	raspberries	750 mL
	Fresh mint leaves	

• Line baking sheet with parchment or brown paper. Using a plate for pattern, draw two 8 inch (20 cm) circles.

• In mixing bowl, beat egg whites and salt until foamy. Gradually beat in sugar until stiff peaks form. Fold in vanilla, bean flour and hazelnuts.

• Divide mixture between circles; spread evenly within outlines.

• Bake in 300°F (150°C) oven for 40 minutes or until puffed and golden brown. Cool. Remove meringues from paper.

• Place one meringue, top side down, on cake plate. Spread with 1 cup (250 mL) whipped topping and half of the raspberries. Top with second meringue, top side up. Spread with remaining topping. Refrigerate for at least 2 hours or up to 6 hours before serving.

• To serve, sprinkle remaining raspberries over top. Garnish with mint leaves.

Makes 8 servings.

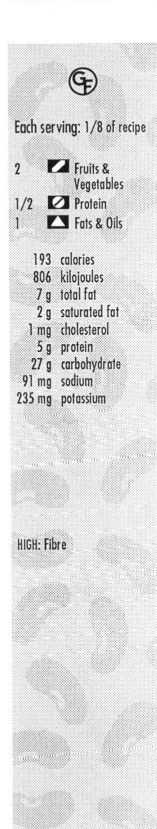

Each serving: 1/8 of recipe

2		Fruits & Vegetables
1/2		Protein
1		Fats & Oils

193	calories
806	kilojoules
7 g	total fat
2 g	saturated fat
1 mg	cholesterol
5 g	protein
27 g	carbohydrate
91 mg	sodium
235 mg	potassium

HIGH: Fibre

STRAWBERRY CREAM ROLL

Once the jelly roll is filled with the strawberry cream it can be wrapped and frozen for up to 4 weeks. By the time it is presented on its serving platter it will be easy to serve.

1	freshly baked unfilled Jelly Roll (p.161)	1
2 cups	whipped topping OR whipped cream	500 mL
1/2 cup	chopped strawberries, drained	125 mL

SAUCE:

3 cups	strawberries	750 mL
2/3 cup	strawberry dietetic spread OR jam	150 mL
1/2 tsp	almond extract	2 mL
	Fresh mint leaves	

• Unroll jelly roll; remove towel.

• Spread evenly with whipped topping; sprinkle with chopped strawberries. Reroll, gently pressing into shape. Wrap in plastic wrap or waxed paper. Refrigerate for at least 4 hours or up to 24 hours.

• Sauce: Set aside 8 strawberries to slice for garnish.

• In food processor or blender, combine remaining strawberries, dietetic spread and almond extract. Process with on/off motion for 2 to 3 minutes or until puréed.

• Unwrap jelly roll; place on serving platter. Spoon 1 cup (250 mL) sauce around it. Slice reserved strawberries; scatter around jelly roll. Garnish with mint leaves. Pour remaining sauce into small bowl.

• To serve, cut into 3/4-inch (2 cm) thick slices. Serve on dessert plate with sauce on the side.

Makes 1 jelly roll and sauce; 16 servings.

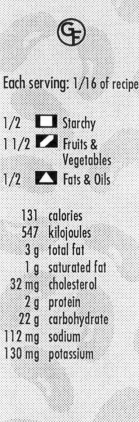

Each serving: 1/16 of recipe

1/2 ▢ Starchy
1 1/2 ◩ Fruits & Vegetables
1/2 ◣ Fats & Oils

131 calories
547 kilojoules
3 g total fat
1 g saturated fat
32 mg cholesterol
2 g protein
22 g carbohydrate
112 mg sodium
130 mg potassium

PINEAPPLE UPSIDE-DOWN CAKE

It may be guilding the lily, but for company, add a dollop of whipped cream or small scoop of ice milk to each serving.

2 tbsp	packed brown sugar	25 mL
6	slices canned pineapple, canned in juice	6
3	maraschino cherries, halved	3
1/2 cup	whole bean flour	125 mL
2 tbsp	cornstarch	25 mL
2 tsp	gluten-free baking powder	10 mL
1/4 tsp	salt	1 mL
1/3 cup	soft margarine OR butter	75 mL
1/3 cup	granulated sugar	75 mL
2 tbsp	corn syrup	25 mL
2	eggs	2
1 tsp	almond extract	5 mL
1/2 cup	milk	125 mL

• Spray 9-inch (1.5 L) round layer cake pan with nonstick coating. Sprinkle brown sugar over bottom; arrange pineapple slices in single layer over top. Place half maraschino cherry, cut side down, in centre of each slice. Set aside.

• In mixing bowl, stir together bean flour, cornstarch, baking powder and salt.

• In bowl, cream together margarine, sugar and corn syrup. Beat in eggs, one at a time, until light and fluffy. Beat in almond extract. Gradually beat in dry ingredients alternately with milk; continue beating for 3 minutes until batter is light colored and very fluffy. Pour over pineapple slices, smoothing top.

• Bake in 325°F (160°C) oven for 30 to 35 minutes or until cake tester inserted into centre comes out clean. Let cool for 5 minutes. With knife, loosen around outside of cake. Invert onto serving plate. Serve warm, at room temperature or chilled.

Makes 1 upside down cake, 8 servings.

VARIATION:
PEACH UPSIDE-DOWN CAKE

• Use 1 can (14 oz/398 mL) peach slices (no sugar added), drained, in place of pineapple slices.

Each serving: 1/8 of recipe

1/2 ☐ Starchy
2 ◩ Fruits & Vegetables
1 1/2 △ Fats & Oils

204	calories
852	kilojoules
8 g	total fat
1 g	saturated fat
55 mg	cholesterol
3 g	protein
28 g	carbohydrate
242 mg	sodium
174 mg	potassium

EXCELLENT: Vitamin D
MODERATE: Fibre

Calculations approximately the same as above.

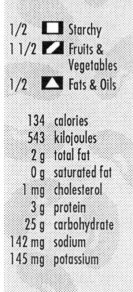

LEMON BERRY PUDDING CAKE

The berries at the bottom of this dessert end up being smothered in a wonderfully tart sauce.

1 cup	raspberries OR blueberries	250 mL
1 tbsp	soft margarine OR butter	25 mL
1/2 cup	granulated sugar	125 mL
1 tsp	grated lemon rind	5 mL
2 tbsp	whole bean flour	25 mL
2 tbsp	cornstarch	25 mL
3/4 cup	1% milk	175 mL
3	egg whites	3
Pinch	each salt and cream of tartar	Pinch
1/2 cup	lemon juice	125 mL

• Sprinkle berries on bottom of 8-inch (2 L) round or square baking dish. Set aside.

• In bowl, cream together margarine and 1/4 cup (50 mL) sugar and butter; stir in lemon rind.

• Combine flour with cornstarch; stir into creamed mixture alternately with milk. Beat until smooth.

• In separate bowl, beat egg whites with salt and cream of tartar until frothy. Beat in remaining sugar until stiff peaks form. Fold into batter until well blended. Fold in lemon juice.

• Pour over berries in baking dish; smooth top.

• Bake in 350°F (180°C) oven for 45 minutes or until tester inserted into centre comes out clean.

• To serve, spoon cake, sauce and berries onto dessert plates.

Makes 6 servings.

CHOCOLATE SOUFFLÉ

The chocolate flavor is so rich it is bound to satisfy the most dedicated chocolate lover. To make it chocolate mocha use cold strong coffee in place of the orange juice.

2 tbsp	ground almonds	25 mL
2 cups	cooked kidney, Romano or black beans	500 mL
3	squares semisweet chocolate, (3 oz /90 g) melted	3
1/4 cup	orange juice	50 mL
1 tsp	grated orange rind	5 mL
1/2 tsp	ground cinnamon	2 mL
5	egg whites	5
1/2 tsp	salt	2 mL
1/2 cup	granulated sugar	125 mL

SAUCE:

1 cup	low-fat yogurt	250 mL
1 tbsp	orange juice	15 mL
2 tsp	granulated sugar	10 mL
	Grated orange peel	

• Spray 4-cup (1 L) soufflé dish with nonstick coating. Sprinkle with ground almonds to coat bottom and sides.

• In food processor or blender, combine beans, melted chocolate, orange juice, orange rind and cinnamon. Purée, scraping down container once or twice, for 1 to 2 minutes or until smooth.

• In mixing bowl, beat egg whites and salt until foamy. Gradually add sugar, beating until stiff peaks form. Stir about 1 cup (250 mL) into puréed mixture to lighten it. Gently fold in remaining egg white until mixture is evenly coloured. Spoon into prepared soufflé dish.

• Bake in 350°F (180°C) oven for 35 to 40 minutes or until lightly browned and puffed. Serve immediately.

• Sauce: In small bowl, whisk together yogurt, orange juice and sugar. Spoon over individual servings of soufflé. Garnish with grated orange rind.

Makes 6 servings.

Each serving: 1/6 of recipe

1/2	☐ Starchy
3	▨ Fruits & Vegetables
1	◿ Protein
1/2	◤ Fats & Oils

266	calories
1111	kilojoules
6 g	total fat
3 g	saturated fat
0 mg	cholesterol
11 g	protein
44 g	carbohydrate
206 mg	sodium
417 mg	potassium

GOOD: Phosphorus, Iron, Magnesium, Riboflavin
EXCELLENT: Folate
HIGH: Fibre

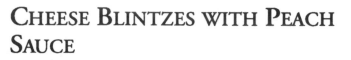

CHEESE BLINTZES WITH PEACH SAUCE

These blintzes are great for dessert when a hearty soup or satisfying salad is the main course. They are also wonderful for weekend breakfasts, company brunches or late evening snacks.

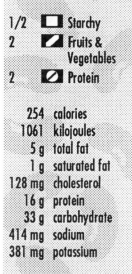
8	Crêpes (p.151)	8
1 cup	1% cottage cheese	250 mL
1 tbsp	granulated sugar	15 mL
1	egg yolk	1
1 tsp	vanilla	5 mL
1/2 tsp	ground cinnamon	2 mL

Sauce:

1	can (14 oz/398 mL) sliced peaches	1
1/2 cup	lowfat yogurt	125 mL
	Fresh raspberries or blueberries	

• Prepare Crêpes ahead. If frozen, allow to defrost in refrigerator or at room temperature.

• In bowl and using fork, mash cottage cheese; beat in sugar, egg yolk, vanilla and cinnamon until well blended.

• Divide evenly among crêpes, placing 2 tbsp (25 mL) in centre of each crepe. Spread into an oblong within 1 1/2 inches (3.5 cm) of left and right hand sides of crêpe. Fold sides (left and right) towards middle over filling; fold top and bottom of crêpe toward middle to resemble an egg roll. Place seam side down, 1 inch (2.5 cm) apart in nonstick baking pan.

• Bake in 350°F (180°C) oven for 20 minutes or until heated through.

• Sauce: Drain peaches, reserving juice for another use. In food processor or blender, purée peaches. Or alternately, in bowl and using fork, mash to saucy consistency.

• To serve, place two hot blintzes on each individual plate. Top with peach sauce; garnish with yogurt and raspberries.

Makes 4 servings.

EXTRAS

Gluten-Free Pasta

Gluten-Free Baking Powder

Gluten-Free Icing Sugar

Playdough

Phil O' Beans

and Other Bean Bags

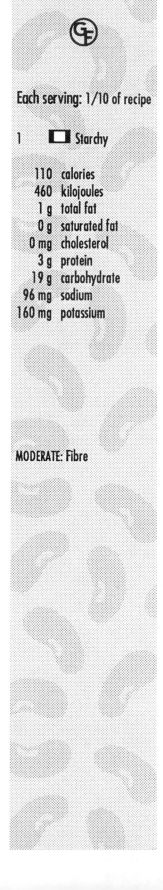

GLUTEN-FREE PASTA

Cook this pasta fresh, after drying for only 20 minutes, in a generous amount of lightly salted boiling water, for about 8 minutes or until taste of raw starch has disappeared. Use the same method for cooking the completely dry, hard pasta but it will take about 5 minutes longer. Use in any recipe calling for pasta. (For lasagne noodles cut the rolled dough into thicker strips.)

1 cup	whole bean flour	250 mL
1/2 cup	rice flour	125 mL
1/2 cup	cornstarch	125 mL
1/2 tsp	salt	2 mL
1/2 cup	water	125 mL
3	egg whites	3
1 tbsp	olive oil OR canola oil	15 mL

• In food processor, combine bean and rice flours, cornstarch and salt.

• In measuring cup, whisk together water, egg whites and oil. With processor running, add in a steady stream to dry ingredients. Process until well combined and mixture gathers into smooth ball.

• Turn out onto surface lightly dusted with cornstarch. Knead for 8 to 10 times.

• With rolling pin, roll out on surface lightly dusted with cornstarch or use pasta maker, rolling until very thin. If using pasta maker, continue to roll until #4 thickness is achieved.

• Allow rolled dough to rest for 20 minutes to dry slightly. With knife or pasta maker cut into thin strips (noodles).

• Arrange in single layer on racks. Let stand for 24 hours or until thoroughly dry.

• Store in airtight containers or bags at room temperature.

Makes enough for 10 servings cooked pasta.

GLUTEN-FREE BAKING POWDER

All gluten-free baked goods – pancakes, biscuits, muffins, quick breads, cookies, cakes – are made using gluten-free baking powder. It is smart to make up a supply of it to keep on hand. Keep handy in cupboard and use within three months.

1/2 cup	cream of tartar	125 mL
1/2 cup	cornstarch	125 mL
1/4 cup	baking soda	50 mL

• In small processor or sifter, blend or sift together cream of tartar, cornstarch and baking soda until well blended.

• Transfer to container with tight-fitting lid; label. Store at room temperature.

Makes 1 1/4 cups (300 mL).

GLUTEN-FREE ICING SUGAR

Use this in any recipe for frosting, in place of the icing or confectioner's sugar called for in the recipe, to make sure the frosting is gluten-free. Dust over baked gluten-free brownies, carrot cakes or muffins, if you wish, for a light finishing touch.

1 cup	granulated sugar	250 mL
1/2 tsp	cornstarch	2 mL

• In food processor, combine sugar and cornstarch. Process, scraping down sides of container frequently, for 5 to 10 minutes or until very, very finely ground and powdery.

• Store in airtight container at room temperature.

Makes 1 cup (250 mL).

PLAYDOUGH

Prepare this modelling dough in advance to have it ready for creative little hands. To help them make interesting designs, allow children to use some of the small utensils from the kitchen such as rolling pin, kitchen knives, forks, spoons, pizza cutter, garlic press, cookie cutters and children's play scissors.

1 cup	water	250 mL
2 tbsp	canola oil	25 mL
3/4 cup	whole bean flour	175 mL
1/4 cup	cornstarch	50 mL
1/4 cup	salt	50 mL
2 tbsp	cream of tartar	25 mL
	Food coloring	

• In saucepan over medium-high heat, bring water and oil to rolling boil.

• Stir together flour, cornstarch, salt and cream of tartar. Pour all at once into boiling mixture, stirring constantly, for about 30 seconds or until ball forms.

• Turn out onto surface lightly dusted with cornstarch. Cool for 5 minutes. Knead 8 to 10 times or until very smooth.

• To color playdough, divide one batch into portions for the number of colors desired, or make a batch for each color. For red, blue, green and yellow, with fork or spoon, work in coloring drop by drop to obtain desired shade. (Combine appropriate colors to make additional shades such as purple, pale blue, coral, etc.)

• Store each color in its own airtight container at room temperature. While modelling with playdough, keep unused portion in its container or covered with plastic wrap to prevent it from drying out.

Makes 1 1/2 cups (375 mL) playdough.

PHIL O' BEANS
AND OTHER BEAN BAGS

To make this jolly chap, you will need scraps of bean-colored, strong fabrics, such as cotton corduroy, velveteen or duck. Or make a "Mr. Jean Bean" out of well-washed denim from discarded jeans. Whichever you use to make this stuffed toy, the kids in your life (any age) will probably love it. Dried colored beans are wonderful for bean bags, whatever their shape, especially for ones intended to be used as weights for door stops or holding down a pile of papers.

1. Cut out one right and one left A; one right and one left B, from the same colored fabric, for bean body; two each of C and D for shoes and four of E for mitts from the same colored fabric as body or contrasting one.

2. From contrasting softer material of knitted T-shirt texture, cut out two strips for legs; two strips for arms.

3. For hat or toque, cut top 6 inches (30 cm) off cuff end from man's colored sock (a discarded one will do).

4. With right sides facing, sew two mitten pieces together for each hand, leaving top edge open; turn to right side.

Phil O'Beans

5. Fold each C with right sides facing, sew down front of boot shape, leaving top and bottom open. Pin or baste, then sew boot sole (D) into place on each boot. Turn to right side out.

6. Fill each mitten and boot with dried beans. At open ends (top) put in a few basting stitches to hold in beans.

7. With right sides facing, sew long sides of leg and arm strips together; turn to have seam inside. By hand or machine, sew legs to boots and mittens to arms with seam-sides inside. Fill both arms and legs with beans. Hold beans in place with a few basting stitches at top of arms and legs.

8. To assemble the body, pin or baste the top edge of each leg to the X on B, with the toes of boots facing to the inside curve of bean. Now, with right sides facing join A to B along straight edge. This attaches a leg to each side of bean.

9. With legs tucked inside and right sides together, stitch two sides of bean together, leaving about 4 inch (10 cm) opening along inside curve of bean. Turn right side out.

10. Through opening, fill with beans until plump. With strong thread and tight stitches, hand sew opening closed.

11. Tuck rough top edge in and stitch arms to body, with thumbs of mittens facing toward the body, where X is indicated on A.

12. In the appropriate places, embroider eyes, nose and mouth. (Or, you may attach buttons or glue-on rolling eyes from a craft store, if you wish, remembering, however, that embroidery is always safest if small children will be playing with finished "toy".)

13. Run line of stitches about 1/2 inch (1 cm) down from the cut edge of sock. Draw together to form top tassle of toque and stitch securely in place. Turn up cuff of sock to form a cuff for toque. Fit at a jaunty angle on finished "Phil O' Bean" and stitch in place.

Phil O'Bean Pattern

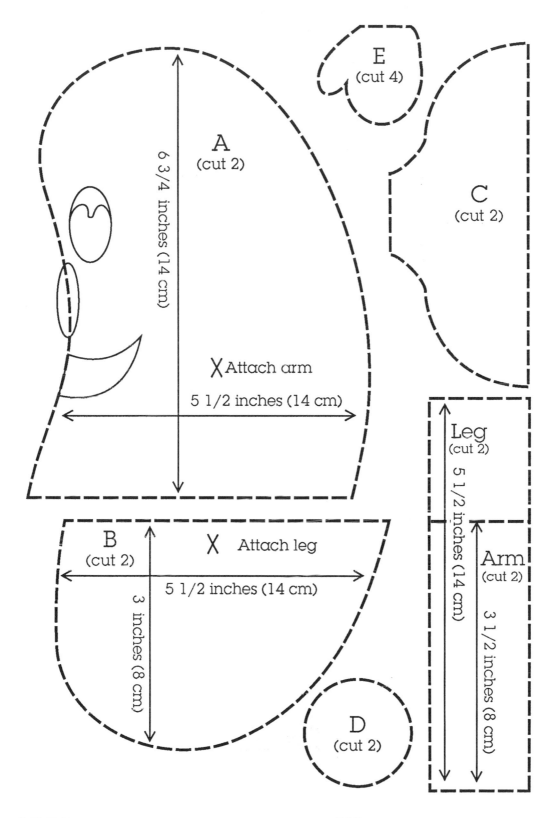

A
(cut 2)

6 3/4 inches (14 cm)

X Attach arm

5 1/2 inches (14 cm)

E
(cut 4)

C
(cut 2)

Leg
(cut 2)

5 1/2 inches (14 cm)

Arm
(cut 2)

3 1/2 inches (8 cm)

B
(cut 2)

X   Attach leg

5 1/2 inches (14 cm)

3 inches (8 cm)

D
(cut 2)

Gluten-Free Whole Bean Flour is available in 2, 5 and 10 kilogram bags at

Grain Process Enterprises Ltd.
115 Commander Blvd., Scarborough, Ontario M1S 3M7
Telephone: (416) 291-3226 . Fax: (416) 291-2159
Toll Free: 1-800-387-5292

or through mail order from

Ontario Coloured Bean Growers Association
Association Office
R. R. 5, Mitchell, Ontario N0K 1N0
Telephone:(519) 348-4141 • Fax: (519) 348-8165

Please Note: Grain Process Enterprises Ltd. is the only source of supply for whole bean flour at publication date of this cookbook. If you would like your grocer, specialty store, health food store or local gluten-free food distributor to stock this NEW whole bean flour, have them call Grain Process Enterprises to make the necessary arrangements.

For information about the Canadian Celiac Association and Celiac Disease please contact:

Executive Director
The Canadian Celiac Association
6519B Mississauga Road, Mississauga, Ontario L5N 1A6
Telephone: (416) 567-7195 • Fax: (416) 567-0710

For more information on the Good Health Eating Guide system or diabetes, contact:

The Canadian Diabetes Association
15 Toronto St., Suite 1001
Toronto, Ontario M5C 2E3
Phone: (416) 363-3373
Fax: (416) 363-3393

QUICK REVIEW

• 1 lb (500g) dried beans = 2 to 2 1/2 cups (500 to 625 mL) dried beans
= 5 to 6 cups (1.25 to 1.5 L) cooked

• 1 cup (500 mL) dried beans = 2 to 2 1/2 cups (500 to 625 mL) cooked

• One can (14 oz/398 mL) beans = 1 1/2 cups (375 mL) drained beans
• One can (19 oz/540 mL) beans = 2 cups (500 mL) drained beans

• Remember to soak and cook beans in about three times their volume of fresh soft water.

• It will take 45 minutes to 1 hour and 15 minutes for cooking depending on the type and age of beans.

• Discarding both the soaking and cooking waters, plus rinsing after each step, will flush away a large amount of the substances responsible for the flatulence that causes beans to be referred to as "the musical fruit" in some circles.

• It is smart to have cooked beans on hand. Home-cooking dried ones is much cheaper than buying canned ones. It takes a little time but very little effort.

• Whole or mashed beans can be refrigerated for up to five days or frozen for up to six months, to be ready for the days when you want to make a dip, salad, soup, main dish. They store well in their dry state, but still, to have them ready in their ready-to-eat form suits the constraints of time when an actual meal needs to be prepared.

INDEX

Comparison of Canadian and American Food Group Systems

American Diabetes Association Exchange System	Canadian Diabetes Association Choice System
1 Starch/Bread	1 ☐ Starchy
1 Fruit	1 1/2 ◪ Fruits & Vegetables
1 Vegetable	2 ✚✚ Extra Vegetables
1 Low-Fat Milk (1 cup serving)	2 ◆ Milk (2%) (2 half cup servings)
1 Lean Meat	1 ⬚ Protein
1 Medium-Fat Meat	1 ⬚ Protein
	1/2 ▲ Fats & Oils
1 High-Fat Meat	1 ⬚ Protein
	1 ▲ Fats & Oils
1 Fat	1 ▲ Fats & Oils

Please note: Our recipes for <u>gluten-free</u> appetizers to desserts are marked with Ⓖ🅕

The recipes that are <u>not gluten-free</u> are marked with 🅖🅕.